204884

GROUND CONTROL

Anna Minton is a writer and journalist. She spent a decade in journalism, including a stint as corporate reporter on the *Financial Times*, and is the winner of five national journalism awards. Finding daily journalism frustrating she began to focus on longer projects for think tanks and policy organizations and is the author of the Joseph Rowntree Foundation's Viewpoint on fear and distrust.

Ground Control emerged from a series of three agenda-setting reports, two of which were published by the Royal Institution of Chartered Surveyors and the other by the think tank Demos. The first focused on gated communities and ghettoes in the US, questioning to what extent these trends are emerging in the UK. The second looked at polarization and culture in one British city, Newcastle, and the third investigated the growing privatization of public space.

She appears regularly on television and radio and is a frequent conference speaker, invited to speak to a wide range of audiences, from art biennials to policemen. *Ground Control* is her first book. She lives in South London with her partner, who is a film maker, and her son.

More details available at: www.annaminton.com

D1387808

ANNA MINTON

Ground Control

*Fear and Happiness
in the Twenty-First-Century City*

PENGUIN BOOKS

PENGUIN BOOKS

Published by the Penguin Group
Penguin Books Ltd, 80 Strand, London WC2R ORL, England
Penguin Group (USA), Inc., 375 Hudson Street, New York, New York 10014, USA
Penguin Group (Canada), 90 Eglinton Avenue East, Suite 700, Toronto, Ontario, Canada M4P 2Y3
(a division of Pearson Penguin Canada Inc.)
Penguin Ireland, 25 St Stephen's Green, Dublin 2, Ireland
(a division of Penguin Books Ltd)
Penguin Group (Australia), 250 Camberwell Road, Camberwell, Victoria 3124, Australia (a
division of Pearson Australia Group Pty Ltd)
Penguin Books India Pvt Ltd, 11 Community Centre, Panchsheel Park,
New Delhi – 110 017, India
Penguin Group (NZ), 67 Apollo Drive, Rosedale, Auckland 0632, New Zealand
(a division of Pearson New Zealand Ltd)
Penguin Books (South Africa) (Pty) Ltd, 24 Sturdee Avenue, Rosebank,
Johannesburg 2196, South Africa

Penguin Books Ltd, Registered Offices: 80 Strand, London WC2R ORL, England

www.penguin.com

First published 2009
Reissued with new material 2012

003

Copyright © Anna Minton, 2009, 2012
Photographs copyright © John Davies, 2009

The moral right of the author has been asserted

All rights reserved
Without limiting the rights under copyright
reserved above, no part of this publication may be
reproduced, stored in or introduced into a retrieval system,
or transmitted, in any form or by any means (electronic, mechanical,
photocopying, recording or otherwise), without the prior
written permission of both the copyright owner and
the above publisher of this book

Typeset by Palimpsest Book Production Limited, Falkirk, Stirlingshire
Printed in Great Britain by Clays Ltd, St Ives plc

A CIP catalogue record for this book is available from the British Library

978-0-241-96090-5

www.greenpenguin.co.uk

MIX
Paper from
responsible sources
FSC
www.fsc.org   FSC® C018179

Penguin Books is committed to a sustainable
future for our business, our readers and our planet.
This book is made from Forest Stewardship
Council™ certified paper.

Contents

Contents

For my father

UCB
204884

Author's Note

Ground Control came out in 2009, in the wake of the financial crisis. Nearly three years later, the UK and the global economy continue to reel from that crisis, yet few column inches are devoted to the possibility of alternative models. I wanted to write this new chapter of the book, focusing on the development accompanying the London Olympics, because in spite of the economic outlook, the Olympics represents the high point of the debt-based model of property-fuelled development which played such a large part in bringing the crisis about.

The book ended on a positive note, suggesting that that the era of TINA – 'There is No Alternative' – was passing, paving the way for a more civic minded and democratic approach to the city. Sadly, there is little sign of that so far. Even so, and despite the excesses catalogued in this account of the Olympic project, I hope that we will begin to talk seriously about alternatives and I hope that this new chapter will play some part in starting that debate.

Although there have been a number of policy changes in the areas investigated by *Ground Control*, in particular the end of the Pathfinder policy explained in Chapter 5, they have not affected the overall thrust of the case the book puts forward, and I have left the body of the text untouched. The book stands on its own, but the new chapter complements and in many ways completes it, with the Olympic development neighbouring London's Docklands, where the story detailed in *Ground Control* began.

Anna Minton, October 2011,
London

The Olympics and the public good

The Great Exhibition and the Festival of Britain are often held up as the inspiration for London 2012. When giving presentations, Baroness Ford, the former banker who is now chair of the Olympic Park Legacy Company, highlights these landmark events. The Great Exhibition of 1851, which left London with a legacy of museums and public spaces, was visited by a third of the population and made millions of pounds which were used to found the Victoria and Albert Museum, the Science Museum and the Natural History Museum. In 1951 the Festival of Britain, another turning point in our national memory, left as its legacy the Royal Festival Hall, one of the finest public buildings in the country. But is the legacy of the 2012 Games really comparable to the legacy of the Great Exhibition? Returning to the issues raised in the first edition of *Ground Control*, this new chapter examines the real legacy of the 2012 Games. Since the book was published, Britain has been rocked by a series of crises, in parliament with the expenses scandal, in the media and police with phone hacking and in the social fabric with the riots of 2011. Each crisis has exposed profound weaknesses in democracy with commentators highlighting the corrosion of the public realm. Sadly, the legacy of the Games is more closely linked to our own time than the public spirit of the Victorians, or the post-war Britons.

If the urban environment we create reflects political realities and provides a litmus test for the health of our society and democracy, then the Games, which are developing a large swathe of East London that includes some of the poorest parts of Britain, are a mirror for our times. 'By staging the games in this part of the city, the most enduring legacy of the Olympics will be the regeneration of an entire community for the direct benefit of everyone who lives there,' the Olympic bid document promised. This new part of London, which is the size of a new town, includes Westfield Stratford City, the biggest shopping complex in Western Europe, a 500 acre Royal Park, which is the first park to be built in the UK since Victorian times, and thousands of new homes.

The Olympic development is the apogee of the story of city change described in this book. It is a process that began in the late 1980s in Docklands and will end nearby with the completion of the largest development Britain has ever seen in Stratford City and the Olympic park. Far from the civic-minded legacy promised, this is the architecture of extreme capitalism, which produces a divided landscape of privately owned, disconnected, high security, gated enclaves side by side with enclaves of poverty which remain untouched by the wealth around them. The stark segregation and highly visible differences create a climate of fear and growing mistrust between people, which together with the undemocratic nature of these new private places, erodes civil society.

This new chapter is not going to repeat my original thesis about fear. That is at the heart of the book and is thoroughly investigated in later chapters. Neither am I going to update all the policy changes which the Coalition government has brought in since 2009. Some are better – on civil liberties – but many are worse – in terms of housing and planning policy and youth services – but in terms of the broad themes discussed in the book, the change in government amounts to little more than re-arranging the deck chairs on the *Titanic*.

Instead, I am going to focus simply on the Olympic development and the impact it is having on local people, the supposed beneficiaries of the Olympic legacy.

Local support is vital to any Olympic bid and London 2012 was no exception. But while the rhetoric of legacy promises has continually emphasized the importance of local involvement the reality has been very different. The failure not only to involve local people in genuine consultation about the changes but to stick to an agreement on local jobs and housing signed by no less than Lord Coe, chair of the

London 2012 Organizing Committee, is shocking not least because it has received hardly any coverage.

It's important to look at this betrayal of local promises alongside one of the biggest changes in government policy that affects local people living in the Olympic area in 2012: the privatization of poor housing. A trend which was emerging when I wrote *Ground Control*, it is now the norm. Like the privatization of our streets, public places and now entire communities, this too has been the subject of hardly any debate.

In *Fool's Gold*, Gillian Tett discusses the problem of 'social silence', whereby whole sectors of society fail to ask questions about disturbing practices. She argues that this is one of the causes of the financial crisis. This problem is compounded by the emergence of 'technical silos', where only experts steeped in technical knowledge can understand what's going on. The real tragedy is that rather than being hidden due to a plot, the burgeoning crises remain hidden in plain sight because of social silence. This is equally true for many aspects of contemporary political discourse in the UK, from phone hacking to regeneration and housing, which is obscured by the jargon of property finance, planning and housing. The process of privatization, which brings with it a confusing multiplicity of competing companies and quangos, ensures that what happens becomes so complicated that it is almost impossible to follow.

What is marked about the Olympic regeneration is that despite the financial crisis there has been no pause for thought in a changed economic climate of the debt-fuelled approach to property finance, which privatizes the public realm in its wake, and which is at the heart of the Olympic project. Despite the series of crises which have defined the last few years there has not been a corresponding shift in the way the financial, political and media elite operate. Instead there is a strong sense that it remains 'business as usual' and that we are just waiting for a return to normal.

When it comes to the Olympics that raises serious questions not just about the economic rationale for the project, but about democratic accountability. The significance of London 2012 is not just, or even mainly, about sport. It is all about the legacy. It is what this legacy will be, and what perhaps it could have been, that is the focus of this chapter. I hope it will help erode the social silence.

The 'regeneration Games'

The chief executives running the Olympic project continually emphasize that the importance of London 2012 for the UK is not sport but legacy. 'Everything will be driven by legacy,' David Higgins, the former chief executive of the Olympic Delivery Authority, repeatedly stressed.[1] A clue as to what this legacy might resemble is immediately available from a look at Higgins's CV. Higgins is the former head of Lend Lease, the Australian multinational property company, where he was chief executive. It was under his leadership that Lend Lease built Bluewater, the UK's second-largest out of town shopping centre. Adjacent to the Olympic Park – much of it built incidentally by Lend Lease – is Westfield Stratford City, the largest shopping centre in Europe, through which 80 per cent of visitors to the Olympics will pass on their way to the Olympic Park. When former London Mayor Ken Livingstone gave his backing to London's Olympic bid, the only precondition he required was that the Games be held in East London. Here was an opportunity for regeneration on a Bluewater scale, which had been planned for years but repeatedly floundered. For the army of employees working for the various Olympic quangos these became the 'regeneration Games'.[2]

The rationale for this approach, pioneered by Margaret Thatcher and Michael Heseltine and later adopted with enthusiasm by Gordon Brown at the Treasury, was that the way to bring prosperity to East London was by creating engines of regional economic growth, based on a virtuous circle of property finance, shopping, spending and rising property values. The financial crisis notwithstanding, this is the high point of an approach which has seen large private centres take over towns and cities around Britain, created as citadels of finance or high-end retail which aim to attract the well-heeled ABC1s of the region rather than the local communities around them. For example, the easiest way to get to Cabot Circus, the private shopping complex in the centre of Bristol, is via the M32 motorway, which leads straight to the Cabot Circus car park. There is no need to visit the city itself and many shoppers don't. It is Bluewater in reverse, with the out-of-town shopping mall now bang in the centre of town. And like Bluewater, there is nothing about Cabot Circus which is rooted in the surrounding environment, reminding shoppers that they actually are in Bristol. Instead, these are consumer hubs on international transport networks that resemble nothing more than airport departure lounges.

In West London's Shepherd Bush Westfield have also opened what, until Stratford City, was the largest shopping centre in Western Europe. 'The public transport infrastructure has been designed to ferry people directly into Westfield then straight out again, rather than to Shepherds Bush itself,' local MP Andrew Slaughter complained, echoing the concerns of many local residents.[3] Stratford City is exactly the same, with a state of the art station, where it is planned the Eurostar will stop in future, exiting straight into the shopping complex via a new bridge, with many shoppers barely noticing they are in East London. The entrance to Stratford City is separated from ground level, and the rest of Stratford, by a large flight of steps. Looking down, curious shoppers might catch a glimpse of the Stratford Centre, a rundown 1970s mall that stands at the feet of the glittering new complex and is almost a parody of 'us and them'. It goes without saying that the vast majority of shops in the new shopping complex are financially far out of reach for local people.

The history of plans for major development in Stratford has more to do with the privatization of British Rail than the Olympic bid and is a complex tale of collapsing deals involving a confusing array of companies. The story began with the privatization of British Rail and the building of the Channel Tunnel Rail Link in the mid 1990s, which saw huge tracts of land passed to private companies. Since then, developers have been trying, and failing, to get a deal together to develop what had been publicly owned land.

In 1996, London and Continental Railways, a company created when British Rail was privatized, won the government contract to build the high-speed rail link between London and the Channel

Tunnel and took over large amounts of land around the proposed new stations at Ebbsfleet, Ashford, Kings Cross and Stratford. At Stratford, Chelsfield, a property company run by Nigel Hugill, which already had plans for an enormous shopping mall in London's Shepherds Bush, signed the deal to develop another huge shopping complex there, along with property company Stanhope, run by Sir Stuart Lipton, who went on to chair the government agency the Commission for Architecture and the Built Environment. He resigned from there in 2004 after an independent audit into conflicts of interest concluded that in future the chairmanship of CABE should not go to a property developer.[4]

Although London and Continental got into difficulties in 1998 and was restructured, Chelsfield's deal remained on the drawing board, but in 2004, just before London won the Olympic bid, Chelsfield was bought out by a trio of companies, including Westfield, the biggest shopping centre operator in the world, alongside Multiplex, the company building Wembley, and the Reuben Brothers, property investors who had made billions in investments in the aluminium industry in 1990s Russia. Then, even though the property boom was at its height, that deal entered shaky waters with the three ill-matched partners unwilling or unable to work together.[5] Around this time London unexpectedly won the Olympic bid, which was based on plans to redevelop Stratford. Now the stakes for this precarious development, suddenly catapulted to the heart of the Olympics project, were much higher. At this point Livingstone stepped in and made clear his desire to see Westfield build the Stratford complex, accusing the Reuben brothers of being asset strippers. Controversially, Livingstone ratcheted up the row with the Reubens, telling them if they didn't like the pressure he was putting on them they could 'go back to Iran and try their luck with the Ayatollahs'. When it was pointed out that the Reubens were actually born in India to Iraqi Jewish parents, the mayor's response was to apologize to the people of Iran for associating them with the Reubens.[6] The Reubens issued a public statement claiming that the comments were resulting in confusion and uncertainty, which threatened the Olympics,[7] while London and Continental Railways described the remarks as 'destructive' and 'offensive'.[8] This ill-tempered row only reflects just how vital this deal had become to Livingstone and to the Olympic project.

Lipton then sold his stake to Westfield, which bought the others out, ending up not just with development rights for the shopping centre but the Athlete's Village and thousands of new homes, rights which it subsequently passed on to that other giant Australian developer, Lend Lease, whose European arm was now run by Nigel Hugill, the former boss of Chelsfield.

At this point the first rumblings of the subprime crash were being heard, putting the entire project in jeopardy, yet again. In tune with the rest of the country, the Lend Lease deal collapsed and Westfield appeared to be in no hurry to begin work on the shopping complex. As the government prepared its £50 billion bail out and nationalization of the banks the Olympic project was also bailed out, with public funding for the project increasing by £5.9 billion – almost three times the original budget.[9] Under the terms of the original agreement, Lend Lease was going to bring in large amounts of private equity to fund the project, but following the financial crisis the company found it difficult to borrow the money.[10] So the government agreed to finance the Athlete's Village and pay Lend Lease to be the project manager. According to the House of Commons Public Accounts Committee less than 2 per cent of the Olympic budget has ended up coming from the private sector.[11]

Meanwhile Westfield, whose billionaire owner was having to fend off fraud accusations for tax evasion to the tune of $68 million in the US,[12] allegations which he strenuously denies in his ongoing court case, also received £200 million of public money from the Olympic Delivery Authority to pay for roads leading to the shopping complex.[13]

There is more to this fiendishly complicated story,[14] but this saga of collapsed deals and government bailouts, characterizes the Olympic regeneration project. As to the amount of money spent by the government, at the time of writing the budget had nearly quadrupled to £9.3 billion. Admittedly this is dwarfed by the £76 billion spent on bailing out the Royal Bank of Scotland, but even in the context of the staggering recent bailouts it remains a very large sum. Needless to say, without such government assistance, the other schemes planned by Westfield and Lend Lease around the country have all come to an abrupt halt.

Describing the Olympic bailout, Paul Norman, a blogger who writes on the Olympics, told me: 'It's an enormous figure and it makes it ludicrous when they talk about bringing it in on time.' Columnist Simon Jenkins noted acerbically that it is 'easy to complete the crazy project on budget if the budget is continuously increased'.[15]

Despite the enormous sums spent the fact that the Olympic venues have been completed on time is considered to be a huge triump for UK plc. The merry-go-round of questionable decisions by an array of different companies and quangos does not end there, as on completion the Olympic village was put up for sale, one of the first parts of the park, alongside the Olympic stadium, to be sold off. When the 500 acre Olympic Park re-opens to the public in 2013 it will be named the Queen Elizabeth Olympic Park. It is the first park to be built in London since Victorian times and the first to be called a Royal Park since then. But despite its Royal moniker and despite a campaign for Royal Park status, led by Newham Council Mayor Robin Wales,[17] the Olympic Park will not be a Royal Park. It will not be run by the Royal Parks Agency but by private companies and the places within it, from the Olympic village to the Olympic venues, will be private. Or at least that was the intention, although at the time of writing it emerged that the sale of the stadium to West Ham Football Club had fallen through. The tender battle between West Ham United and Tottenham Hotspur, was a saga in itself, ending with the collapse of the deal.[18]

Earlier in 2011, the Wellcome Trust, Britain's biggest charity, had made a £1 billion bid to buy the park and the village, aiming to create a global hub for scientific research and innovation – 'a Silicon Valley for Europe' – focusing on health, technology and sports science, in conjunction with two universities, and including a museum, social housing and the creation of 7,000 jobs.[19] But this substantial investment in Britain's future was turned down by the Olympic Park Legacy Company on the basis that amongst other things it did not offer 'value for money' to the taxpayer.[20] Instead, the Legacy Company opted to sell the Olympic village to a consortium led by the Qatari royal family, which offered a higher price for the village.[21] Rejecting the Wellcome Trust proposal, the plan now is to sell off separate bits of the park piecemeal, to different bidders at different times. The argument is that this is the best way to make the most money from the park, although the debacle over the stadium does not bode well. Contrast this approach with 1851 when the Great Exhibition opened. In that year the Crown Lands Act was passed, creating London's eight royal parks by transferring the parklands owned by Queen Victoria – which include Hyde Park, Regent's Park and Richmond Park – into public ownership at a time when the control of public places was being transferred from aristocratic landlords to democratically elected local government.

Today's Olympic Park was never going to be a Royal Park or a public park. But at least the Wellcome Trust bid, which would have ploughed all the profit it made from the village into the park, was a genuinely public spirited proposal to invest in Britain's future. It is amazing that despite the utter collapse of the commercial case for the Olympic development the bottom line remains the only consideration the Olympic decision makers are prepared to consider.

How local promises were broken

While the acronym-laden quangos and the property multinationals are central to the 'delivery' of the Games, the support of local people for an 'East London Games' is acknowledged as a key factor in London winning the bid.

At the end of November 2004 Amber Charles, a fifteen-year-old East End schoolgirl, was flown to Switzerland to hand the London 2012 candidature file into the International Olympic Committee HQ in Lausanne. This was obviously a PR opportunity for London's bid, but it also reflected an upsurge of genuine local support for the Olympics, led by the community organizing group, London Citizens, which was then known as TELCO – 'The East London Communities Organization'.

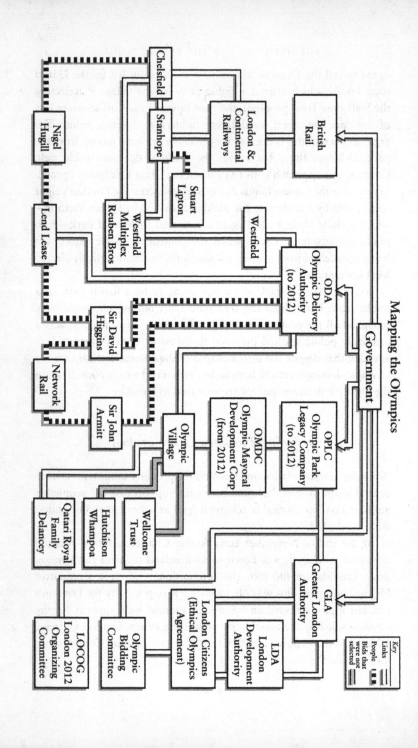

Mapping the Olympics

Key

Links

People

Bids that were not selected

Public support is considered critical to any Olympic bid. In recognition of that the London 2012 bidding team, under Seb Coe's direction, approached TELCO and asked them to publicly back the bid.[22] With a membership of thousands throughout the East End, including around 80 community and religious groups, the group was in a position to quickly mobilize support. An activist with TELCO at the time remembers a series of heated meetings to discuss whether the organization should lend its support to the bid. 'I remember those conversations. Would our council tax go up? Would we have to pay for it? We remembered Docklands – that didn't go well for local people. I remember a particular meeting in a Methodist church in Stratford. It was a real deliberation on what was happening outside our control and how much we could control. The consensus was that the bid was going ahead with or without us so however sceptical we were we thought if with our involvement we could have a number of people's guarantees then we were quite happy with that. After that we became integral to the bid,' she recalls.

The upshot was that TELCO, in consultation with its members, drew up an 'Ethical Olympics Agreement' which included six 'People's Guarantees' relating to affordable housing, education, health and employment. Among the pledges was that £2 million should be set aside for a construction academy in Leyton with 30 per cent of construction jobs set aside for local people and the Lower Lea Valley designated a 'living wage' zone. As for affordable housing, a Community Land Trust, which ploughs profits back into the development, would build homes for local people.[23]

The agreement was signed in 2004 by Lord Coe, then chair of the Olympic Bidding Committee, Mayor of London Ken Livingstone and John Biggs, deputy chair of the London Development Agency (LDA). As a result of the agreement Coe told the *Evening Standard* that the Games were now 'eminently more winnable'.[24]

But once London won the bid TELCO found the relationship changed dramatically. While the LDA, which is responsible for upholding the Mayor's pledges on the Games, held regular meetings with them the ODA, which was not in existance when the agreement was signed, refused to meet them or acknowledge the ethical Olympics pledge on the grounds that the quango had not been in existence when the agreement was signed. In desperation TELCO decided on collective action, picketing ODA chief David Higgins on his way in and out of breakfast meetings. One TELCO employee remembers standing outside the ODA in the rain handing out cake. 'We said this is your piece of the cake, how about ours? After that he did talk to us.'

Although the negative publicity did lead to a series of meetings with Higgins, the ODA has refused to honour the ethical Olympics pledge, claiming it is 'illegal to dictate the terms of contracts struck under open tender'.[25] A director with London Citizens, closely involved with the organization's Olympics work, says: 'LOCOG and the ODA did not understand the legitimacy of who TELCO was representing. At the beginning of the bid there was a reciprocal relationship based on an understanding of both parties' concerns. After the bid, when new agencies took over, there was far less willingness to carry it on as a relationship. My view is that there was a real, genuine opportunity for things to happen. TELCO was never critical of the Olympics as a concept at the start, and when you consider the work that went into that agreement . . . I think it is a scandal. London Citizens does not support any political party or affiliation. It has never given its "branded" support to anything other than bringing the Games to East London for the legacy it will create. The responsibility that should be felt is huge.'

When I went to meet John Biggs at his office at the GLA he told me it was a failure of collective responsibility. 'In my view for the ODA to say "this happened before our watch" is disingenuous. The ODA ought to be seen to be bound by agreements the LDA made. But the ODA is accountable to the Olympic board. If it is not delivering that is down to the Mayor and [the minister responsible for the Olympics.] This agreement has been failed by a [confusion] of many interests. The problem is everyone has been mesmerised to an extent by delivering the games on time', he said.

Father Tom O'Brien, whose parish covers Bethnal Green, told me that the chance to make this a games for East London has been missed. 'They've missed an opportunity. It wouldn't have cost much while it was TELCO votes which won the games', he said.

The clearest symbol of this, for him, has been the row over the route for the marathon, which will not run through East London.

The organizer of the marathon, David Bedford, who also runs the London marathon, which does go through East London, went onto resign from LOCOG and accused the organization of 'appalling' handling of the affair in failing to consult local people over the plans to change the route.[26] Instead, the marathon will run three laps of a circular route in Central London, passing tourist attractions like the Houses of Parliament, Trafalgar Square and the Tower of London, with the finish line not in the Olympic Stadium, but on The Mall. This is despite the fact a marathon finish in the Olympic Stadium is actually an International Olympic Committee (IOC) requirement for bidding nations, and was included in London's bid.

The reason given by LOCOG is 'operational issues', specifically that road closures would risk disrupting other competitions and that the security 'lockdown' surrounding the final mile of the route to the stadium would make the event inaccessible to spectators. The impact of the very high levels of security around the Games will be discussed later in this chapter and no doubt did play a part. But as far as local people are concerned the suspicion is that the decision has more to do with London's image and branding, projected around the world. 'They don't want grotty parts of East London. The preferred image is projected by going through the centre,' a London Citizens activist said. Biggs agreed: 'They wanted the telegenic stuff for the world networks.'

A private new town

The aspiration for the Queen Elizabeth Olympic Park is to create a new part of London. In an inspired piece of marketing a new postcode of E20 has been created for the area spanning the Olympic Park and Stratford City, which is the same postcode as that given to the fictional district of Walford in the soap opera *EastEnders*.

Within the park up to 11,000 new homes in five adjoining districts are planned, which is effectively the size of a new town. The difference with the rest of London is that it will be a private new town, or more accurately a number of privately run places. Just as the Olympic Park is not a royal park but privately run, these new communities will not be accountable to local government but will be privately governed by separate companies.

These are fundamental changes of great importance to local people. But yet again, despite the rhetoric of local consultation, local people have not been consulted in any meaningful way and when they ask questions no information is forthcoming. A London Citizens director who has been involved in the consultation process is highly critical of the Olympic Park Legacy Company's 'roadshow' approach to consultations carried out by private contractors. He believes that 'The reason they do these consultation sessions is so that they can present their current thinking. But it's very much done and dusted. There's no real check on progress, no option to recall. There are no answers given to questions people put such as "what do you mean by affordable housing?" and "who will I be paying my council tax to?" ' he says.

In contrast London Citizens have carried out their own consultations, involving feedback from thousands of local residents, which found that the question of governance was very much at the top of local concerns. 'The park is intersected by three boroughs but all services are going to be run by the Park and administered by the Park, yet the Park is not accountable to the people who live there. It is bizarre that in that area people will be paying council tax without real community representation. These are the concerns that came out of the consultation but questions like that haven't been broached successfully', he says.

This was also my experience when I tried to put these questions to the Legacy Company, which is the body that currently oversees the park, although it will be replaced by a Mayoral Development Corporation after the Games. Unfortunately I was unable to find out more about the implications of the private ownership of the area because the Legacy Company was unwilling to discuss it with me. After weeks of unanswered emails I was asked to submit a list of questions. A press officer responded that 'our Executive Directors are very busy and in terms of the level of detail you want to go into it is too early to tell'.

Baroness Ford, chair of the Legacy Company, has often talked of the company's role as evolving 'a great London estate' in the manner of landowners such as Grosvenor.[27] In interviews Ford has said she aspires to create a great estate in the tradition of London's Belgravia or South Kensington, two of the capital's most affluent areas.[28] The 'Homes' section of the Legacy Company website – with the strapline 'Inspired by the best of London's heritage' – is accompanied by a picture of an elegant Georgian terrace.

Quite apart from the suitability of creating Belgravia in the heart of Newham, this is misleading on a number of levels. When advocates of privately owned estates point to the Georgian squares and terraces built by the Dukes and Earls who controlled London in the early nineteenth century, they omit to mention that this was a pre-democratic model. Today the Georgian streets and squares are part of the fabric of the city, but what is no longer visible is that these places were once barricaded and closed to the public. Chapter 2 of this book details how, as democracy took hold and central and local government grew in power, the estates were opened up to the public. It is also misleading to imply that today's property multinationals create places that have even a passing resemblance to the Georgian terraces in any way except for the fact that they are privately owned.

While the Legacy Company claimed not to know the details of the future governance of such a large part of London, the situation at the Athlete's Village – which, confusingly, is not part of the Legacy Company's remit – may shed some light on what will happen in the future. As the ODA's Paul Hartman told me, the village 'will be privately owned to maintain with the community, the environment they wish to live and work in'. So it is clear that this will be a private estate, but the mulitiplicity of quangos, agencies, special purpose vehicles and private developers involved makes it very difficult to determine who will be accountable for its future governance.

Samantha Heath, from London Sustainability Exchange, has been involved with the Athlete's Village from the start. She explains what happened: 'When this was designed there were no proper governance procedures. The governance of the streets and how the rubbish would be disposed of – these were issues right from the start. We had no councillors to go to, it was very spurious who the governance authorities were going to be. Lend Lease is just in there as a builder.

The issue is we need to get the governance right from the start. Who owns the streets? We need to know that from the beginning', she says.

Without such basic information it is very difficult to plan for the provision of integrated services, from policing to rubbish collection, let alone democratic accountability. But because these places are commercial products, sold to the highest bidder, often the owner is not in place at the beginning, and even if they are the estate will very likely be sold on to another owner. In 2011, six years after the Athlete's Village was conceived and when it was virtually finished, a consortium led by the Qatari royal family bought the site, following a competitive tendering process. They are now responsible for its governance, although they will very likely outsource this to an estates management company.

At a conference I went to about the legacy of the Athlete's Village, even Nick Williams, head of 2012 at Newham Council, was reduced to saying: 'There are too many agencies. There's no overall governance of this area that makes it coherent.' It did not inspire confidence when he went on to say that the Athlete's Village would 'set the tone' for all the Olympic-related development.

Heath sees no conspiracy to undermine democracy, rather a failure to understand the processes at work. 'They don't see the implications of it. They don't see the relevance. It's more about officers and individuals who can't take on broader contexts. The reason why it's a mess is because of the unintended consequences. I'm sure that Newham Council does believe that its councillors are the community representatives but what locus do they have in this environment?', she wonders. At the same time, she feels that local consultation on all aspects of the development was particularly poor as, contrary to the rhetoric, the Athlete's Village was seen as 'a new quarter', unconnected to the local community. 'Engagement with the community was pretty sparse', she says.

As for the Legacy Company, that will turn into the Mayoral Development Corporation in April 2012, run by the same staff but with considerably greater powers, in particular planning powers which will stretch over a far larger area. Swamped by coverage of the Olympics, this extension of planning control has received little attention, although it means that local people will not to be able to turn to elected councillors if they are unhappy with plans for new development, mirroring what happened in Docklands under the Development Corporation set up in the 1980s.

The area which falls under the remit of the new Mayoral Development Corporation will span not just the Olympic Park, Athlete's Village and Stratford City but 'a wider area including Hackney Wick, Fish Island and, south of the Olympic Park, areas of Stratford, Three Mills and Bromley-by-Bow'.[29] This means that a very substantial part of East London will be characterized by new private fiefdoms accountable only to the blurred mass of quangos which are replacing democratically elected local government.

The miserable demi monde of housing

If Stratford City is a world away from much of Newham, East Ham is right in the middle of it. I had arranged to to meet 'Pete', who works for the council, there. Pete – not his real name – was risking quite a lot by agreeing to talk to me about his job and it had taken a few weeks of phonecalls to arrange the meeting. 'I can't be seen to be talking to you or I'll be given a roasting. The council try and lockdown the message. That's just the way local government is, especially with the Olympics', he told me.

A typical day's work will see Pete walk into a two-bedroom house 'and find 20 to 30 men in there, sleeping four to five to a room. The record is 38', he says. The most recent problem in Newham has been the proliferation of hundreds of illegal 'supersheds' put up in back gardens. 'It's mostly legal and illegal immigrants', Pete says. 'People accept it – it's crap but it's cheap, but there's the cost of the social consequences – on health and mental health. The owners do what they like to the properties to maximise the rent. A lot of them are first generation. It's okay to do that in Dakkar but it's not okay here. Now it's becoming the norm', he says.

Newham, where most of the Olympics will take place, includes 13 of London's 15 most deprived wards. Nearly half the population live below the poverty line and 70 per cent of children live in low-income households. The majority of the population is born outside the borough and transience is very high with a 60 per cent 'churn' in housing each year.

Chapter 6 of this book details the untold story of housing and tracks how the government started to use the private rented sector to house the poor. Now, under changes proposed by the Coalition the private rented sector is set to take over housing for the poor.[30] Shelter describe the reality of living in private rented housing in Newham as a miserable *demi monde* of no tenancy agreements, landlords with false identities, little chance of getting deposits back and people forced to live in sheds, garages and even fridges.

'People are living in the backs of shops, in basements in kebab shops and in sheds. You see a betting shop or a chicken shop and there'll be a room above it with ten or twenty people,' says Marc Lancaster, community outreach advisor at Shelter. 'People have even been found in commercial fridges, where the meat is stored. And they're paying rent for it. I actually wondered if I'd dreamt that.'

One man's experience is typical of the kind of conditions Pete sees all the time. Two weeks before his wife was due to give birth the couple woke up to find the bed covered in debris – the ceiling in the room they were renting had fallen in. When the husband started to pressure the landlord to carry out repairs he responded by initially changing the locks and then removing the door to the room, effectively evicting the couple and leaving them homeless. 'He removed the door so we had to leave,' the husband says.

Just ten years ago, private renting was a marginal, though significant, part of the housing picture providing accommodation in often appalling, and appallingly expensive, conditions. But by the late noughties the private rented sector had moved into the mainstream of social housing provision due to the lack of social housing available. Even so, although it was becoming commonplace to house benefit claimants in private rented housing it remained a very serious concern for politicians with a report commissioned by the government in 2008 describing this part of the private rental market as the 'slum' rental market at the 'very bottom end' of the sector.[31]

Today, the private rented sector accounts for a third of all housing in Newham, which is a proportion set to increase rapidly as the changes kick in. 'Most poor people are in the private rented sector. We don't house people anymore. We signpost them to private renting. At the moment the waiting list for a three-bedroom council house is 16 years so there's no choice,' Pete explains. What concerns Shelter most of all is that despite the abuse and illegality rife among private landlords, Grant Shapps, the housing minister, has emphasized that the private rental market does not need regulation, claiming it is already over-regulated. Following the previous government's damning review new regulations were proposed including a National Register of Landlords and compulsory written tenancy agreements. But Shapps has made it clear that he believes 'the current system strikes the right balance', promising that 'the Government has no plans to create any burdensome red tape and bureaucracy'.[32]

For a great many people in Newham and the neighbouring Olympic boroughs of Tower Hamlets and Hackney the main impact of 2012 on their daily lives will be the further marketization of housing for the poor, which is being introduced as the Olympic preparations come to a close. The cuts in housing benefit, which come into force in April 2012, will affect the 40 per cent or so of private renters in Newham on benefit and have caused controversy, with Conservative London Mayor Boris Johnson likening them to 'Kosovo-style social cleansing' of poorer people from inner London.[33] Research by Cambridge University confirms his fears that only a handful of outer London boroughs will be affordable to those on housing benefit, as benefit will now only cover the bottom 30 per cent of market rents in an area, rather than the average. The parts of London likely to remain affordable are clustered into distinct blocks in outer London, including 97 per cent of Barking and Dagenham and 76 per cent of Newham.[34] 'It's going to drive all the poor people this way and to Barking and Dagenham,' Pete says.[35]

This is the context for the Olympics legacy, which has at its heart promises to create thousands of affordable homes for local people. On paper the masterplan for the park promises up to 11,000 new homes in five new neighbourhoods, 35 per cent of which will be affordable.

How many of those will eventually be built is uncertain, but what is certain is that the Athlete's Village will provide nearly 3,000 new homes in 2013. 'That's massive – it's effectively shipping in a whole new community. But it raises the big question of who moves into those homes,' says Rachel Orr, campaigns manager at Shelter.

Of those homes, half will be affordable. While that might sound straightforward, it isn't, as the always slippery definition of 'affordable housing' has changed yet again. Definitions in this area have been hard to pin down for a long time, since the state effectively stopped providing council housing, a process tracked in Chapter 6. Council housing then made way for 'social housing', the new term for subsidised housing provided largely by housing associations, which cost significantly less than market rates. Now the changes brought in by the Coalition government mean that housing associations can charge up to 80 per cent of market rent for 'social housing'. 'In London there's a huge difference between social rent and 80 per cent market rent,' Orr explains. For example, a three-bedroom property in an outer London borough could cost £126 a week in social rent, but at 80 per cent of market rent that would be £390. 'This is the product that's replacing social housing,' she says.

These are the death throes of social housing, which is morphing into renting at a slightly lower market rate, while the private rented sector takes over as the main provider of housing for the poor. As to what it means for the Athlete's Village, it is unlikely that much of it will be affordable to people in Newham, desperately in need of housing. Pat Turnbull, from the New Kingshold Residents and Tenants Association, describes how local residents find the legacy claims laughable. 'We have a severe housing shortage in all the local boroughs. We have people in their thirties living with their parents, so much overcrowded accommodation and terrible conditions in the private rented sector – all of which are going to get worse with the changes in housing policy. Then you have this pristine money-making development going up but only a tiny percentage will be for local people. It will be for select people,' she says.

For Orr the problem is that the legacy executives have failed to appreciate the reality of where they are. '[They] are so focused on the

Olympics legacy – it's as if it's happening in a different world, but it's happening in Newham,' she says. 'It's almost as if the Olympics housing legacy is in a bubble. People still seem to talk about the Olympics legacy as if none of the cuts to housing and benefit policy here have happened.'

In many ways, while the Olympics might be nearby, it is literally happening in a different world, with the Olympic Park and the Athlete's Village physically disconnected from the rest of Newham, separated by the railway and roads which cut the development off from the rest of the borough. Walking down East Ham's High Street North, Pete says: 'The Olympics has got nothing to do with it. It's completely sealed off. There are kids here who can't go out of their postcode. They've never been to Oxford Street. They've never seen the sea. That's what poverty does to you.'

A new settlement with the 'public good' at the centre

This chapter has already documented the entirely private nature of the Olympic regeneration, predicated on the hope of rising property prices and land sales. But if London 2012 seems to be a far cry from the public spaces and civic minded trusts in perpetuity of the Victorians there is one new development which could not be more in tune with the legacy of 1851, not least in terms of its location on London's Exhibition Road.

Chapter 8, which investigates alternatives to the model of debt-fuelled private places, looks at the emergence of 'shared space' which removes all the barriers, railings, crossings and even traffic lights from major thoroughfares. The consequence, counter intuitively, is that the risk of accidents decreases and places become safer as the impact of taking away external controls means that interaction between people increases. The Dutch traffic engineer behind the concept, Hans Monderman, was well aware that the implications of his idea went far beyond questions of traffic, impacting on civility in public space and trust between strangers. 'Eye contact and the consultation between civilians in public space is the highest quality you can get in a free country,' he said.[36]

Since *Ground Control* was published, shared space has been introduced in a number of parts of London, including Oxford Circus and Exhibition Road, which has been effectively rebuilt as a public place where people and traffic co-exist without controls. According to the London Borough of Kensington & Chelsea, 'the project will transform Exhibition Road into one of the most important public spaces in London and a major new cultural venue for the 2012 Olympics.' What is surprising about this scheme is that it is genuinely public.

Daniel Moylan, a flamboyant Conservative politician who sports orange-rimmed spectacles, is the key figure behind Exhibition Road. For him, a factor central to the success of the scheme is that it is public, adopted by the local authority. 'When local authorities adopt a highway it remains absolutely clear what the position is – it is effectively public land in every way. It is a structure that works,' he says. Moylan, who is now deputy director of Transport for London, is also partly responsible for one of the more positive aspects of the Olympics – to make London 2012 the first 'public transport' games.

But although the advent of shared space in some parts of the UK has coincided with London 2012, the Olympic developments themselves are characterized by exactly the opposite, with exceptionally high levels of security. Indeed, the UK's track record in security and surveillance was considered a key strength of London's bid. Once London won the bid, Mayor Boris Johnson described the security operation to the Culture, Media and Sport Committee. He said that 'broadly speaking, there will be quite substantial security and protection around the main Olympic venues of the kind that you would expect, and you will be seeing more detail about that nearer the time, but it will be not unlike what they did in China.'[37]

'Island security' is the popular term among 2012 security practitioners, who talk of 'locking down' the Olympic Park. Since 2007 the site has been a 'sterile zone' which has been 'sealed', encircled by an eleven-mile blue perimeter fence which is electrified in parts. When I visited in 2010 I was told to bring my passport and the number of security checkpoints, bag searches and biometric checks I had to pass through were considerably more stringent than those required for the Houses of Parliament. To back up the 'island security', peripheral buffer zones will be set up, including police helicopters, fleets of CCTV vehicles, road checks and stop and search.[38] This security 'lockdown' surrounding the mile to the stadium was the reason why the organizers said the Marathon should be rerouted through central London as the event would be inaccessible to spectators.

According to calculations, nearly £1 billion is being spent on the largest security operation in the UK since the Second World War, with around 7,000 private security guards, in addition to the police, employed by the different venues, carrying out CCTV monitoring, stewarding, access controls and magnetic detector bag searches.[39] Following the Tokyo and Seoul Olympics the security legacy was one of permanent private policing. In London, private security will in any case be a feature of all the Olympic developments, as they are all privately owned and privately controlled, but other security innovations introduced during the Games are also set to become a permanent part of the landscape.

Chief among these is the use of 'Drones', the unmanned spyplanes used in Iraq and Afghanistan and modified for civilian use in Los Angeles in 2005. Drones are already being piloted by a number of British police forces, but the deployment of both civilian and military (RAF) Reaper Drones to monitor the Olympics is viewed by surveillance experts as likely to be 'a major catalyst' to a national rollout.[40]

What is particularly marked about the very high levels of security planned is just how little debate this generates. Drones hit the headlines when it was reported that the Merseyside Police Force was flying them without a licence, but the story disappeared after Merseyside promised that was an administrative error and pledged to get a licence. The spread of CCTV over the last fifteen years, despite the lack of evidence that it helps reduce crime, has also been characterized by a muted debate, especially compared to other countries. Similarly, the very high levels of security surrounding the Olympics and accompanying regeneration is not a part of the national debate. Instead, it feels unpatriotic, subversive even, to question whether so much security is necessary, as if to do so might provide succour to terrorism.

Contrast that response with the last Olympics in Vancouver. There, concerns about the consequences of the 2010 Olympic winter games – dubbed the 'surveillance games' – reached such a pitch that a group of academics signed the 'Vancouver statement', deploring the overuse of security technologies at the Games as responsible for fuelling a climate of fear. The statement, signed by more than 40 academics from five different countries, pointed out that contrary to the spirit of the Olympics, 'recent games have increasingly taken place in and contributed to a climate of fear, heightened security and surveillance and that has this has often been to the detriment of democracy'.[41]

Part of the reason for the silence surrounding security is the extent to which high levels of security have taken over so much of our public life in the UK, with all public buildings, in particular schools and hospitals, now built within defensible enclosures, surrounded by CCTV and high wire fences, with entry permitted only by remote-controlled access. Chapter 4 details how this approach took hold, through the spread of the police-backed design policy, 'Secured by Design', which ensures that planning permission for all new development is contingent on very high levels of security.

Nonetheless, the contrasting trends of security and shared space show that even if there is little vocal debate around the subject there is interest in creating inclusive, genuinely public places among some British policymakers. Daniel Moylan was also responsible for assisting the Mayor with his 'Manifesto for Public Space', published at the end of 2009. This states explicitly that the adoption of streets and public places is 'an important principle' which should be negotiated in all new schemes, to counter the 'corporatisation' and 'growing trend towards the private management of publicly accessible space.'[42]

As the Mayor has planning powers in London this is an important policy statement, which can be enforced. Although it has come too late to affect the Olympic developments it has the status of legislation and should ensure that from now on streets and public places in London are adopted by local authorities and remain genuinely public. But despite this, Moylan is not confident that all local authorities will abide by the Mayor's Manifesto for Public Space because many 'have given up' their democratic responsibilities. 'They don't want to adopt roads because of the cost,' he says.

Because there has been so little development recently, bar the Olympics, it is not possible to test the impact of the Manifesto, but the London Assembly recently published a review of public space which implies that the growing private ownership of public space is an inevitability and that the best way to ensure democratic rights is for local authorities to negotiate agreements with developers to ensure public access.[43] So, in this way democratic rights to the city, such as the right to political protest in public places, would become conditional on agreements with developers.

In the policy areas covered by *Ground Control*, the government has given up its democratic responsibilities, handing over responsibility for the public realm and for housing of the poor to the private sector. Another factor, with echoes in other areas of domestic policy, is that the government does not want to see regulation or intervention, claiming that the self regulation of, in this case private renting, will suffice. Meanwhile, although the economic rationale for this way of doing things has collapsed, the intention is not merely to return to business as usual as soon as possible but to pursue a model which is even more extreme than the previous one. This is the phenomenon of 'Tesco Towns', with the superstore now responsible for creating entire communities, including hundreds of homes and schools, not to mention streets and public places.

Spenhill, the regeneration subsidiary of Tesco, is planning 'district centres' in Gateshead, Kirby, West Bromwich, Bradley Stoke, Shepton Mallet, Seaton in Devon and in Bromley-by-Bow in East London and Woolwich and Streatham in the south. In Bromley-by-Bow the proposed district centre, which overlooks a dual carriageway, was heavily criticised by the Commission for Architecture and the Built Environment for an application to build hundreds of homes overlooking the A12 Blackwall Tunnel, while the new school would be tacked onto the Tesco delivery yard, which would mean that children would have to cross the car park to get there. Despite CABE's criticism, the scheme received planning permission. Following the damning review Tesco did go back to the drawing board but CABE's design review did not approve their revised application either, recommending it should not get planning permission.[44]

Sir John Sorrell, the former chair of the Commission for Architecture and the Built Environment, described how this was the next wave of development. 'Our concern is not only the quality of this kind of development – which is generally very poor – but the way in which architecture and places are created in the image of the retailer.'[45] In every one of these places the local authority has been very keen to get the proposals through, often in the face of huge public protest accompanied by the kinds of dirty tricks and subterfuge that are well documented in later chapters. When local government refuses to reflect the engagement of the voting public and to support democratic processes can anything be done? Local democracy should ensure that councillors who support unpopular proposals are voted out, but when decisions are not made locally that can't happen. These failures in local democracy are mirrored by the recent failures in parliament and the situation is not helped by the trend in contemporary politics, hit by scandals and crises, to conclude that both the state and the market have failed. It is this space that the vague notion of the 'Big Society' is attempting to occupy.

One answer, which is rarely explicitly acknowledged, is to abandon democracy and the ideal of citizenship. This is exactly what is being facilitated by the continuing private takeover of parts of the city. Developer Crispin Kelly explains. 'The idea that public space needs to be managed and mothered by the state is left over from the notion that when we go out in public we are exercising our role as citizen. In fact now we are largely going out for entertainment and shopping, and the codes developed for shopping centres have turned out to deliver both what the punter wants and the investor needs: safe, clean and orderly places. Now these codes can be applied more widely.'[46]

A combination of the marketing power of the companies involved, the technical complexity of the areas under discussion and the power of social silence means that this vital debate is rarely heard. It is particularly disturbing that this is peculiar to Britain, with a far more lively debate on these subjects in the US, Canada and continental Europe.

The only way to counter this trend, in every aspect of our politics, is for a new constitutional settlement that will put the idea of the public good back at the centre of the public realm. When it comes to the physical public realm, the concept of the 'public good' or 'public benefit' was quietly removed from planning legislation in 2004, with no discussion or debate. Chapter 2 describes how this happened. It contrasts the situation with the US, where a similar change followed a Supreme Court Judgement in 2005. However, over there it caused a huge national outcry, with protestors camping on the White House lawn to the point where former President George W. Bush personally intervened. The consequence of that campaign is that a large number of states have now revoked the legislation. In other European countries, such as France, the public good remains at the centre of planning policy, with the 'Declaration d'utilite publique' ensuring that public benefit is at the centre of a proposed project.

If the public good was the benchmark test for new development, the concept would be at the heart of the legal system when it comes to the public realm and so many decisions about Olympic regeneration would have been made differently, paving the way for a public-spirited legacy which really was in tune with the Festival of Britain and the Great Exhibition. The Wellcome Trust's proposal for the Olympic Park would have stood a better chance of success and the pledges signed as part of the Ethical Olympics Agreement would have been met. A planning system based on the public good would be able to enforce the Mayor's Manifesto on Public Space and would stop the rise of 'Tesco Towns' in their tracks when they are overwhelmingly opposed by local communities. But in all the government's discussions of 'localism' – which is rooted in the idea that local people should make local decisions – the concept of the public good has failed to get a single mention.

The legalistic response of the ODA, that it did not have to abide by the ethical Olympics agreement because it is 'illegal to dictate the terms of contracts struck under open tender', would not hold water if planning for the public good, in the interests of the community as a whole, was at the centre of planning policy. One of the main effects of privatising places is the proliferation of hundreds of agencies, quangos and competing companies which is not only confusing and bureaucratic but that also fractures the public realm into atomised, disconnected units, which makes the creation of holistic plans for places much more difficult. The government is planning to introduce neighbourhood plans, but as the guiding principle of the new National Planning Policy framework is that planning 'must not act as an impediment to growth', there is little chance that these plans will defend the public good.[47]

As we continue to live in a representative democracy, where we elect councillors to local government and MPs to parliament, promoting the notion that both the state and the market have failed is not only intellectually lazy but undemocratic. The problem is that the market has squeezed the notion of the public good out of the state, with the result that local government is failing to represent the wishes of local people. This can only be countered by putting the public good back into the centre of the legal system regarding the public realm. Reinvigorating local government and local democracy, not to mention national democracy, is a harder task. Without the correct legal tools it will be almost impossible.

PART ONE: THE CITY

The George, Isle of Dogs, London

I

Docklands: The Birth of an Idea

This book was conceived in a boom and written in a bust. It is about the emotional impact of an environment created during the 1990s, a period when Britain's unregulated economy built an architecture of boom and bust. Apartments in gated developments, security, private streets and plazas are its motifs, sitting side by side with enclaves of poverty. In the 1980s, when I was growing up, this cityscape, fuelled by the soaring value of private property, or 'real estate', as the Americans would say, barely existed in Britain. Now, a generation later, this way of doing things, which was pioneered in London's Docklands, has taken root in towns and cities around Britain, changing the physical fabric, the culture and the government of the places we live in. It's an approach that owes a lot to American ideas, yet has a peculiarly British twist.

In 1979, when Mrs Thatcher came to power, Britain's industrial base was in the throes of collapse. All around the country industrial heartlands were in decline, nowhere more visibly than in Docklands. Once the largest port in the world, Docklands was reduced to a largely derelict wasteland, bereft of its economic base and identity. Tens of thousands of jobs were lost, factories were abandoned and the riverfront was crumbling. In 1989, as the Cold War came to an end and the political economist Francis Fukuyama declared 'the end of history', Canary Wharf, the emblem of Thatcher's free-market revolution, was going up.

The foundations of the landmark tower, One Canada Square, the tallest building in Britain, were laid at the height of the 1980s' boom. It followed the deregulation of the financial markets, which was the catalyst for the exponential growth of the global financial services industry in Britain. The 1980s established the physical, technological and regulatory framework for an unfettered financial services industry in the UK, to replace the failing industrial economy. This 'new' economy was powered by the abolition of exchange controls and the 1986 deregulation of the stock exchange, an event known as 'Big Bang' because of the increase in market activity. It not only changed the culture of the City of London for ever, it brought with it a boom in property development which created a new corporate architecture. Small firms, with their personal connections, made way for global investment banks, which required very large electronic trading floors, trading in abstract and complex financial instruments like options, derivatives and futures. As the 1980s progressed, 'Big Bang' architecture saw two new financial centres emerge: in Docklands, and at the nearby Broadgate Centre, also in east London.

These places were quite unlike any others in Britain. Not because they were centres for international finance, but because they were privately owned. The Canary Wharf Estate and the Broadgate Centre are private property, in the same way that a country estate, a shopping mall or someone's house is private property. The rules that govern the rest of the city do not apply. Rather than being unconditionally open to the public, like the rest of the city, it is up to the owner to decide who is allowed in and what they are allowed to do there. As a consequence, private-security guards police and control the area, making sure the rules are enforced.

Alongside the private estates where employees went to work, shop and enjoy themselves in waterfront bars and restaurants, a new type of high-security living behind gates and walls mushroomed across Docklands. It introduced a way of life based on living in gated communities; very popular in America, it was virtually unknown in Britain. As former warehouses were turned into waterside apartments overlooking the old docks, Docklands became one of the earliest places to build large numbers of gated developments, providing homes for the high-earning professionals who worked in the neighbouring steel and glass towers. Because much of the area remained among the poorest and most deprived in Britain, the gates and high security were marketed to offer reassurance to the finance professionals who were the pioneers of the new economy, living on the frontline.

For Mrs Thatcher and Michael Heseltine, who was instrumental in kick-starting Docklands as secretary of state for environment, the deprivation of the area was a central justification for what was being created. The development slotted in perfectly with one of the defining concepts of Thatcherite economics: 'trickle-down'. This is the idea that the creation of wealth in an area will 'trickle down' to the poorer parts which need it the most.

'Trickle-down' justified the new private estates, which are underpinned by the idea of being very profitable ventures in themselves, pulling in high rents and billing high service charges. Most important of all, they promised to transform places by increasing not only their own property values but those in the surrounding area, bringing in so much wealth that it somehow flows out of the gates of the gated properties and 'trickles down' to the surrounding poor. This was the idea of 'regeneration', a word which came into use during the 1980s, and means 'rebirth' in Latin. Rather than the more prosaic 'redevelopment', it conjures up the image of the phoenix of Canary Wharf and the new economy rising from the ashes of Docklands and Britain's industrial past.[1]

Yet despite the pioneering zeal of their supporters, when they were built Broadgate and Canary Wharf were controversial, perceived as high-security enclaves of wealth surrounded by some of the poorest communities in Britain. They were also exceptional places – areas where business modelled the area in its own image in what are, after all, finance districts. Now, a generation later, what began specifically to serve the needs of business has become the standard model for the creation of every new place in towns and cities across the country. Previously, the government and local councils 'owned' the city on behalf of us, the people. Now more and more of the city is owned by investors, and its central purpose is profit. The credit crunch may have slowed the sell-off, but every former inner-city industrial area is trying to emulate this model, from the waterfronts of Salford Quays and Cardiff to the controversial demolition programmes of the old industrial northern cities. This is the architecture of post-industrial New Labour, a government which witnessed the largest amount of construction in Britain since the post-war period. But just as the tower blocks and arterial roads of the industrial 1950s and 1960s sliced through cities and communities and failed to stand the test of time, the consequences of many of these grand schemes are disturbing. Because this book is based on a journey around Britain, Docklands, where the architecture of extreme capitalism first began, seems like a good place to begin to ask how this happened.

Does Trickle-Down Work?

I worked at South Quay in Docklands during the mid to late 1990s, when it was a half-built, windswept place, with a smattering of shops and the absence of any life at all after 6 pm. Ten minutes' walk away, the main centre at Canary Wharf was barely more lively. A decade later, emerging from Canary Wharf, one of the most breathtaking stations on the London Underground, it was clear that Docklands had changed again. Although the station favours concrete rather than marble and chandeliers, in its sheer confidence, with its vaulted ceilings stretching up, it seemed, to the sky, it reminded me of the grandeur of Stalin's Moscow Metro.

Coming up out of the magnificent station I found myself in Reuters Plaza, a new pedestrianized square bounded by the pub chain All Bar One and the restaurant chain Carluccio's. Electronic tickertape was running across one half of the square, giving me the latest information on international share prices, courtesy of Reuters. To the north of the square, overlooking Carluccio's, was a large plasma screen tuned to Reuters' financial television news. It was lunchtime and, despite the collapse of a number of banks, the place was busy, as people hurried to buy their sandwiches, rushing back to work or to meetings, talking on mobiles and blackberries as they went. I decided to buy a sandwich, too, and made for the shopping mall at Canary Wharf, where upmarket sandwich bars jostled with luxury brands.

With the lunch hour over, it quietened down and I saw that a number of new roads had been built. A security guard in a motorized buggy trundled past me, his uniform emblazoned with Canary Wharf Estate on the back. More guards could be seen walking around.

I remembered why some of my colleagues had told me they particularly liked working at Canary Wharf. One was fascinated and somehow pleased by the fact that all the lifts in the Tower were equipped with a power point, located in the same place in every lift. Another friend told me that she liked commuting to Canary Wharf because the Jubilee Line carriages always stopped in exactly the same place, so she knew where to stand on the platform.

Canary Wharf is a high-tech environment, a self-contained complex where shops and bars and restaurants provide employees with everything they could want, without them needing to go further afield. South Quay, which is where the IRA bomb exploded in 1996, is half a mile away. Part of the second phase of development and not quite at the hub of things, it is home to a similar mix of media and financial services groups, based in smoky-glass buildings and watched over by large amounts of security and surveillance. So it was only after leaving the big private enclave at South Quay's Harbour Exchange Square that I was able to get a feel for how new Docklands is knitting together with the rest of the area.

Walking down towards the Isle of Dogs from Harbour Exchange Square, it seemed to me that South Quay had spread. But when I reached Crossharbour, which is the next stop on the Docklands Light Railway, a sharp dividing line between new Docklands and the old communities on the Isle of Dogs became clear. On one side of the road, by the station, are newly built office blocks and a host of construction sites, while on the other side is a dilapidated housing estate. In between is the George pub, which flies a flag of St George from its roof, and seems to mark a boundary point, set in the shadow of the skyscrapers, on the corner of one of Millwall's housing estates. This pub could not be more different from the All Bar One of Reuters Plaza, and the contrast between the two sides of the road could not have been greater.

The George is a typical East End pub, which maintains the traditional division between the 'working men's bar' and the 'lounge'. I can guarantee that when I walked in on a Friday afternoon, no one from the offices opposite was drinking there. Carrying on down from the George into Millwall, I could see the towers looming. To my right was a low-rise 1960s' estate, badly in need of repair, with peeling paint flaking from the windows and doors. The people were entirely different, too. In place of the blackberried professionals in a hurry were a few mothers, some white, some Asian and veiled, pushing prams. A group of teenagers larked up the street.

Further on, I came across a small parade of shops, which included a newsagent, betting shop, electrical shop and hairdresser. In the off-licence at the end of the parade all the goods were barricaded behind perspex walls and the cashier dealt with customers through a grilled window. In the electrical shop I met Alan, who, at sixty, has lived on the Isle of Dogs all his life. Tight-lipped, he told me, 'It's all altered – I don't know hardly anyone, most people have gone.' In the hairdresser's I spoke to Pat. 'I've lived on the island for thirty-seven years, it's just gone from docks and council property to conglomerates and private buyers,' she said. 'What I wish they'd done differently is made things more affordable for the locals,' she said, adding, 'Local people don't get a look in where jobs are concerned.' In 1993 unemployment on the Isle of Dogs was running at more than 25 per cent, feeding into support for the British National Party and the subsequent election of BNP councillor Derek Beacon. Elected on a ticket of jobs and homes for local people, it was the first time the far-right party had won a council seat in Britain. Though Beacon served only one term, the divisions in the area have become ever more pronounced, with the local workforce lacking the skills to work in the new financial services industries. And the segregation is not limited to jobs, filtering through to every aspect of people's lives. When I asked Pat whether she used the shops at Canary Wharf, she admitted, 'I don't like going there. It always gives me the fear.'

In Disraeli's famous polemic *Sybil*, written in 1845, he talks of 'two nations' who are as 'ignorant of each other's habits, thoughts and feelings as if they were dwellers in different zones, or inhabitants of different planets'. Walking around the Isle of Dogs, I felt the environment was a different planet to the hi-tech, protected enclave up the road, where people really were as ignorant of each other's habits and way of life as if they were dwellers in different zones. It was also clear that none of the wealth from the neighbouring skyscrapers had found its way on to Millwall's housing estates or into the pockets of their residents; parts of the Isle of Dogs are among the poorest areas in the country, according to the government's Index of Multiple Deprivation. Millwall lies in the borough of Tower Hamlets, where 23.5 per cent were without work in 2007, a figure which is likely to be much higher today.[2]

Rather than wealth trickling down, it had spread, from Canary Wharf to South Quay to Crossharbour. But rather than helping those who need it the most, it has rubbed right up against them yet entirely ignored them, creating a segregated and disconnected patchwork. At the same time the spreading effect has continued to displace the original community, as property prices ensured new homes remained unaffordable for locals, forced to move out further east to boroughs like Barking and Dagenham, or deeper into Essex. In Docklands, which is part of one of the most ethnically diverse boroughs in the country, this inadvertently fuels racial tensions, as white families, fearful of the acute shortage of housing, look resentfully at Asian neighbours in council housing. 'Paul', who didn't want to be identified, told me: 'We're becoming a minority and people think they're getting the short end of the deal.' Explaining, Paul said, 'People don't want to live in a ghetto,' by which he meant a white ghetto, but, looking around me, it felt that what he was really describing was a ghetto of poverty surrounded by the untouchable wealth of the global financial élite.

Trickle down hasn't worked in Docklands or in any of the other places I'm going to visit on this journey where the same model of economic growth based on increasing property values has been rolled out. Yet this model endures because of the high rates of growth it brings in good times, even if the benefits are very unevenly spread, entrenching enclaves of poverty as well as wealth.

Perhaps another reason is wish-fulfilment. The idea that creating wealth in an area will cascade down to help the poorest communities is pleasing and seems logical – it sounds like something that should work. But when all the evidence shows that this fails to happen, those in favour of this growth model fall back on 'TINA', the acronym for 'There is No Alternative'. This largely forgotten term was once a well-known and much-loved Thatcherite mantra, deployed in the same vein as other resounding calls to arms, such as 'The Lady is Not for Turning'.

Yet TINA, and the architecture of the new economy, is a fallacy. It forecloses the option of far more balanced, healthy change. It is undermining democracy and creating fractures in the nature of civic society. This book is not an argument against change, but it is an argument against the type of change we have pursued, laid out in Docklands more than twenty years ago.

The Story of Docklands

The new Docklands developed slowly. During the late 1980s angry communities on the Isle of Dogs watched as the foundations of the first skyscrapers were laid. It couldn't have been more different a couple of generations previously, in the heyday of the docks, when the West India and East India Docks, St Katharine's Dock and the Royal Docks were symbols of Britain's industrial economy and the trading might of the empire. The West India Dock was the first to open, in 1802, bringing coffee, sugar and rum from the West Indies, and as the empire expanded and grew in power so did the docks. Then as now, Canary Wharf, which was a large cargo warehouse until the mid 1960s, was at the centre.[3] Historically, the East End of London has always been the poorest part of the capital, but, the docks were a commercial hub. At its height the Port of London Authority employed 100,000 men, but by the time Mrs Thatcher came to power, those days were almost over and the West India dock closed in 1980.

How did Docklands move from being a place of abandoned wharves to a humming global financial centre? The answer lies in a series of policies pursued by the Thatcher government from its earliest days in power. These policies, affecting property and planning law, paved the way for New Labour's approach to our cities.

The academic Sir Peter Hall explains that the essential concept was 'the American one of leverage',[4] where public money is spent with the aim of pulling in private investment and increasing property prices. The way this was done in Docklands was through the creation of a very 1980s' type of quango, the Urban Development Corporation, or UDC, brought in by an Act of Parliament in 1980. These quangos – that 1980s' term for 'quasi non-governmental organizations' – were organizations funded by public money from the taxpayer even though they were unelected. Very powerful bodies, they were also parachuted into Merseyside, Tyneside and a host of other large industrial areas.

Although the UDCs were very much of their time, the principles they enshrined, of leverage and increasing property values, have defined policies towards cities ever since. This has been particularly the case since New Labour came to power and the Treasury began to play such a prominent role in policies towards property.[5] One of the main reasons why they were so powerful was because of the Conservatives' mistrust of left-wing local authorities. The UDCs were a way to bypass them. The consequence was that, rather like the New Town Corporations of the post-war period, they had almost total control over their designated area, with all the planning and economic development powers of local government, the ability to buy and sell land and to spend millions in public money without discussion or debate. The difference, of course, is that where the New Towns were led by the public sector, these quangos were chaired by property developers.

One of their most important powers, which is obscured by the complex and technical language of planning law, was called 'land assembly', which included 'compulsory purchase powers'. This meant huge tracts of land and property could be joined together, creating enormous new areas. This was achieved by taking over all the public-sector land in an area and buying up homes and local businesses – by force if need be. Handing over these powers to the private sector was something of a novelty at the time. A generation later, it is essential to the creation of new private places.

In Docklands, the result was an area of eight and half square miles which functioned outside the normal planning laws of the country, with no recourse to local democracy. This was why, despite opposition from local communities and politicians, it was able to radically transform the area so quickly. In contrast to the decade of indecision and inactivity which followed the effective closure of the docks, the Corporation got things done, assembling thousands of acres of land and setting up an enterprise zone on the Isle of Dogs, giving investors and developers massive tax breaks as well as freedom from planning restrictions.

The Corporation's own official history describes, with an element of pride, how the area ripped up the planning system, recounting that 'it was breaking all the rules'.[6] Finally taking decisions about the future of Docklands was much needed; Brian Robson, director of the Centre for Urban Policy Studies at Manchester University, wrote that 'the "miracle" of Docklands is miraculous only because it has taken so long to materialize'.[7] Yet the way it was done was questionable and faced huge opposition, not only from local people, but from MPs and commentators across the spectrum. Nigel Spearing, the local Labour MP in Newham, exclaimed, 'The whole of Canary Wharf needed less planning scrutiny than a change of use from a newsagent to a fish and chip shop,' while commentator Simon Jenkins wrote that the Corporation resembled a colonial edict 'imposing emergency rule on a defeated tribe'.[8] Chris Shepley, who was President of the Royal Town Planning Institute during the late 1980s, was also an outspoken critic. 'I thought it was an unplanned solution. There was no design ethos to it – anything went. I thought at the time, and still do, that was wrong. There were more or less no planning rules,' he told me.

In Docklands, the leverage effect of public money, tax incentives and freedom from planning laws had the desired effect, pump-priming land values and starting a property boom which is often described as a gold rush. The aim had been to attract property developers and build an office district to rival the City, creating a property market where there hadn't been one before.

It worked, and property prices soared as the billions spent in public money were almost quadrupled by the amount of private money pulled in.⁹ For the American consultants employed in Docklands, schooled in the new architecture and hoping to create a 'mini-Manhattan' on the Thames,¹⁰ things were going well, although critical MPs feared that at best the place would be a finance district cheek by jowl with housing estates.¹¹

Then the crash of the late 1980s hit. Bob Barlow, a marketing consultant who worked with Barratt Homes and other developers in Docklands for twenty years, described the bipolar atmosphere of the time: 'In the late 1980s it was like the Yukon gold rush in the whole Docklands area. Places such as Limehouse were totally overheated and developers were building orange boxes and practically giving away free Porsches with them. It was exciting, but it was frightening. Then the whole thing went belly up.'¹² By 1992 the Canary Wharf Estate itself had gone bust and its owner had to file for bankruptcy.

By 1997, when New Labour came to power, Docklands had recovered and was considered such an exemplar by Tony Blair that he chose to host his first Anglo-French summit on the thirty-eighth floor of Canary Wharf Tower. Today, notwithstanding the global financial collapse, it is one of the world's foremost finance and media centres. Whether it provides a sustainable economic model for creating places and whether it creates a healthy psychological environment are different questions altogether.

Private Lives

Bow Quarter was one of the first Victorian factories converted into a gated community. Once the Bryant and May matchmaking factory, it closed in 1979. By 1988, just as the foundations of Canary Wharf were being laid, the disused factory, which is a listed building, was being converted into a luxury gated enclave of 700 apartments with its own gym and swimming pool, supermarket, bar and restaurant.

Nearby Canary Riverside is another gated community with twenty-four-hour private security, private gym, tennis courts and swimming pool. These private estates are at the luxury end of the market and were initially a new phenomenon to which very few people aspired, bar Mrs Thatcher herself, who bought a home in a gated development in 1985, while she was still in office. Today gated living is so common in Docklands that the majority of new homes include gates and electronic surveillance.

The ultimate private living and working environment in Docklands is ExCel, which includes an exhibition centre as big as Earls Court and Olympia combined, six hotels and 2,000 homes on its hundred-acre 'campus', which spans the length of the Royal Victoria Dock. Privately owned by a Malaysian conglomerate and run by a private company, ExCel is not just an exhibition centre but a private community.

With two and a half miles of corridors, the conference building is huge, something of a disadvantage if you arrive, as I did, at the wrong end. When there are no exhibitions on, walking from one end to the other reminded me of nothing more than an empty airport, with no one but security guards milling about. Piped pop music filtered in from unseen loudspeakers. I finally reached the workshop I was attending in one of the hundreds of seminar rooms, but later the sense of disorientation returned when I left the building with colleagues to find we had taken a wrong turn off one of the corridors, emerging into an area which was disconnected from the rest of the complex, rather like coming out of a car park on the wrong storey and finding no way of reaching ground level.

If the building feels disorientating and disconnected from its environment from the inside, it's no less alien from the outside, where a number of roads, clearly marked 'private', link ExCel into the motorway network for quick access to central London. But like the other transport link, the Docklands Light Railway, the motorway is on a different level from surrounding local communities in Canning Town, making it a very difficult place for local people to reach on foot, even though it is right next door. Such a lack of connection with the surrounding environment may seem hard to justify. Yet because ExCel hosts arms fairs such as the Defence Systems and Equipment International conference, it is clearly more than a happy coincidence. Explaining, ExCel's estates manager was keen to tell me that the site can, if necessary, be surrounded by a 'ring of steel' to make the entire place 'a completely secure site'. ExCel was designed and completed before the terrorist attacks of 9/11, but it is easy to see why, as terrorism has ratcheted up the political agenda, ExCel's focus on security – and the disconnection from the surrounding environment that comes with it – is seen as more and more of an advantage.

Living and working in high-security private environments enables wealthy professionals to move almost seamlessly from office to luxury waterfront apartment or from conference centre to airport with minimal contact with the surrounding environment. The problem is that, even if the journey to and from work involves driving from one secure car park to another, there will be times when contact with the outside world cannot be avoided. When this happens, new research is highlighting that people who are normally insulated in private environments become unusually anxious. On the other hand, those on the outside, like Pat on the Isle of Dogs, fear the new private places, suspecting they are not meant for the likes of them.

Counter-intuitively, there is also mounting evidence that far from promoting the feelings of reassurance and safety promised in the developers' brochures, it is the blatantly security-conscious environments themselves which are responsible for growing levels of fear, for those behind the gates and those outside. Fear creates unhappiness. Part of the argument of this book is that this changing landscape is one reason why levels of unhappiness are higher in Britain than ever before, comparable only with the United States.[13]

2

The Death of the City

Coming out of White City tube station in west London's Shepherd's Bush, Television Centre, the modernist BBC building, dominates the landscape. Built on the cusp of the 1960s, it brings to mind black-and-white television and a time when public-service broadcasting ruled the airwaves, with its mission to inform as well as entertain, courtesy of public-spirited documentaries and a man at a desk with a microphone. On the other side of the road an enormous box structure looms, emblazoned with the logo 'Westfield' in a jaunty red script. Westfield London, the biggest shopping centre in central London, which opened in 2008, is another place which reflects its function and its time, built towards the end of a decade when property development and shopping radically changed every British town and city.

During the eighties, alongside the 'Big Bang' architecture of Canary Wharf and Broadgate, the phenomenon of out-of-town shopping centres was the architectural signature of Thatcherism. Places such as Bluewater in Kent, Lakeside in Essex, Meadowhall in Sheffield, the Trafford Centre in Manchester and the MetroCentre in Gateshead opened as a result of Mrs Thatcher's loosening of the planning system, a policy which was later reversed, because of the damaging effect it had on high streets in towns and cities. What has happened under New Labour is that, to find a way around planning restrictions, shopping centres have moved wholesale into the centre of cities. Westfield London is one example, but what is increasingly common is the creation of open-air property complexes which also own and control the streets, squares and open spaces of the city. Like Docklands, which was able to assemble a huge area of land because of the powers of the UDCs, these new places are able to take over large parts of our cities using similar powers.

East Village, Madison Square, Liverpool

Liverpool One, the huge new private shopping complex in the centre of Liverpool which covers thirty-four streets in the heart of the city, is the biggest so far. Today, every town and city is home to these new places, large and small, built on brownfield sites and owned and run by property companies. A brownfield site is the technical term for land, normally in cities, which has previously been used by industry, unlike the virgin land of a 'greenfield' site. Their main distinguishing feature is that, like Canary Wharf and the Broadgate Centre, these parts of the city are privately owned and privately controlled, which gives them quite a different feel from the rest of the city. In their defence, politicians and developers point out that people like these places and flock to shop there, but they are also raising a challenge to a type of public life, public culture and democracy in British cities which has been taken for granted for the last 150 years.

Before Liverpool One was completed, I met one of the developers in charge of the project. He explained to me that the aim was to create more Bluewaters, but this time within the city. 'I think what's been going on for the last five or six years is that people have been visiting regional shopping centres like Meadowhall and Bluewater and finding them much cleaner and safer than other parts of city centres. They don't care about the legal niceties, they just wonder why some parts are managed better. Our desire is to use the same principles applied to the major shopping malls, such as Bluewater, but in the context of the city centre,' he said.

When I went to visit Westfield London, I wanted to see what impact Westfield, an Australian property-development company, had on the architecture and the look and feel of this part of Shepherd's Bush. The company is also in the process of recreating a far bigger part of the capital to the east, at Stratford City, one of the main sites for the 2012 London Olympics. Like Liverpool One, Stratford City will not be a covered shopping mall but effectively a private city within a city.

Westfield London is big. It's the third-largest shopping centre in the UK, behind Bluewater in Kent and the MetroCentre in Gateshead. But apart from its size, which is apparently equivalent to thirty football pitches, it is remarkably similar to any other shopping centre I've ever been to. There were lots and lots of shops and acres of pristine marble floors, but little to distinguish this place from any other or to remind me that I was in west London, with Television Centre outside the doors and down-at-heel Shepherd's

Bush Green down the road. A friend who lives nearby told me more and more of the small tatty shops which fringe the Green have been forced out of business by the new mall. In Westfield London I didn't feel as if I was in Shepherd's Bush but, just as at ExCel, more as if I was in an airport, behind the departure gates, in that transnational shopping area, a place which is neither home nor abroad.

Stratford City is a far more ambitious project, but the principles Westfield has applied in Shepherd's Bush are the closest guide to what can be expected by the time it is completed in 2011. At the time of writing, work had started on this enormous place but was far from completion, so, Westfield London apart, the best way of getting a feel for what it would be like was the view from the top floor of Holden Point, a tower block overlooking the building site. A viewing platform had been built there, with a specially constructed toilet, created for the queen's use when she visited.

With the wind whistling around the twenty-first floor, I looked down at the tiny matchstick figures of construction workers and mechanical diggers below, and listened as the tour guide outlined the vision for the future. 'The shopping centre here will be bigger than Bluewater,' she said. To the right the international train station was clearly visible and to the left she pointed to a huge area for the 'very large retail park', including hundreds of shops, cafés and restaurants, and thousands of homes, which will include the accommodation for the athletes' Olympic Village.

According to Westfield, Stratford City is 'the largest retail-led development in the UK, probably in Europe'. When I went to see one of the developers at the company, he described it to me as 'the last big site in London', where 'you can start to see a small town'. With its seventy-three hectares of former railway land, it is, like Docklands, the ultimate brownfield site. Over the last fifteen years entirely new places have been created in these former industrial areas all over Britain, but of all these, because of its sheer size and its association with the Olympics, Stratford City is the flagship. As the developer said, 'It's the first time we have done anything like this.'

It isn't the first time for London, though. By 2011 London, like most British cities, will be intercut with similar places, from Paddington Basin in the west – an enormous privately owned place the size of Soho – to the huge new development at King's Cross. Dotted around are a great many far smaller places which are run along similar lines, from Regent's Place in Euston to Cardinal Place in

Victoria. Similar developments have gone up or are planned all around the country in old industrial cities and seaside towns, regional centres, commuter towns and market towns, in Preston, Crawley, Leeds, Sheffield, Liverpool, Wells. The consequence is the creation of a new world, where town and city centres are becoming little more than shopping complexes, albeit without actual walls – places which are described by their critics in America as 'malls without walls'.[1] On the surface these places may not sound like they have that much in common with the creation of finance districts like Canary Wharf and the Broadgate Centre, but in essence they are almost identical.

Who Owns the Streets?

What has happened in the newly created places all around Britain has parallels with the early nineteenth century, before the advent of local government. Before local democracy took hold, much of the capital was owned by a small of group of private landlords, members of the aristocracy who were mainly dukes and earls. The Earl of Bedford controlled Covent Garden, the Earl of Southampton had the Bloomsbury Estate, and the Duke of Westminster ran the whole of northern Mayfair, Belgravia and Pimlico.[2] Today, the Duke of Westminster runs Grosvenor, the property company which owns and controls Liverpool One, but this direct link to the landlords of old is becoming the exception to the rule. Multinational property corporates are now the most likely owners of large chunks of British cities.

According to an article written in 1856 in the *Saturday Review*, the growth of London was down to 'the simple unchecked competition of rival estates sent into the market to hustle against each other'. The landlords were effectively master planners who could determine the whole social, economic and architectural character of a neighbourhood. According to the writer Donald Olsen, there were good ones and bad ones. In contrast to the contemporary drive to make the maximum profit out of places, because of their great wealth and high social position, the landlords of old were able 'to plan without a continual preoccupation with immediate financial returns', concentrating on the long-term future of their estates instead.[3]

What we don't see today is the degree to which these parts of London, which include some of the finest Georgian and early Victorian squares, were fortified by hundreds of gates, bars and posts. Now some of the most open and public parts of the city, great efforts used to be made by the landlords to protect those inside the gates from the outside world. The estates employed their own private-security forces and, in one particularly well-guarded patch on the boundary of the Bedford Estate and disreputable Camden Town, there were five sentry boxes. The Bedford Estate used uniformed ex-prison officers to patrol their enclave and when a fight over entry into the area broke out, leading to a death, the coroner is recorded as saying that government conduct was 'disgraceful in allowing these squares and places to be closed to the public'.[4]

These comments reflect a general tide of public opinion which started to turn against the private estates with their gates, private roads and private streets, an opposition which swelled as local government grew in power. By 1864–5, after two major parliamentary inquiries, 163 miles of road were passed over to local-authority control and 140 toll bars were removed. By the 1880s, anger at the remaining restrictions caused the *Daily Telegraph* to denounce the 'persistence on the part of a few great landowners in a selfish and tyrannical policy' and proclaim that 'the noble obstructors of the queen's highway have enjoyed that fantastically feudal privilege quite long enough'.[5] Since then it has been common practice for local authorities to 'adopt' the streets and public spaces of the city, meaning that whether or not they actually own them, they control and run them.

As control over streets and public places moved away from the landed gentry to democratically elected local government, local authorities also began to build up the amount of land and property they owned, although the pattern of landownership in Britain has always been and remains incredibly complex. Property experts estimate that today local authorities are, after the Forestry Commission, the second biggest landlord in the country,[6] but a typical pattern of ownership in most British cities would include a mix of property owned by the local authority, institutional investors, small and large businesses and individual property owners.

As the twenty-first-century corporate estates take over large parts of the city, the last decade has seen a huge shift in landownership, away from streets, public places and buildings in public ownership and towards the creation of new private estates, primarily given over to shopping and office complexes, which, while not actually gated, feel very much like separate enclaves. At the same time, control of the streets is being handed back to the estates, reversing the democratic achievements of the Victorians.

This is a very significant shift. Land and property which has been in public hands for 150 years or more is moving back into private hands. It is difficult to find out exactly how much land is being sold off, because, unlike the United States and most of Europe, Britain does not have a proper record of what is owned by whom. When I asked a solicitor from the Land Registry about this I was surprised to hear him say, 'We are often asked, "Who owns Britain?" and people are astonished and shocked when we say we don't know.'[7] What is well known is that the sale of what are described as 'local-authority assets' is a major plank of government policy, with a government target of sales of £30 billion by 2010 and billions of pounds in sales already recorded.

Who controls the roads and streets is, as the Victorian protestors were well aware, enormously important to how cities function. Today there has been no public debate about the selling of the streets at all. Instead, as ownership of British cities goes back to private landlords, the process of removing public rights of way is buried in the arcane language and technical detail of one of the most obscure parts of planning law, which is normally the province only of highways departments. To try to understand it, I went to see a planning lawyer at a top City law firm. He explained to me that the private estates are able to abolish traditional rights of way through a process known as 'stopping-up orders'. This changes the legal basis of public highways, which may have been there for centuries, making them public no longer. Bringing home to me just what a significant change this is, he told me that there is an adage in highway law which says 'once a highway always a highway'. 'It's a common-law right which goes back to before the Conquest. It's one of those things about being a free-born English person,' he said. In many British towns and cities, this common-law right is being quietly removed.

Compulsory Purchase and 'Public Benefit'

Although there are parallels with the old nineteenth-century landlords, there are differences too. One of them is that the rise of these estates is the consequence of specific policies towards planning introduced as a result of the government's enthusiasm to create places like this.

The main policy concerns what is known as 'land assembly', or 'compulsory purchase', which was so important to the creation of Docklands. Compulsory purchase is a crucial piece of legislation, but, like so many aspects of planning law, most people have never heard of it. Over the last ten years the detail of this body of law has changed significantly, enabling the big private landlords to buy up all the land and property in a given area by forcing businesses and property owners to sell if the landlords are able to prove that the development will be of public benefit. The big change was brought in by an Act of Parliament in 2004. It altered the definition of 'public benefit', by placing far greater importance on the economic impact of a big new scheme, rather than taking into account the effect on the community. This change is very similar to recent legislation passed in the United States.

My pinstriped planning lawyer agrees that the legislative change that took place in 2004 is very important, but although he supports the private estates, the way he described how the government had put together the legislation shows how it was slipped in through the back door. 'There was no Big Bang legislative change, because the way this government does legislation is very crafty. They publish an Act and then they say, we'll fill in the details later through guidance and statutory instruments,' he said. So, while the legislation may not look very significant when it passes through parliament, by the time it becomes law, the addition of utterly obscure guidance and statutory instruments, which few people have noticed, ensures it is rather different.

Much of this book considers the effect of American policies imported to Britain. When I compared this legislation with its American counterpart, I was surprised to find that while it has raised no debate here, across the Atlantic it sparked off major national protests. In the US, compulsory purchase is called 'eminent domain', and when a Supreme Court Judgement brought about changes almost identical to Britain's 2004 Act, it was front-page news, protestors camped outside the home of one of the judges, and former President George W. Bush intervened. The issue, as in Britain, centred on the meaning of the 'public good', with the Judgement changing the definition of the 'public interest' to emphasize economic growth over community benefit. Critics claimed that misinterpreted the Fifth Amendment, benefiting large corporations at the expense of small businesses, homes and communities. Most US states are now considering legislation to curb the Judgement.

In the US the sanctity of private property is enshrined in national culture to such an extent that the rights of small property owners are far more closely guarded. As a result, when it comes to land and property, we are going much further than the Americans in our rush to privatize the city. Over here, it is very difficult to fight a compulsory purchase order when it is imposed by the local council, even though the story of every large new development project has an enormous human cost, as Chapter 5 on the housing market renewal policies of Britain's industrial cities shows. The legal importance of compulsory purchase remains under the radar for most people, bar those in the housing market renewal areas or people living near the sites of proposed infrastructure projects like the new runway at Heathrow. Even so, although the issue has failed to tap into the national consciousness in the same way that it has in America, planning battles around the demolition of parts of the city are routinely fought and the same questions are always debated. These debates are usually characterized by those in favour of development as the protests of nostalgic NIMBY conservationists who oppose all change, but the real issues go to the heart of the question of what kind of cities we want to live in.

At Spitalfields market in east London a campaign group known as SMUT – Spitalfields Market Under Threat – fought vociferously to save the old market from demolition, gathering 25,000 signatures in a bid to preserve what they described as an essential community asset. In 2002 they argued, 'Spitalfields residents do not want their market replaced by a soulless office development, a windswept corporate plaza and chain stores.'[8] In the end they lost their battle after thirteen years and the property company Hammerson built exactly the type of corporate plaza critics didn't want, next door to the tiny rump of the old market which was allowed to remain. The new development, which is patrolled by security guards with 'Spitalfields Estate' emblazoned on their jackets, promised to retain a market, but the official-looking market pitches and the pristine cleanliness, quite out of character with a real market, couldn't be more different from the old market next door. Eric Reynolds, a property developer who was at the centre of the campaign to save Spitalfields, feels 'the atmosphere has changed and it has become an extension of the Broadgate Centre rather than an extension of Brick Lane'.

The development in Liverpool of Liverpool One faced a similar planning row and public inquiry. The row focused on the survival of Quiggins, an indoor market of fifty or so arty shops and boutiques which had been a cultural icon in the city for a generation, launching the careers of musicians, designers and playwrights. In her statement presented to the inquiry, Claire Curtis Thomas, the MP for Crosby, said: 'What it [Liverpool] does not need is to become nothing more than another bland, characterless, sleek aggregation of top-brand stores. It must surely try to preserve the best of old Liverpool, and the unique quirky individuality that has nurtured so much talent over the years and deserves the chance to go on doing so. The vast and growing support for the retention of Quiggins offers hope that this spirit is alive and that it will survive into a future that will see Liverpool regenerated, prosperous, but still its inimitable and special self.' As to the proposals to privatize the streets, which were not specifically debated at the public inquiry, she added: 'We view with very real misgiving the associated proposals to privatize the thoroughfares of the new area and police them with so-called security-guard "quartermasters" in what appears to be a bid to sanitize the area.' The pleas went unheard, the site was forcibly purchased and Quiggins was demolished to make way for Liverpool One.

In a piece called *The Emotional City*, architect Adam Caruso describes the impact of compulsory purchase. 'While planning authorities may argue about façade materials and the survival of medieval street patterns in the master plan, several city blocks that once housed thousands of tenants and was in the ownership of hundreds are now controlled by one owner backed by international financial institutions. Do not be fooled by the medieval street pattern, the well-maintained squares, the lunch-time activities, these developments constitute a serious erosion of democracy and the public realm. This process is taking place all over London and in all major cities.' He goes on to say that 'land assembly' is 'one of the most direct and destructive manifestations of the current economic regime of the city'. In contrast he points to continental European cities which are 'important physical repositories of a place's history' with the result that, without being a museum, 'the city is a manifestation of a particular living culture, of reality'.[9]

The opening of Liverpool One was planned to coincide with the city's year as Capital of Culture in 2008, with the shopping complex the symbol of Liverpool's contemporary culture and reality, shrunk down to a monoculture of shopping and spending. Quiggins was nowhere to be seen.[10]

The Decay to Renaissance Story

While the growth of entirely private places in British towns and cities has much in common with Victorian patterns of landownership and reflects the scaling back of local democracy, the way the Labour government describes what happened in cities over the last decade is quite different. It talks of a 'renaissance'.

The familiar story which is often told is that during the 1970s and 1980s inner cities became dangerous places, where crime and violence were rife and middle-class families fled to the suburbs in search of safety and security. It was a trend which appeared to have come to Britain from America, where it was more pronounced and where the racial overtones created the term 'white flight', leaving inner cities hollowed out and populated by poor blacks. It is true that as industry left large parts of our cities empty, unemployment and crime rose steadily. In 1981 the Specials released their seminal single, 'Ghost Town', about urban blight. There were riots across Britain. Inflation was running at more than 20 per cent.

By contrast the late 1990s have been characterized as a time of 'urban renaissance'. People flooded back into Britain's towns and cities, to live, work and enjoy themselves in the new dockside and riverfront places which opened up in former industrial areas all around the country. In fact the first phase of this 'renaissance' began during the 1980s in Docklands, Liverpool and Newcastle under the auspices of the Urban Development Corporations. Old industrial areas, from St Katharine's Dock in London to the Quayside in Newcastle, saw warehouses and factories converted into new 'mixed use' developments, combining offices, balcony apartments, restaurants, bars and, most likely, an art gallery or perhaps an iconic piece of architecture or public art. The Quayside in Newcastle, a place of dilapidated wharves and virtually a no-go area in the eighties, was transformed into a mix of bars, upmarket hotels, apartments and a contemporary art gallery in the old Baltic Flour Mill.

While much of what happened in Newcastle has been positive, the whole story is not so straightforward. The poverty and deprivation of communities lying just behind the Quayside remains unchanged. In many cases original communities are much worse off, where they have been faced with demolition and forced to move elsewhere. It's the same all around the country, from Leith in Edinburgh, cheek by jowl with Pilton, which is one of the poorest parts of Britain, to Cardiff, where local communities are divided from the regeneration of Cardiff Bay by a dual carriageway. In Butetown, just a few hundred metres separate the uniform new-build apartments of Lloyd George Avenue from the steel-shuttered shops and rundown housing of Bute Street.[11]

It is true that there were serious problems in Britain's inner cities during the 1980s. But the failure of high streets in towns and cities also had a lot to do with that other landmark Thatcherite policy towards property and planning, the removal of planning laws to allow the building of out-of-town shopping centres, such as Bluewater and the MetroCentre. This process of development, with out-of-town supermarkets and inner-city deprivation, sits in contrast with what happened in cities in continental Europe, which have never needed an 'urban renaissance'. In France and in other European countries, poverty is concentrated in the suburbs; cities suffered from the same decline of industry yet active steps were taken to safeguard healthy city life. In Italy, France and Germany legislation had been passed to restrict large stores and favour smaller shopkeepers.[12] In Britain things got so bad in the end that the policy of encouraging out-of-town superstores was actually reversed in the mid-1990s by the unusually far-sighted Conservative secretary of state, John Gummer. So it was out-of-town development, as much as decline in industry, which contributed to the perception of a rotting inner city.

What really happened is far more complex than the appealing message that, following years of urban decay, the 'urban renaissance' transformed city life. The decline of the inner city and the 'renaissance', which is based on discredited 'trickle-down' economics, were not so straightforward, because trickle-down produces a very uneven pattern of growth, even when the boom and bust cycle is in an upswing.

Economically Viable?

Part of the 'decay to renaissance' story of the city is that during the 1970s, as the post-war industrial economy faltered, there simply wasn't the money to allow local government to invest properly in cities. So the private sector came to the rescue, persuaded by the incentive of large amounts of public money to inject private funds into new property development.

The financial crisis of 2008, which was fuelled by a combination of policies on property, finance and shopping, has pulled the rug out from under this argument. Speaking soon after the banking collapse, as retailers started to go bust, Lord Young of Graffham, Conservative secretary of state for trade and industry during the 1980s, told the BBC's *Today* programme: 'The world has changed. In the eighties it was the end of the industrial era. Now it could well be the end – or a big change – in the financial-services era. We're seeing tens of thousands of jobs go every week. Week after week we're seeing retail businesses go down.'

Now, the question is whether this economic model of development based on property values and property speculation, with the aim of generating the maximum amount of profit out of places, is such a good one after all, or if it is in fact part of the problem. This is a business model based on debt, like so much of the contemporary British economy, and, like so many aspects of the financial crisis, it is largely incomprehensible to all but the most technical of experts. The new private developments recently built or under construction are 'highly leveraged' – which means, in layman's terms, that they are based on huge loans and large amounts of debt; billions of pounds of investment have been borrowed and ploughed into these new parts of the city on the basis of predicted rises in property values.

The cycle works feverishly well when the market is hot, with property developers reaping enormous profits, but when it cools speculators and banks lose out and the market collapses, which is what has happened all around the UK. Hardest hit was the part of the property economy known as 'buy-to-let'. In virtually every British town and city the majority of the new apartments which dominate the new private developments were bought by investors who aimed to let them out, earning a stream of income. By the time the boom was at its height, buy-to-let, which will also be looked at in Chapter 6, was giving way to the new phenomenon of 'buy-to-leave', where investors were buying properties even before they had been built, with no intention of renting them but simply for speculation, to sell on as property prices continued their inexorable rise.

I went to Liverpool a good eighteen months before the crash and even then someone said to me, 'This could be the biggest bubble since the South

Sea.' Not long after, the consequence of the crash left tens of thousands of these flats empty in towns across the UK, with northern cities such as Liverpool, Manchester and Leeds suffering particularly badly. Toby Lloyd, a regeneration consultant, described 'the glittering towers of empty flats and the shopping centres' as 'a perfect representation of the boom we've just gone through. It's a hugely debt-orientated leveraged model of development. We saw an insane expansion in the credit market.'

A banker I spoke to told me just how high the levels of debt were. Describing a discussion he had with a property tycoon on a private jet on the way to a meeting, he said he asked the tycoon what he thought the market would do, but the businessman only looked at him blankly and said, 'I don't know – I'm not the one who's driving the market. You're the guys who are lending 75 per cent of the price – I'm only putting in 25 per cent of my money.' At that point the banker said he realized that what was happening was unsustainable. In the good times, the more investors are allowed to borrow from the banks, the higher their profits will be, as they can spread large amounts of debt – also known as 'gearing' – across many schemes, all of which are likely to see increases in property values, multiplying profits many times over. Fuelled by lack of regulation in the banking system, a risk-taking culture involving huge debts saw the banks lending the lion's share of the money for billion-pound schemes, with the unprecedented amounts of debt contributing to soaring property prices. The property industry has always relied on rising property values, but the sheer scale and availability of debt meant prices became ridiculously inflated.

When the boom turns to bust, because the schemes are based on the premise of inexorably rising land and property values, deals fall apart. Investors can't pay back the loans and banks become reluctant to lend, finding that the huge rises in value forecast for the future have vanished into thin air and that they have lent far more than they can afford. This is the reason schemes around the UK are on hold. As for many other half-finished projects, the government is likely to bail them out with large injections of public money. But this is an approach to planning our cities which is underpinned by borrowing, debt and large speculative increases in property prices, which means it contributes in no small part to the boom and bust economic cycle.

Estate Management

The first phase of the 'renaissance', which began in the 1980s, did not necessarily create private estates, except in the finance districts of Docklands and at the Broadgate Centre. But the next phase, during the late 1990s, went much further and fuelled the growth of entirely private places all around the country, which are now the template for all new development.

The City planning lawyer said, 'These are areas where the Englishman is allowed as a privilege not as a right. It also has the beneficial effect that behaviours can be controlled.' Like the early nineteenth-century estates, today's 'malls without walls' are private property, which means that the landlord has the power to decide what rules and regulations apply in the places they control. They are run in a very different way to the rest of the city, which should be relatively easy to understand but remains opaque, mired in jargon and complex legal arrangements, as well as the reluctance of the big landlords to point out the changes that private ownership involves. Often they claim the developments are not even privately owned because they tend to be leased from the local authority. Invariably, though, that is a mere technicality, because the lease lasts for hundreds of years – 999 is standard – which is effectively for ever.

What they all have in common is the emphasis on security and safety which is part of what criminologists describe as the 'mass private-property thesis'. This argues that as malls, multiplexes, campuses, shopping centres and the business districts spread, the growth of private security is a given.[13] But when it comes to the details of how these places will actually be run, which is what determines their character, the information is rarely available.

Often something can be found in the obscure 'Estate Management Strategy' of the company. This is the biggest clue to the look and feel of places, dealing with questions of who owns the streets and how they plan to police them. But this type of information is barely in the public domain and is not in any of the mountains of marketing information available. It is not so much that 'people don't care about the legal niceties', as the developer in Liverpool said, it's more that they haven't been told about them.

During the public inquiry in Liverpool, security within Liverpool One received unfavourable publicity, with criticism that traditional rights of way

Cardinal Place, Victoria, London

were to be replaced by 'public realm arrangements' policed by private guards known as 'quartermasters' or 'sheriffs'. Subsequently my repeated attempts to contact Grosvenor, requesting more information about the nature of these 'public realm arrangements', were met with a blank. I presume the 'quartermasters' must have had legal status because they were mentioned in the public inquiry, but Grosvenor would not return my calls on the matter. When it came to Stratford City, had I not known exactly what I was looking for, I would never have found it among the thousands of pages of documents which made up the planning application.

After much searching, I finally unearthed the 'Stratford City Site Wide Estate Management Strategy' and began to get a vague idea of how the 'site wide security regime' would work. The section entitled 'Ownership/Control' stated that the Estate Management Company 'will keep overall ownership/control' and 'be responsible for organizing patrol, surveillance and response'. In the section called 'Access Principles' the first principle was the non-specific assurance that 'the public will generally have access to the site except where there are good reasons for restricting access', although there was no indication of what a good reason might be.

With no definition of a 'good reason' and with the knowledge that the London Olympics will be the largest security operation ever undertaken in the UK, it seems almost certain that Stratford City will be one of the highest-security private places yet built. Major sporting events have a long history as a testing ground for new security technologies and it has already been announced that Unmanned Aerial Vehicles, or UAVs, also known as drones, will be used during the Olympics. The drones, which are used by the military in Iraq or Afghanistan, are fitted with electronic eavesdropping equipment and high-definition cameras and were adapted for civilian use in Los Angeles in 2006. Dr Kirstie Ball, who is a specialist in surveillance, predicts that after the Olympics, drones, which are already in use in parts of Liverpool, will become a permanent fixture in London.[14]

It is very likely that drones will fly over Stratford City, although the Estate Management Strategy doesn't actually say so, favouring non-specific language and merely stating that the company will be responsible for a security 'response', which could mean just about anything, to anyone.

The little steel plaques emblazoned with the words 'Private Property', which are often found where street signs might once have been, are another small clue as to how the private estates are run. Outside the old County Hall building, on London's South Bank, a small yet prominent sign states the area is owned by Shirayama Shokusama Co. Ltd. Often the plaques include a list of behaviours which are not allowed, such as skateboarding or rollerblading, alongside the name and telephone number of the company which controls the area and a statement that twenty-four-hour CCTV is in use. Although there is rarely any mention of it, a whole host of other behaviours are also invariably banned, including filming, political activity such as handing out leaflets, demonstrations, busking, begging or selling the *Big Issue*. In some places even eating a sandwich or taking a photograph is forbidden. John, the photographer who shot the pictures which accompany the book, was told he would not be allowed to take photographs at Paddington Waterside, one of the new private places in London, unless he could guarantee the images would represent residents and management in a positive light. Explaining the type of atmosphere he hoped to achieve, the developer connected with Stratford City told me he wanted to 'make sure it was up to the standard of any private office lobby', which seemed to me to be a strange aspiration for a large part of central London marketed as a busy, diverse and 'inspiring' place.

The absolute minimum level of security on every private estate I've visited has been round-the-clock private guards and blanket CCTV coverage. CCTV, with its counter-intuitive effect of increasing fear of crime, considered in Chapter 8, only really took off throughout Britain in the early 1990s, but before that it had been used in business premises and shopping centres. So it has seemed like a natural extension for today's open-air malls without walls to expand their CCTV networks to 'cover every inch of the site', as I was proudly told in Liverpool One. Similarly, the uniformed private-security guards who have long patrolled commercial property premises have emerged into daylight and are now on the streets of the new private estates, although there is ongoing controversy about the involvement of criminal gangs in many security firms, despite attempts to regulate the security industry.[15]

Such a high level of security is not simply down to the fact that commercial private property goes hand in hand with private security. It is also heavily influenced by the role of insurance and risk, which is very different in private and public places. The arrival of an American-style compensation culture and the fear of litigation is already something of a cliché, with ludicrous health-and-safety restrictions much mocked, such as when a country council

local authority power

proposed banning hanging baskets in case they fell on someone's head. But the truth is that, although local authorities and private landlords are equally liable, the new private places are far more conscious of risk and do everything in their power to create environments which are as safe as it's humanly possible to be.

Bill Gloyn, who is chairman of European real estate at insurance broker Aon, explained that this is because local authorities are normally willing to pay out millions of pounds in compensation, while the private estates, which aim above all to make a profit, are not. Even if the private estates were happy to allow compensation claims, the banks lending the developers the money and the insurance companies may not be willing to allow them to take the risk. 'Insurers like to see developers taking as many measures as possible to avoid a claim and they're taking an increasing interest in risk controls being put in place in developments,' Gloyn said. The consequence is that the private estates are far more 'risk averse' than the public parts of the city. This creates a very different atmosphere and public culture, which is now at the heart of all new development.

I thought about risk and insurance in public places when I went to Venice and was sitting having a drink at one of the many canal-side tables. Watching the water by the canals is incredibly relaxing. As I sat there enjoying myself, I suddenly realized I wouldn't be able to do this in England, because the canalside would be fringed by metal railings to prevent anyone falling into the water. For strollers, shoppers, employees on a lunchtime break or people out in the evening, that creates a clinical sterility which means these places bear more resemblance to an office lobby than a thriving part of the city which is full of life. But it's not just a question of atmosphere and taste: there are psychological dangers as well in creating places which have too much security and as a result are too safe and too controlled. The problem is that these environments remove personal responsibility, undermining our relationship with the surrounding environment and with each other and removing the continual, almost subliminal interaction with strangers which is part of healthy city life. The consequence is that people are left far more frightened when they do have to confront the unexpected, which can never be entirely removed from daily life. These are themes which are explored in more detail in Chapter 8.

A marked effort has been made to make Liverpool One architecturally striking, with Grosvenor employing twenty-two different architects. But as with Westfield London, when I went there, I found that despite the relatively interesting architecture, there was nothing about the place to remind me of where I actually was – I could have been anywhere in Britain or America with a high-end shopping centre with hundreds of upmarket shops. The careful branding of the bins, benches and bollards dividing the complex from the rest of the city kept reminding me I was in Liverpool One, as did the uniforms of the private-security guards and cleaners, but although I had been told that the design of the complex faithfully followed the original street pattern, I couldn't see any street signs.

Hans Van der Heijden, a Dutch architect who was working on the restoration of the neighbouring Bluecoat Arts Centre while Liverpool One was being built, said he believes that this feeling of disconnection with the rest of the city is deliberate. 'Liverpool One does not have a wall. Its wall is invisible, but yet it is clearly marked by the stylistic discontinuity in the architecture. With all its steel and glass Liverpool One establishes a contrast with the historic brick city of warehouses.' His personal experience, working on a project to preserve a historic building surrounded by Liverpool One, has not endeared him to the development. He claims that Grosvenor 'simply hated' any reference to the past. 'For Liverpool One the historic harbour and warehouse architecture was not acceptable as inspiration for their retail architecture, which is about newness and tries hard not to use any historical precedents. Our client thought in terms of meeting his building with its socio-cultural context, while Liverpool One thought in terms of imposing their ideas on land readily available for construction.' The consequence was 'endless quarrels' over the extension to the Bluecoat and unexpected problems when it was discovered that the neighbouring streets had been privatized and that permission was needed to use them. Van der Heijden felt the experience contrasted sharply with his work in Holland, but in the UK it is standard practice to request permission to use streets which are under private control.

He feels Liverpool One has created this brand identity based on upmarket shopping, which has little to do with the actual city, because the aim of the development is 'a self-contained shopping mall serving a regional market – and not the city of Liverpool'. I talked about this and the emphasis on private security over a drink with someone who works for Liverpool city council and he agreed: 'They're doing it because they're anxious they won't attract the disposable income of the Cheshire set. This is for ABC1s,' he said, implying the complex was for the social group equated with the middle class by market researchers, not for the majority in what is one of the poorest places in Britain. Liverpool is the most deprived district in the country, according to the government's Indices of Multiple Deprivation.[16] Hundreds of millions of pounds have been poured into the city as a result of Liverpool One and the year as European Capital of Culture in 2008. Yet because skill levels remain low, income levels and employment have not improved.[17] Liverpool has the highest number of working-age people with no qualifications and in 2007 the city came top for numbers of people on unemployment-related benefits in a league table of twenty British towns and cities.[18]

As I had done in Docklands, I wanted to get an idea of whether people in in the city feel that Liverpool One is not for them but for the affluent of the region, so I went out to Norris Green, a run-down estate about a half an hour's bus ride from the centre of Liverpool. There I was quickly reminded of Pat, who had said that the shopping centre at Canary Wharf wasn't for the likes of her. In Norris Green I met John, who said, 'In terms of what's going on in the city centre, people out here don't relate to it. They say, "The city centre's nothing to do with us." The money isn't touching them at all. People can't understand who's going to shop in all those fancy stores.' Darren Guy, who is one of the founding editors of *Nerve*, a grassroots arts, culture and social issues magazine, said, 'I'm all for regeneration but the type of regeneration they're talking about is a bit of a con. It's just economic boosterism for the centre.'

Liverpool One includes apartments and restaurants but is mainly devoted to shopping, and, despite the recession, when I visited in the run-up to Christmas 2008 it was fairly busy. Down in London, Paddington Waterside, a private enclave the size of Soho, is all about office blocks and waterside apartments, with few shops and fewer people to be seen, although there is a very similar feel of sameness and sterility. In this case, however, the sense of disconnection from the rest of the city is even greater.

The entrance to this massive eighty-acre place is round the corner from Paddington Station. Paddington is a busy and bustling part of London, with a multitude of small shops run by the multi-ethnic community and crowds going to and from the mainline station. But despite the size of Paddington Waterside, it's impossible to find and invisible from the main street. Eventually I stumbled across a small, pristine entrance and walked gingerly into a large empty square, surrounded by glass office blocks and balcony apartments, overlooking the canal. Just as I hadn't been able to see this place from the street, there was no sense from inside the development that the busy street or Paddington itself even existed.

Inside Paddington Waterside it was very quiet, almost empty and closely monitored by CCTV, which had the effect of making not only us, but the occasional stranger walking through seem very noticeable and out of place. Outside on the street, while I was aware of the hubbub, I didn't notice anyone in the passing throng and although it was busy no one stood out as strange or threatening. As we walked along one of the steel-fringed canals, my companion said, 'It could be Canary Wharf, it could be anywhere – it's a personality-free zone.'

These places are not inspired by the culture of where they are but by the idea that the economy will prosper if they meet the economic needs of the region. A place like Paddington Waterside is not rooted in the real, noisy characteristics of where it is, but in the convenience of its location for multinational companies, with the new high-speed rail link running from Paddington Station to Heathrow in just fifteen minutes. In fact as far as the transient professionals living and working there are concerned, it is likely that the developers think it is a positive advantage that they have created a place which bears no relationship to its immediate, more diverse surroundings.

Whether or not people like these environments, which bear more relationship to an airport than a local high street, is arguably a matter of taste. The real problem is that because these places are not for everyone, spending too much time in them means people become unaccustomed to – and eventually very frightened of – difference.

3

'Clean and Safe'

Why New Labour Fell in Love with Manchester

Every time I've been to Manchester, the city has been different. The first time was in 1990, soon after the Berlin Wall came down and long before the property-fuelled expansion trialled in Docklands took hold in Britain's industrial cities.

This was the Manchester of Tony Wilson and the Hacienda, Joy Division and New Order, clubs and music venues spilling out of empty industrial buildings. 'Madchester', the trendy university of choice, was grimy with Victorian soot and slightly dangerous. Areas like Hulme were increasingly colonized by students. I remember standing around in a dank basement warehouse somewhere at the height of the acid-house craze, with most people on ecstasy.

By the time I returned during the property boom, the city was unrecognizable. The old Hacienda nightclub had closed down and had been converted into Hacienda Apartments, and Tony Wilson, always a man who rode the zeitgeist, was on the board of Elevate East Lancashire, one of the government's 'market renewal' agencies. It wasn't only the hoardings everywhere promising 'more luxury apartments' in one converted old mill after another, or the marketing suites on every street corner, it was the sheer number of cranes and the noise of the building work, with the sound of pneumatic drills in my ears wherever I went.

Later still, once the recession hit, the cranes stopped working and many of the newly built apartments were empty. Beetham Tower, where footballer Phil Neville bought a penthouse, includes a five-star Hilton Hotel and twenty-two floors of apartments. When the financial crisis hit in 2008 it was half

Exchange Square, Manchester

empty.[1] From the mid nineteenth century, when Engels wrote *The Condition of the Working Class in England*, based on his experience of industrial Manchester, this city has been the bellwether for social and economic change in Britain. In ten years and in 100 years from now there will be more radical changes, reflecting the state of the British economy and society.

The centre of the city, which had been bombed by the IRA in 1996, had also changed beyond all recognition, becoming one enormous shopping centre. Alongside shopping, the city's ambition to reinvent itself as a centre for the global financial services industries initially went from strength to strength, with investment banks Kleinwort Benson, the Bank of New York and Citigroup all opening offices. Manchester, it seemed, had transformed itself, via 'Madchester', from industrial grime and decline to 'the' British city outside of London.

Manchester seemed the perfect example of a city which symbolized the trajectory of progress proclaimed by the government, from urban decay to urban renaissance, and it was soon anointed New Labour's favourite city. The love affair reached new heights when the party broke with ninety years of political tradition, abandoning failing Blackpool in favour of the upbeat image of Manchester as a more suitable venue for its annual conference in 2006. The icing on the cake was when Richard Florida, the American economist who coined the term 'the creative class', declared Manchester the UK's most creative and enterprising city.[2]

Today the property, shopping and financial services economy in the city has gone through the same boom and bust cycle described in the last chapter. Accompanying that, however, is another far less publicized story, which is not directly about decay and renaissance, growth or recession, but about the decline of local democracy and the rise of private government.

It's a story which goes hand in hand with the fate of one of Manchester's emblems of democracy, the Free Trade Hall. Built in 1840 on the site of the Peterloo Massacre, and long regarded as a public building of great political and cultural significance, its democratic credentials were cemented by a long history of political meetings and rallies which featured Gladstone, Disraeli, Lloyd George and the suffragettes. After the Second World War it also became a concert hall, hosting the Hallé Orchestra, and playing a pivotal part in Bob Dylan's career and in the history of punk rock.

But in 1997, despite fierce opposition from Manchester's Civic Society, the city council sold the building to property developers. It's now part of a national hotel chain and is just one of many landmark parts of the city which are owned by business and removed from the public life of the city. Much of Piccadilly Gardens, which was given to the people of Manchester 'in perpetuity', has suffered a similar fate, with an enormous office block, 'One Piccadilly Gardens', now home to the Bank of New York.

The Free Trade Hall, on the site of Peterloo, has always reflected Manchester's public, political and cultural life. As that building left the public realm, a far wider and more profound change to the city's democratic life was just beginning, as the city council handed control over central Manchester to a private company funded by local businesses and chaired by the main property developers in the city.

Since 2000 the centre of Manchester has been run by a private company called Cityco, which is very similar to the Business Improvement Districts (BIDs) which have sprung up in towns and cities all around Britain in the last few years. This new way of governing has been brought to the UK from America and marks the beginning of private government and the decline of local democracy. I decided to come first to Manchester to look at how this process works, because Manchester's approach is, as usual, right in the vanguard, pioneering Cityco before legislation for Business Improvement Districts had even been introduced in the UK. Sitting in a Danish bar overlooking Piccadilly Gardens, Kevin Ward, who is professor of geography at Manchester University and an expert on BIDs said, 'Manchester is at the leading edge of these changes because it already has business signed up to such an extent.'

The problem is that creating companies, funded by business, to run our cities is linked to a new culture of authoritarianism and control, which has also been imported directly from America – again with a British twist. It's a culture which has helped Manchester gain the dubious accolade of ASBO capital of Britain, as a result of its enthusiasm for excluding certain people and certain activities from the city centre; a newly sanitized culture is leaving behind Manchester's northern, industrial heritage and music history. In its place the city made a very self-conscious attempt to emulate the US. It even changed the name of one its central streets from York Street to New York Street.

Improving the Trading Environment

'The trading environment is the public realm and the public realm is the trading environment.' So I was told when I went to a conference about BIDs. A Business Improvement District is a company which charges a levy – sometimes called a tax in America – on local businesses and uses the revenue to do everything it can to improve the 'trading environment' in a particular area. The policy has been copied directly from America, where more than 2,000 BIDs criss-cross the country, with sixty in New York alone. This journey across the Atlantic taken by American ideas, from policies on welfare to zero tolerance, is described by academics as 'fast policy transfer' or 'policy tourism'.

BIDs are a way of running the city which is based on the type of management models taught at business school. It relies on a set of instructions organized according to the pyramid structure made famous by the positive psychologist Abraham Maslow, who is often described as the father of management psychology. Maslow's 'hierarchy of needs' created a diagram relating to what was needed for human survival, with the first layer of the pyramid centring on basic physiological needs such as breathing, food, water, sleep and sex. Subsequent levels focused on safety, love and esteem, culminating in self-actualization at the peak. Maslow was keen for psychology to move away from the study of neurotics and towards a more positive look at exemplary people, such as Albert Einstein and Eleanor Roosevelt, and his theory offered what looked like a map to achieve personal growth. While it has been criticized for lacking a scientific research base, the 'hierarchy of needs' pyramid remains central to management training and motivational psychology.

When it comes to the BIDs pyramid, which is geared towards creating the optimum trading environment, the first layer on which the whole structure depends is the creation of a clean and safe environment, so just as man needs to breathe and eat to survive, these parts of the city have to be clean and safe. The next layer is 'transport and access', the level up is 'marketing and branding of the area' and the apex is the creation of a 'memorable experience for visitors'.

Making sure the city is kept 'clean and safe' sounds like a pretty good idea. After all, who would want to live in a dirty and dangerous city? But behind this deceptively simple and appealing promise is a completely different way of looking at places: just like a shopping mall, from which the BID model was developed, the overriding aim is to become a profitable business. One manager of a BID in a busy part of London explained, 'It's all about the bottom line. We're a commercial organization which retailers invest in to improve the retail environment. It's nice to make it clean, but we're not doing it for the community agenda, we're doing it for the bottom line.' Echoing his words, another told me, 'Primarily the aim is to improve the bottom line for businesses in our area.'

Treating the city as a private business, accountable to property developers and retailers rather than local electors, has huge implications for public life, public culture and democracy. It creates places which are quite different from the British cities of the last 150 years, focused on revenue and commercial rather than innate value. And like the private estates of the last chapter, they have strict rules on who and what is or is not allowed in the area, enforced by teams of uniformed private-security guards and closely watched by large CCTV networks. A manager of a business district in a small British city explained to me that the pyramid of principles translates on the ground as 'a team of daytime and evening ambassadors who liaise with police, big, state-of-the-art cleaning equipment, camera-based footfall counting, nearly 300 CCTV cameras and a twenty-four-hour control room, and 32 per cent of the budget on marketing'.

In America BIDs have swept across the country over the last fifteen years and, according to the New York University Law Review, they are having a significant impact on government, 'changing the way America governs its shopping districts, commercial areas and downtowns'.[3] The neo-Conservative American commentator Heather MacDonald, who is a great supporter, writes: 'The BID movement is one of the most important developments in local governance in the last two decades,' and praises it for providing 'a vital and dynamic West Berlin to city governments' sclerotic East Berlin'.[4]

But although there are thousands across the country, they are very controversial, sparking protests and opposition in many cities, with claims that local government, branded by writers like MacDonald as 'East Berlin', is being eroded along with local democracy. Opponents, who are very vocal, also fear that, like the private estates, BIDs create 'new communities of like incomes with the power to tax and the power to enforce the law' and are 'becoming a separate city within the city'.[5] Their approach to social problems, in particular homelessness, has also aroused concerns and during the mid 1990s criticisms in New York reached such a pitch that the *New York Times* splashed a major investigation on its front page alleging that employees of the Grand Central Partnership BID were beating up homeless people – allegations which the BID denied.[6] But despite high-profile American concerns about private government, the loss of democracy and the displacement of social problems, shortly after New Labour got into power the government decided to bring the policy to Britain. Here, however, there has been nothing like the debate which took place in the US, showing that once again, just like the protests over eminent domain, the arrival of American property policies in Britain actually causes far less disquiet in the UK than it does there.

Kevin Ward explained to me that the idea of BIDs had been floating around in UK policy circles since the early 1990s, but really only started to be seriously considered by the government after a study of New York by the London School of Economics, which concluded that BIDs had been 'highly effective' and were 'consistent with the spirit of the age in Britain'.[7] Subsequently, in 1997 a group of senior MPs, including John Prescott and Richard Caborn, who was then planning minister, went on a brief study tour of New York's Bryant Park BID, concluding from their visit that BIDs were successful in the US and could work in Britain.

The 'ultimate visit' which sealed the deal, according to Ward, was when Dan Biederman, who had been director of three BIDs in New York, came to London. He founded the Bryant Park Corporation, going on to work at the Grand Central Partnership and forming the Thirty-fourth Street Partnership, running the three largest BID companies in Manhattan during the 1990s.[8] In 2003, following the interest from New Labour politicians, he came to Britain and was whisked straight to Number Ten. 'A number of Americans came over, including Dan Biederman, who said he'd got a product he could market in the UK. He met government and leading retailers – the impetus came from him,' a senior executive with a major high-street chain told me.

BIDs are not limited to the US and first started in Canada, but British politicians made it quite clear that it was the American model we were copying. The Office of the Deputy Prime Minister stated 'Business Improvement Districts are "New York-style schemes".'[9] A manager of a BID in the UK explained how this 'fast policy transfer' had worked. 'Our company was formed on the basis of the US BID model after a series of visits to the US by local-authority officers,' he said. Another added, 'We use the New York Mayor's office documentation as the model.'

Although the principles are the same, there is one difference between the American and British approaches: in the US property owners pay the BID company, while here tenants do. The reasons why are rooted in the arcane nature of British property law rather than in any ideological difference: to make landlords pay would require a land registry of property owners, which Britain does not have. Because of this democratic deficit, getting tenants to fund the BID seemed much simpler.

In academic debates about the privatization of public space, the privately owned places of the previous chapter are described as 'pseudo public space', because while they are actually private, they do let the majority of the public in. Places which are run by BIDs or private companies like Cityco, on the other hand, are seen as 'pseudo private space' – streets and open spaces which are publicly owned but are actually privately controlled. It can all become terribly confusing, with the same multiplicity of agencies, organizations and companies which characterize 'public-private partnerships', overlapping and blurring the lines of accountability.

What is clear is that these places are, in many ways, interchangeable with the private estates of the last chapter, despite the differences in landownership, because they are run according to very similar principles. Where private estates gather service charges, BIDs collect revenue from local businesses and aim to make the maximum profit out of places according to the Clean and Safe model, with the goal of pushing up property values in the area. When I met the developer involved with Liverpool One, he agreed, telling me that BIDs were another means of creating 'malls without walls' inside cities. 'One way society is doing something about it [making places clean and safe] is through BIDs; what we're doing in Liverpool is through leasehold arrangements,' he explained.

'Clean and Safe'

This slogan is used repeatedly by politicians and is a perfect fit with the 'decay to renaissance' story. It sounds so appealing, because who could possibly object to cleaning the streets and making sure places are safe? But what it really means for places is a far more controlled, shopping-mall environment, based on high security and a commercial street-cleaning operation, which aspires to make the streets of the city as clean as any office lobby.

Walk into any British town or city today and there will be more uniformed private-security guards, rangers, wardens and 'ambassadors' than ever before, as a result of the most profound changes to the police since the *Dixon of Dock Green* days. In 2002, when David Blunkett was home secretary, he introduced 'the wider police family', which allowed 'for the exercise of police powers by persons who are not police officers'.[10]

This new 'police family' includes security guards and other undefined 'authority figures' in shopping centres, privately owned places, business districts and residential areas, who can act alongside the police and issue fixed-penalty notices as long as they have accreditation. A review of these 'authority figures', who patrol places stopping and questioning people about their comings and goings, was commissioned recently, and at the time of writing extending their powers to issue fixed-penalty notices for a far wider range of offences is being considered.

When Blunkett introduced this shift away from the public police and towards private security, he described it as an attempt to drive fear of crime down, and claimed that his opponents had forgotten about the realities of crime and disorder. In fact his loudest critics have been from within the police itself, who do not support the spread of private patrols and prefer to see their own community support officers on the streets. But the managers who run business districts prefer to hire private security firms because they can control them more easily and get them to focus on what business, rather than the public, might want. 'If we want the community support officers to monitor a certain business, they won't. They are answerable to the Metropolitan Police, not to us,' a manager in central London told me.

Business Improvement Districts around the country are clear that, like the private estates, they want only some of the public. In exactly the same way that Liverpool One aims to attract 'ABC1s', managers of business districts are quite open about the same aspiration. 'High margins come with ABC1s, low margins with C2DEs. My job is to create an environment which will bring in more ABC1s,' one told me. So, Clean and Safe is really about far more than safety, it's about creating places which are for certain types of people and certain activities and not others. Exclusion is either covert, by making people feel uncomfortable, or overt, by banning them, with the list of un-desirables spanning far more than the usual suspects of beggars and the homeless to include groups of young people, old people, political protes-tors, photographers, really anyone who is not there to go shopping, or at least to sit in a Starbucks and have an expensive latte. It is no coincidence that Manchester, which operates one of the most vigorous Clean and Safe poli-cies is also the ASBO capital of Britain.

When we think of CCTV, we probably think we're being watched by the government, or the police. In fact, CCTV is often monitored by private com-panies. Every business district operates along the same lines. When I visited the CCTV control room in Coventry, which is part of CV One, the city's BID, I was told that the camera network would be expanding to 700 cam-eras, even though Coventry is a small city, with a comparatively low crime rate. While I was there a security guard radioed in a concern to the CCTV operator, his voice crackling over the radio, to say that a photographer had been spotted carrying a tripod. I watched as a number of cameras were trained on the photographer, monitoring his progress as he walked down the street. 'We have issues about people taking photographs and videoing,' the operator explained. Moments later the radio crackled again to say, 'We have a problem with some young people hanging around.' The relevant camera zoomed in on what looked like students from the university, waiting outside a shop.

The operator described the different types of camera at his disposal, including 'talking cameras', with a loudspeaker through which he could issue instructions straight on to the street; the 'high-rise camera' – 'they're seven-teen storeys up and can get right into doorways'; 'metal mickeys', 'a small ball type camera which cost £2,285 just for the lens'; 'the dome' – 'their particular advantage is that you can't see where they're looking'; and the standard 'shoe-box camera', which is the older technology with a slower zoom. New tech-nology coming soon would mean that they would be able to 'click on somebody and the system will do its best to follow them with all the cameras at the same time'.

When I asked why, given the low crime rate in Coventry, the city was plan-ning to more than double its CCTV network, he agreed that crime was low but said, 'From our point of view one crime is one crime too many. If we can deter or detect a single crime, it's doing the job it's designed to do.' As to debates about civil liberties and a Big Brother surveillance society, he believes 'people are not that bothered'. Putting forward the standard defence for all manner of invasions of privacy, which is that if you have nothing to hide you have nothing to fear, his colleague said, 'They don't bother me because I know I'm not going to do anything wrong.'

In many ways they are right. Most people are 'not that bothered' by the cameras, often welcoming their arrival in the hope they will feel safer. Before I started researching the increase in security, I didn't notice CCTV much either. Professor Clive Norris, deputy director of the Centre for Criminological Research, believes that 'it is about much more than crime. It enables people to be tracked and monitored and harassed and socially excluded on the basis that they do not fit into the category of people that a council or shopping centre wants to see in a public space.'[11] Rough sleepers, *Big Issue* sellers, teenagers or anyone vaguely unkempt are the groups the cameras target, not to mention photographers, as I discovered when I was in Coventry. When it comes to surveillance, the UK has gone much further than the US; CCTV is not common in American cities, although its use is growing. Britain, on the other hand, has the most CCTV in the world, with more cameras than the rest of Europe put together.

When it comes to cleaning, the aim is to keep the streets of the city as clean as the shelves of a supermarket, with teams of cleaners and sweepers and state-of-the-art cleaning equipment. Cityco, for example, invested in a £20,000 chewing-gum removal machine and oversees a £75,000 street-washing programme. In Coventry the enthusiasm to get rid of chewing gum is such that 'gum targets' have been introduced, which are 'disposal devices . . . covered with a printed, removable gum sheet on which the chewer deposits used gum'. The gum sheets carry a message campaign to 'motivate the user to dispose responsibly'. Campaigns against litter have always attracted widespread support. But there is a fine line between encouragement and enforcement; how long will it be before dropping gum becomes a crime? In many places dropping litter already is an offence, with stories hitting the headlines of a mother dropping a morsel of her daughter's sausage roll on the pavement and facing a £75 fine.[12]

The effect of having so many different types of cleaning teams, security guards and ambassadors is an environment with lots of different officials in uniforms, some even equipped with 'head cams' – special caps affixed with a CCTV camera. Echoing David Blunkett, Roger Barberis, the director of policy at Cityco, explained: 'The idea is we have a family of people out there.'

Reclaiming the Public Realm

Cleaning up litter, grime and disorder are the priorities, but the problem with this is that in the drive for perfect cleanliness and order, places are also cleaning out many of the people. Alongside Clean and Safe, another phrase, 'reclaiming the public realm' frequently fell from the lips of British politicians while this new raft of policies towards cities was being put in place. Like Clean and Safe, this phrase also originated in New York, under the mayorship of Rudy Giuliani, and, again, the flipside of this cheery message is a public culture of control and zero tolerance. In 1994 Giuliani issued Police Strategy No. 5, which was dedicated to 'reclaiming the public spaces of New York'. In it he identified the homeless, panhandlers, prostitutes, squeegee cleaners, squatters, graffiti artists, 'reckless bicyclists' and unruly youths as the major enemies of public order and decency, ordering the police to pursue a policy of zero tolerance against them,[13] and providing the city as a whole with principles similar to those of individual BIDs.

Although New Labour was still in opposition, Jack Straw, who was then shadow home secretary, adopted Giuliani's rhetoric following a visit to New York in 1995. On his return he made his own famous speech promising to ban those same 'squeegee merchants' and laying down the foundations of what was to become the 'respect' and antisocial behaviour agendas, looked at in Part Three.

Moving beggars and the homeless out of New York was at the centre of Police Strategy No. 5 and resulted in the *New York Times* investigation which alleged that 'goon squads' working for the Grand Central Partnership BID regularly beat up the homeless to get them to leave Manhattan. The *New York Times* wrote:

Bubba, Big Black, Kizer and Red are the street names of four men who have said they served on squads that beat up the homeless. They said that in recent years, while working for the Grand Central Partnership, they and others threatened, bullied and attacked homeless people to force them from doorways, bank vestibules, plazas and sidewalks all over Manhattan.

'We beat people at Sixth and Waverly,' said Ernest Montgomery, a 6-foot 4-inch amateur boxer known as Bubba. 'We beat people at Tudor City. We beat people at 51st and Third. We beat people at 86th and Third. We beat people at Herald Square and Greeley Square. We beat people at the Roosevelt Hotel ...' They said that although the administrator never explicitly told them to beat people, he used phrases – 'do whatever you have to do' and 'hold a nonverbal conversation' – that they interpreted as authorizing the use of force.'[14]

By 1997, according to Neil Smith, professor of anthropology and geography at the University of New York, 100,000 homeless people had retreated to the outskirts of New York City, to coastal scrublands, boardwalks, highways and the fenced-in areas around airports.[15] Nor was this strategy limited to New York, with business districts from Cleveland to San Diego banning the homeless from city centres. In a research report into San Diego's business district, a manager describes the 'clean and safe' programme:

There are two types of safety ambassadors. And I'd better be careful in this. One group are greeters. They walk around downtown in pairs and give directions, hand out maps, assist. They're not safety. They're welcome ambassadors, so to speak, and they all wear nice uniforms and caps, and, you know, you can tell that's who they are. There's another part [who] are the safety ambassadors that are a little meaner, a little rougher-looking, so to speak. They stay out of the public view a little bit more. But they're not leg breakers. Without being leg breakers they're the guys who will get in the face of homeless people ... you don't want to mess with them, that's what it amounts to.[16]

So where do the homeless go once they've been moved on? In San Diego the solution has been several 'sprung structures' which resemble giant tents, erected on out-of-the-way streets to house 7,000 homeless people.

Beating up the homeless and housing them in giant tents may seem a far cry from the British experience, but similar trends are at play in the UK. A manager in central London told me, 'Our guys don't physically grab them, but other Business Improvement Districts do.' A security guard who had worked for two different business districts added that his previous employer did use violence, although that is not permitted by law. Describing the climate at his old job, he said, 'There's a way of doing things there where you follow a line, you don't think for yourself. Here we don't deal with wrestling people to the floor. We're not supposed to touch and wake up homeless people because that's considered assault, but where I used to work, they do that, they're more "hands-on".'

In another city centre an outreach worker told me how the business district had reorganized the local homeless population, ensuring they were 'moved on' during the day, before returning at night. 'We used to see lots of homeless in the city centre but now we don't see them during the day. But they come back at night,' she said. A security guard explained that this was because planning permission for a hostel in the city centre had been refused. 'The issue we've got at the moment is where do we put them? Technically we should be moving them on, but where do I take them?' In London, the Corporation of London attracted negative publicity when it emerged that street cleaners were waking up homeless people between 2 and 3 am and forcing them to move on, before drenching the area where they were sleeping with cold water, allegedly to clean the streets.[17]

But it's not only beggars and the homeless who are targeted by these efforts to 'reclaim the public realm', with curfews prohibiting young people – and in some places anybody at all – in downtown areas in American cities, policies which overlap with aspects of the antisocial-behaviour agenda looked at in Part Three. For example, in Cleveland's Public Square a curfew after 10 pm, mainly aimed at young people and the homeless, prohibits anybody from gathering. Terry Schwarz, who is a senior planner at the Cleveland Urban Design Collaborative, says the consequence is that downtown is 'a ghost of its former self. Public Square has a grand, heroic scale but it has too few people to make it feel active and vital . . . the space feels lonely and underutilized most of the time.'

Terry Schwarz believes policies like curfews and bans simply treat the symptoms of social problems and not the causes, an approach that permeates all the legislation concerning antisocial behaviour. In Britain rough sleeping barely existed before the late 1980s. But by 1989, all along the Strand, in the heart of London's theatreland, homeless people were bedded down in one doorway after another. This sudden flood of people on to the streets was a result of the crash which followed the 'Big Bang' and the consequent housing crisis, when thousands of homes were repossessed. Benefit cuts and policies on mental health also played a role, with the 1980s witnessing the closure of the old mental asylums, replaced by what became known as 'care in the community'. Pressures on the NHS, which hit mental health particularly hard, meant that rather than being cared for in the community, many with mental health problems slipped through the net – and on to the streets.

Since then many attempts have been made to deal with the problems of rough sleeping, which ebb and flow but remain a new reality, compounded by drug and alcohol addiction. At the same time the number of official homeless – families, children and individuals in poor-quality emergency accommodation – is not far off 100,000,[18] despite continuous government promises to slash the numbers. Former soldiers from the armed forces, often with mental-health problems such as post-traumatic stress disorder, make up a disproportionate amount of the homeless population, alongside young people who have recently come out of the care system, and economic migrants.

The real causes of homelessness can only be dealt with through a combination of alternative policies on housing and mental health, looked at in Parts Two and Three. Homeless charities working with local councils are the main players in this complex area but as Business Improvement Districts spread around the country, they have started to take on a pivotal role, as they do in the US. Because BIDs are companies focused on the 'bottom line' rather than organizations geared towards providing social care, they are unlikely to be best placed to solve these problems, even though they often claim to work in tandem with homelessness charities. What happens all too often, in the US and the UK, is that a 'hands-on' approach to the homeless simply sees the problem 'moved on' – which is a way of tackling social problems on the basis of nothing more complex than 'out of sight, out of mind'.

The other group most often affected by CCTV and the control policies of BIDs are young people. Roger Barberis told me that Cityco doesn't seek to give young people ASBOs 'because they are the customers of the future', although he said that some young people had been prosecuted for skateboarding, which is another banned activity. 'They have been prosecuted, but only when they were baiting the street-crime wardens – I don't think that's authoritarian or unreasonable,' he said.

Perhaps the most potentially disturbing bans are restrictions on political protest and the right to protest, with Manchester again in the forefront. In 2004 Marks & Spencer began gathering evidence against pro-Palestinian and anti-Iraq-war protestors handing out leaflets outside their branch, hoping to obtain an ASBO against them which would ban them from the area. At the time, Mike Rawlings, Cityco's city-centre security advisor, who was in favour of the ASBO, told the *Manchester Evening News*: 'Marks & Spencer has been collating information and looking at trying to issue and enforce ASBOs. The situation is ongoing. A lot of what is happening is a great nuisance to the company.'[19]

But Hussain Al-Alak, chairman of the Iraq Solidarity Campaign in Manchester, felt what was happening was closer to intimidation. 'There is a feeling of persecution. It is unbelievable that one little protest is causing so much hoo-ha and so much scandal.' Peter Rothery, a lawyer and member of the council's Lib Dem opposition added, 'Anyone has a right to protest in a free society.'[20] In the end the protestors were removed after being found guilty of obstructing the highway.

So, the idea of 'reclaiming the public realm' is a partial one, with only some of the public – namely consumers with money to spend – encouraged to be there. Others with no money, from the homeless to groups of young people and political protestors, are removed. But it's not only groups seen as actively hindering shopping which are discouraged. The lack of comfortable benches and public conveniences means that older people, mothers with young children, families and couples can no longer sit and watch the world go by without paying for the privilege. When the Business Improvement Districts talk about the virtues of making places 'clean and safe', what they don't mention is that in the process they are cleaning out many of the people. This new public realm is not really public at all.

Toytown

One of the biggest problems the new 'clean and safe' parts of the city wrestle with is how to make places exciting. All too often they are strangely sterile, soulless and lacking in atmosphere, as the drive to create new places pays little attention to real historic and cultural identity.

Instead, a new identity is self-consciously created with the carefully themed branding of areas reflected in the new names of places, the street furniture, signage and the uniforms of the various officials. A piece from the *New Yorker* described branding the Times Square business district, where jump suits and caps are bright red to match the trash cans, while t-shirts and logos are purple to match the plastic bin liners. Similarly in Britain, carefully colour-coordinated uniforms, street furniture and signage are designed to give places a visual identity which will reinforce their brand and make them stand out. This type of identity is even more marked in the private estates, with the colour of the stone for the pavement sharply delineating one zone of landownership from another.

The contradiction is that while the managers of business districts want to create a 'buzz' and an atmosphere, they plan entertainment very carefully. Street theatre and buskers are auditioned and their performances timetabled and choreographed to take place in certain designated spots, which means that the unexpected rarely happens. One of the most magical experiences I ever had in a city was in Riga in Latvia. I was wandering around the old town when I heard a saxophone from around the corner and, following the sound, found the musician playing alone in a snow-covered square. The pleasure of the experience was that it was so unexpected, unlike the feeling that buskers today are placed in strategic spots, which takes away the joy of the moment of discovery.

The branded signage, helpfully pointing the way to attractions, alongside the ambassadors giving out leaflets and asking passers-by if they know where they're going, subtly removes the freedom to just wander around and linger in places, perhaps coming across a saxophone player like that, or even getting lost and encountering a different experience. In 2007 a research project published by the social-policy research and development charity, the Joseph Rowntree Foundation, used forty-six observers to look at how people actually use public spaces, finding that one of the most important functions of public space is to allow people to 'do nothing'. This was described by the authors as 'an essential role which shouldn't be eradicated', in contrast to the growing micro-management of activities which threatens to design out lingering and wandering around.[21]

I talked about this with a manager of a Business Improvement District who explained:

We probably are a bit controlling in your terms, but we want quality control. We do audition our buskers and we even let Scots pipers in, but I'm afraid we control all that – they have to book into our diary. I don't think we'd ever apologize for wanting that control because it would reduce quality and safety. We prefer planned creativity. There's a trade-off between public safety and spontaneity. What you want is a few surprises, I agree with that, so we add in unpredictability with lighting schemes and water features, anything that adds to the quirkiness of what happens when you walk around as a consumer. We make huge efforts to import vitality.

This is a completely different way of looking at the city, where the local character of a place, with all the eccentricities that make it special, is all but removed. In this new environment ASBOs are issued for activities such as preaching in the street, with Phil Howard, a well-known local character, removed from London's Oxford Circus for proclaiming his message of 'Don't be a sinner, be a winner'. Lamenting his removal, the *Guardian* described him as 'a London landmark, a red-faced Big Ben or shouty Nelson's Column'.[22] The result is that, despite the emphasis each place puts on creating a unique destination, they all tend to be strangely similar, and not just because they are home to the same high-end chain stores. Even the names of these places are the same, no matter where they are, with prefixes and suffixes such as 'One', 'New', and 'West End' cropping up with monotonous regularity, while 'Exchange' is the word of choice for numerous Exchange Squares and Exchange Places around the country.

Writing nearly forty years ago, the French sociologist Henri Lefebvre predicted that the consequence of treating places simply as a product to sell to consumers would create units of near identical places,[23] produced according to the same tick-box recipe. The conundrum is that sameness is dull, yet these places have to provide a 'memorable experience' to attract visitors. So they micro-manage a programme of activities and put on festivals to draw people in and increase 'footfall'.

The obsession with treating places as products also encourages fake environments. Historic places are known to be popular and so, while the real history may have been sanitized or entirely demolished, fake historic quarters are created, such as the Printworks in Manchester. The former Victorian printing press, which once printed the *Daily Sketch* and later the *Daily Mirror*, was badly damaged by the IRA bomb and rebuilt as an entertainment complex of chain bars and restaurants and a multiplex. 'Step inside and you're confronted by a theme-park-style recreation of a New York street,' writes the latest edition of the *Rough Guide to England*.[24]

Many identikit shopping areas and themed historic quarters are popular, and their critics are dismissed as elitist snobs who consider themselves too good for the chains. But opposition to 'Disney' type environments is not only about the merits of small shops versus chains. It also feeds into the contemporary obsession with finding places which are 'real' and 'authentic', with the irony that this is exactly what the Business Improvement Districts are trying to achieve for themselves in their aspiration to be distinctive and unique. Yet the way these places are marketed and sold only makes them more and more similar and less and less 'real'.

At the same time the feeling of an invisible hand directing what is going on, combined with the guards and the 'electronic eyes' of hundreds of CCTV cameras, changes and deadens the atmosphere. The manager who told me she liked 'planned creativity' also said, 'I like Disney. It's great and it's fun. But you are aware all the time that Big Brother is behind it.' The consequence of running places like this is that it removes all the imagination and creativity from city life, both for the managers controlling events according to a fixed schedule, and for the participants who are unable to depart from the script.

'Bugger Democracy'

Just as the private estates of the previous chapter are not democratic, so streets and public places which are publicly owned but controlled by organizations run by business leaders are not democratic. The rules are decided by those businesses, rather than by residents who have elected local representatives through the democratic process. Which begs the question, what and who is a city for? We are losing the concept and fabric of our cities, gaining instead clearly demarcated districts.

One manager declared that it was precisely the undemocratic nature of the approach which is the unique selling point, because it means 'you can get things done' without getting bogged down in the competing needs of different groups. As we walked around his area, he occasionally stopped to scrape a piece of chewing gum off the pavement, before exclaiming: 'Bugger democracy. Customer focus is not democratic. You ask the customer what they want and you deliver it. The citizen is a customer and the aim is to respond best to the needs of the customer. The second it becomes involved with politics, it becomes diluted down and the pure vision of the customer is lost.'

In the US the controversy about whether business districts are replacing local government and undermining democracy is vocal and outspoken. Here the subject is rarely mentioned. And when it is, it is mired in the confusing discussions about 'partnership' which characterize the relationships between so many 'public-private' organizations and government. For example, the founding chairman of Cityco was also the head of Bruntwood, Manchester's biggest property developer, and the current chairman is the joint chief executive of Argent, the company redeveloping Manchester's Piccadilly Place, but because the board members also include the leader and chief executive of the council, Cityco has some democratic accountability, although the lines are unclear.

This blurring of democratic accountability is as confusing as the status of today's new type of public space, open to the public, but only on certain conditions. The writer Ken Worple, who took part in the Joseph Rowntree Foundation's research into public space, said that he believes 'there is a problem defining certain kinds of shopping space as public space because of the strong rules regarding entry, inclusion and exclusion'. The research concluded that 'public spaces are regarded as democratic because everybody can use them', which means that if the 'reclaimed' public realm is no longer space everybody can use, we need to worry, not only about the state of our cities, but about the state of our democracy. This was a spectre which Henri Lefebvre raised forty years ago in his book *The Right to the City*, when he asked, who is the city for?[2][5]

Supporters of this new type of public space point out that many people like it, flocking to the shops, events and festivals, and while it is true that some of these places remain empty, many are busy. When I gave a presentation on the subject as part of Architecture Week, I was rebuked by a policy expert: 'If the criticism is that designers are producing soulless shopping mall environments, who are we to criticize – we must ask the people who use them.' The problem is there is no means of asking either those who use them or those who don't or can't, because this way of creating places has not been part of the political debate, with few people aware that cities are now run by a mix of private companies and individual private landlords. And if anyone does begin to question it, the inevitable response is to fall back on 'TINA' – there is no alternative.

If the popularity of central Manchester is evidence enough that many people like these places and vote with their feet, a proper debate also needs to take into account the displacement of social problems into other areas and the polarization of cities. During the period that Manchester reinvented itself as a property and shopping mecca, it continued to witness growing poverty, with wealth manifestly failing to trickle down to the 30 per cent on housing benefit, rising to 50 per cent in some areas. Manchester males have the lowest life expectancy in the UK, and more than half the population lives in the 10 per cent most deprived wards in Britain. Even if they felt welcome there, these people do not have the money to enjoy the city centre.

Kevin Ward, like many American academics, draws parallels between the rise of business districts and of gated communities as ways of organizing city life. 'The underlying rationale is very similar to gated communities – it's "keep people out who don't belong",' he said. Another manager of a business district said, 'Am I going to pretend part of the response isn't to displace the problem elsewhere? No, I'm not. The whole business of BIDs is moving the problem on, either by putting homeless people in a hostel or making sure they go somewhere else. In the US they've moved them out of state or to the non-BID areas of Manhattan.'

Lefebvre argued that each historical period produces the kind of public space, and therefore public life, which reflects the political realities of the time. Right from the start questions of access and exclusion have always been associated with public space, with the ancient Athenian agora open only to free men, who were citizens, and denied to foreigners, women and slaves, who made up at least half the population. The public spaces of the city, its streets and open squares, is also associated with political protest and revolutionary struggle – from the streets of Paris in 1789, 1871 and 1968, to Tiananmen Square. But in today's new public spaces, which aren't really public at all, political protest is banned.

If this new type of public space was limited to a handful of places in each city, it could be one of many alternatives. Instead it is the only model on the table. Because Manchester was bombed so badly in 1996, it was able to recreate the city centre comprehensively and get there quicker than other towns and cities around the country, placing it right in the vanguard of the current model of private government, property development and shopping. But in the process it has foreclosed the possibility of any other type of change, which could have been more healthy, inclusive and sustainable in the long term.

To the apoplexy of the city council, the veteran Labour politician and MP for Manchester Gorton, Gerald Kaufman, spoke out and said that he believed that after the bomb Manchester 'missed the opportunity to rethink the whole future of the city for the twenty-first century . . . I have just received a glossy brochure from Manchester City Centre Management Company [the former name of Cityco]. It claims that "a programme of major project completions have changed the character of Manchester for ever". What a daft boast! The character of Manchester is great – a historic city inhabited by sturdy, independent, generous-minded citizens. What was needed was a reconstruction programme that would express that historic character in a new, exciting way.'[26] Instead they got upmarket chain-store shops and a multiplex with an IMAX screen.

The spread of private companies like Cityco and business districts reflects a significant and largely unrecognized transfer of power away from local government and local democracy. 'For all the private-public partnerships of the 1980s and 1990s, we still had city government running the show. Now this is changing,' Kevin Ward said. This is a shift which has only taken place in the last few years. It's not that the Manchester of the mid 1980s, with its high unemployment and derelict warehouses, didn't need to change. But was there really no alternative to this?

PART TWO: THE HOME

The 3 Towers, Dalton Street, Manchester

4

Secured by Design

How Gated Communities Came to Britain

Driving towards large wrought-iron gates. I zapped the remote control and slowed, watching as the gates glided open before me. I drove through and as they clicked shut, the space inside felt snug and safely enclosed. I've been to a few gated communities, and not only for research: some acquaintances and a cousin of mine moved into them. The first time I remember hearing of anyone living in this kind of environment was in the late 1990s, when some friends moved into a flat in an old Victorian primary school.

The stereotype of gated communities is of luxury living and wealth, where the super-rich can live in peace and exclusivity, protected by security and high walls from the riff-raff outside. They are not only an American phenomenon: they flourish in countries with extreme wealth inequalities and social divisions, such as South America, South Africa and parts of south-east Asia, India and China – societies where the architecture of extreme capitalism has made its mark. In Rio inhabitants of armed, gated compounds commute by helicopter so they can avoid the streets and barrios of the city. But in Britain, the truth is that most gated developments are surprisingly ordinary. In many areas the majority of new properties built recently include gates and high security. It is also increasingly common for public housing to be built with walls, fences and ubiquitous CCTV.

This phenomenon, virtually non-existent until the first gated developments in the newly emerging Docklands, hit the headlines when Mrs Thatcher bought a home in a gated development in Dulwich during the 1980s. It made the news because she was one of the first to choose this kind of lifestyle. At the time, Liberal Democrat MP Simon Hughes described her choice as 'symbolic of the two nations created by this divisive Conservative government.'[1] Yet this type of high-security living was not a common feature of the British landscape under the Conservatives. It only took off well into the New Labour decade. Before that these were 'uncommon places for uncommon people'.[2] It is hard to get accurate figures but by the twenty-first century, there were many thousands of these developments,[3] especially at the extremes of the social spectrum – in areas both very wealthy and very deprived, nearly all new development is gated. When he was home secretary, David Blunkett was a particularly strong advocate of gated communities in poorer areas, issuing calls to 'make available to the many what is currently available to the few'.[4]

Why has this new high-security lifestyle come to Britain and what does it feel like to live in a gated community? The assumption remains that it is a superior choice if people can afford it, reflecting both prestige and fear of crime, which is emblematic of the growing divide between the haves and the have nots. While true in part, of far greater influence have been the American design policies on 'defensible space', which is why gated housing is common not only for luxury mansions but also for public housing. 'Defensible space' is a policy dating back to the 1970s which has increasingly influenced the design of property in Britain. Over the last decade this approach has really taken off thanks to a government initiative called 'Secured by Design', which is strongly supported by developers, the insurance industry, the police and politicians. Combined with the private government of places, this policy is bringing gated living to Britain in a big way – whether you choose it or not.

The Stereotype of Luxury Living

Although gating is commonplace these days, the stereotype of extreme wealth and luxury living behind the gates does have some basis in reality, and certainly influences popular thoughts about gated living. No discussion of this way of life can be complete without a visit to an enclave of such exclusivity that it's home to an array of premiership footballers, oligarchs, non-doms and billionaire financiers. In parts of Surrey, which are within easy commuting distance of London, this type of architecture is common, mirroring the creation of unprecedented wealth in the City and the astronomical salaries and bulging bonuses which characterized the financial sector before the financial collapse. I first looked at the spread of gated communities before the recession and the brazen promotional material from one of the local estate agents made this link clear, with a typical glossy brochure emblazoned with the words: 'The City has had a good year. The majority of our buyers come from London and the home counties. Sell Sell Sell.'[5]

St George's Hill, built by the developer W. G. Tarrant in the 1920s, is the oldest and most exclusive of all, surrounded by the beautiful wooded countryside around Weybridge, full of shady lanes overhung with branches. Ironically, this most private of places is built on a site made famous in British history by the Diggers, who set up camp here in 1649 and issued a call to the common people of England to pull down the enclosures – the fencing in and private ownership of land – and cultivate common land. In 1999, to commemorate the 350th anniversary of the Diggers, land rights activists, led by environmentalist George Monbiot and the campaign group The Land is Ours, returned and attempted to erect a memorial to the Diggers,[6] before being ejected by court injunction.[7] Today, St George's Hill, which is built around a world-famous golf club, has the feel of a high-security country club and has erased all mention of its historical occupants. Simon Ashwell, a local estate agent with Savills, had agreed to show me round, and as we drove into St George's Hill – a car is essential to this lifestyle – he told me how it was the most sought-after and prestigious address of all, describing it as 'the daddy' of gated estates.

We drove up to the entrance, clearly marked 'private property', and stopped at the sentry box, where a uniformed guard asked our business. Simon said we were visiting a property inside and the barrier, which has automatic number-plate recognition, was duly raised. Once we were in, we drove slowly through what resembled a large country estate, with secluded detached mansions set far back in their own parkland. It was lush, green and deserted as we drove down the winding private road, with Simon pointing out various homes which belong to 'Russians, the owners of football clubs, chief executives of banks, hedge-fund managers and sporting personalities'. My main impression of the houses was that they were incredibly large but mostly designed in a similar way, with the majority favouring a newly built neo-Georgian or Tudorbethan style. Simon explained that a lot of the original Tarrant properties have been pulled down because what is more important for purchasers is buying land here and then building new homes according to their own specific, very high specifications. Strangely, although each billionaire buyer presumably has highly individual tastes, most of the mock-Georgian piles looked the same, favouring the same columned entrances and wrought-iron fences.

Because of the status of St George's Hill and its popularity with an international elite of super rich, Simon explained that it was least affected by the downturn in the property market. 'St George's Hill has stepped out of the property market. You look at wealthy people now who are international and they have to have a home in London,' he said, explaining that if they have a family, they often prefer to come out here. To illustrate his point, he described a chat with the wife of a Russian client. When he told her that the area was very handy for local airports, she immediately assumed he was referring to Farnborough for their private jet, rather than nearby Heathrow or Gatwick.

I had expected to see homes which were quite unlike anything I had ever seen before, and I wasn't disappointed. Simon pointed out mansions with indoor swimming pools and home cinemas, fitted out to the highest specifications and with the latest technological wizardry providing the highest security available, from cameras mounted on poles and internal and external split-screen CCTV, to complex remote-controlled locking, alarm and lighting systems. The house we visited was simply the biggest I have ever been to, although Simon assured me that it was quite average for St George's Hill. Leading off from one of the downstairs living areas, which was the size of a small assembly hall, was a 25-metre indoor swimming pool inlaid with marble. 'Anything over three and a half to four million needs an indoor pool,' Simon said.

'I liken it to cars,' he said, explaining that for many of his clients this type of home is the ultimate in 'boys' toys'. This type of property is nearly always bought by men, although it is normally women who buy houses. Prices for the most expensive homes were upwards of £10 million, with one home on sale for £14 million. 'At this level homes are not "need" purchases – you don't "need" to spend so many millions to put a roof over your head,' Simon said. 'This involves so much money that only men are going to buy it. And like in a car, they want all their toys, so there's more and more technology in them.' It can't be any coincidence that these buyers also favour cars which resemble mobile gated homes; Sports Utility Vehicles like the Humvee – a design based on the American tank, the Hummer – offering their owners a similar combination of security and technology were parked in many of the drives.

The properties at St George's Hill also tend to be 'double gated', which means that, to the consternation of some residents who like the 'community' idea of living in a gated community, each individual home is surrounded by its own gates and private-security systems, within the wider gates. At a neighbouring gated community, Burwood Park, Simon told me how this had caused a major conflict, because 'double gating' is against the covenants – rules and regulations, in plain English – that residents have to sign up to, although many chose to ignore this, to the fury of others. 'The covenants say you can't have gates and borders to the property should be green – shrubs and hedges – but most people have their own gates. They fall out with the residents' association and get planning permission from the council. When I started working here, this didn't happen,' he said.

The analogy Simon drew with buying a car made me wonder: if the purchase of every possible security innovation, from double gates to split-screen CCTV, feels like an upgrade, then where will it end? When I suggested, half-jokingly, that panic rooms would be next, I didn't really expect him to agree and tell me that he had already seen a few. 'Panic rooms are starting to come in. I have seen a few "retreat rooms", a lockable room within a home, but I haven't seen the full thing yet, with food, where you get oxygen pumped in, but you will get that,' he said.

Although Simon was confident that panic rooms would enter the market, I don't think he believes they will become much more than a niche product. Instead he predicted that more and more cameras and private-security companies working for individual properties will be 'the next wave'. He described to me one particular house covered in cameras, inside and outside.

Before I did a viewing, the wife of the owner said to make sure I took my shoes off upstairs, though not to bother with downstairs. Afterwards the owner phoned and said, 'You have to take your shoes off in my home.' I explained and he was fine, but then I wondered, how did he know? I've got lots of houses with cameras all the way round, with the split screens. You think, why? I don't know why they want to do it. It's like a toy and they want to show that they've got it. You really don't need that level of security here at all, and, even if you did, what are you going to do with it? What could you do if you saw two men in balaclavas coming across the lawn?

Whether the next stage is more cameras or private-security companies that look after individual homes, for estate agents like Simon it goes without saying that there is going to be a next stage. The desire for security is not a need which can easily be satiated: the more security people have, the more they want. Not long after my visit to St George's Hill, I read about a new development at One Hyde Park in London's Knightsbridge, where penthouse flats were designed with bullet-proof windows, iris scanners, specially purified air, panic rooms and a security system believed to have been designed in consultation with the SAS.[8] But, no matter how much military hardware is installed, the aim of creating a maximum-security environment to make people feel safer is doomed to failure because, as I explore later, security is as much an emotional as a physical state.

The 'Ultimate Heritage Asylum Conversion'

When gated communities first started to take off, they often sprang up in old public buildings, such as converted schools, hospitals or churches. Another acquaintance of mine, John, moved into a former Victorian poorhouse, prized for its security. The development included the original building that once housed the destitute: this was the most expensive place to buy. Virginia Park in Virginia Water is a large walled estate built around what was once Holloway Sanatorium, one of the grandest of the old Victorian asylums, commissioned by the philanthropist Thomas Holloway and designed by the architect W. H. Crossland, who also built neighbouring Royal Holloway College. Iain Sinclair, who visited Virginia Park as part of his walk around the M25 for his book *London Orbital*, described it as 'the ultimate heritage asylum conversion'.[9]

Holloway Sanatorium has always been an evocative location for me because my father worked there as a psychiatrist. The hospital closed in 1981 as part of the government's asylum closure programme and I vividly remember my parents coming home from the auction selling off what remained of the patients' unwanted furniture. They bought a large oak chair which is still in the hall.

There is no mention of the history of Virginia Park in the glossy estate agents' brochure, which trades on its prestige and advertises 'A Magnificent

Lifestyle in a Parkland Setting'.[10] This was one of the most upmarket of all the asylums, incarcerating the mentally ill among the aristocracy. Patients used to bring their own furniture and servants, and the story goes that Queen Mary once came for tea. Mental hospitals seem to be particularly well-suited to life as gated communities, built, as they were, with high security in mind to keep the inmates in. This one, which was intended for the very wealthy and surrounded by a thick, high wall, is particularly apt, centred on the gothic grandeur of Crossland's Sanatorium, which is a Grade I listed building.

I wondered what my dad would make of it all and asked him if he'd like to go back and visit the place with me. He had no particular nostalgia for the old Sanatorium, which was taken over by the NHS in 1948, although it maintained some of its status as the Priory of its day. He described it as 'not one of the best hospitals but not one of the worst either' and told me how he was pleased to leave the leaking roof which meant a pool of water used to collect in the corridor outside his consulting room.

Today the 24-acre estate, which had very large grounds and a cricket pitch, is filled with clusters of detached homes and townhouses in the shadow of the original hospital. After the estate agent had shown us around a four-bedroom house on the market for £1 million, she took us into the old hospital, now converted into apartments, to show us the 'facilities', for which residents pay a £3,000 annual service charge.

The curved stairway leading to the Grand Hall made me think of a gothic *Brideshead Revisited*, with deep red and gold hand-painted panelling inlaid on the walls and the ceiling. The staircase opened up into the perfectly restored hall, with a stage at one end and room to seat hundreds. But although the brochure promised a programme of events, including concerts, plays and balls, planned by the Residents' Association Social Committee, the hall lay empty because, we were told, the Social Committee failed to get off the ground. Instead the magnificent space, which has a massive gilt hammer-beam roof and was once a large library, is unused. As I looked at the shafts of light which came in through ornate arched windows, illuminating the frescos and gilt walls, the air seemed to hang thick with memories as well as dust.

Next we visited the old patients' dining room, where my dad used to have his lunch, which is now a luxury indoor pool in another splendid setting with a hammerbeam roof – which means it is the only Grade I listed swimming pool in the country. That was empty, too, but apparently does get some use.

The final and strangest stop was the chapel, half converted into a sports hall. When we walked in the estate agent gasped and said, 'What a shame,' as we looked up at the stained-glass windows and vaulting roof which surround the linoleum floor of a badminton and basketball court. 'It feels very weird. It doesn't feel right. You look up and it feels right and then you look down and it doesn't,' she said, before explaining to us that her father-in-law is a vicar.

As the security guard raised the barrier and we drove out of the estate, my dad explained to me that Royal Holloway College, which is just a couple of minutes down the road, had wanted to buy the building to use it for its facilities and to provide much-needed student accommodation. But it was unable to match the price offered by Octagon, the developers. Octagon have restored the building – with a lot of funding from English Heritage – but the consequence is that a great public building, which was once owned by the NHS, is no longer part of the country's national assets and a resource like the Grand Hall lies unused, when Holloway's sister building would have benefited so much from it. No one laments the passing of the old asylums, but, like the neighbouring college, this was a public building personally funded by Thomas Holloway as a 'gift to the nation'.

In towns and cities across the country the great civic achievements of the Victorians – hospitals, schools and churches, often built to enhance public life and civil society – are no longer part of the public life of the city at all, instead sold off to the highest bidder and turned into housing developments surrounded by gates, as if to emphasize their removal from the public realm.

'It's the House We Wanted, Not the Gates'

St George's Hill and Virginia Park are the stereotype of what gated communities are all about, offering luxury facilities and thick, high walls. These places are 'uncommon places for uncommon people', set in the shadow of a Victorian architectural masterpiece or a world-famous golf course. Yet life behind the gates of most gated developments is surprisingly ordinary.

Monica is a journalist, aged fifty-six, who lives in a gated development in a pleasant house with a glass conservatory. Over a cup of tea she told me, 'The truth is, when we moved, gates were not one of the factors we were looking for. It never entered my head to see gated complexes. We saw lots of places that weren't right and when we saw the house, that was what we wanted to buy, not the gates. We would have bought the house anyway and I imagine that applies to a lot of people.' With the impact of extra security seen mainly as 'a bonus', as Monica said, rather than an essential, that is not enough to explain the soaring numbers of gated developments. Equally important and very much part of the hard sell is the idea of prestige and exclusivity which is immediately made clear by a trawl through any estate agent's literature, with gated developments variously described as 'exclusive', 'prestigious' and 'impressive'. For this cocktail of security and prestige developers add 5–10 per cent on the price, which purchasers are willing to pay, not least because they see the innovations as an investment, tapping into Simon's idea of an 'upgrade'. He feels it is a mix of 'expectations, peer pressure and snobbery'.

This appeal to snobbery and status is just as important in run-of-the-mill gated estates and, to show me what impact gates have on the surrounding environment even in very ordinary places, Simon took me to see a partially gated estate in a suburban cul de sac. Starting with the smallest houses, which were modest starter homes closest to the entrance, the homes grew in size and value as the cul de sac wound round. As the houses grew larger, a gate and wrought-iron fencing stood between us and the bigger homes. 'The gates make your home look more impressive and more valuable,' Simon said and I couldn't help but agree. 'You'd be amazed by how many people, even wealthy people, stop at a gate,' he continued, making me think how gates frame places, picking out the space and highlighting it. While a frame is an appropriate way of drawing attention to a picture, places are not gallery spaces, and gates, like frames, make the space outside the gates seem less important, so the non-gated part of the cul de sac suddenly seemed less desirable. That, of course, is part of the point. 'It's marking your territory, it's impressive,' Simon said.

Snobbery and the status conferred by gates is part of the attraction for some people, but others find it embarrassing. A study of the Bow Quarter in east London found that a number of residents mentioned the 'embarrassment' they felt at living in a gated community.[11] Monica told me: 'I'm not essentially an elitist sort of person. Sometimes when I'm driving in and out of the gates I have a slight twinge of embarrassment. I don't want anyone to think I'm some sort of grand personage.'

Monica, who moved into her gated development in 2001 almost by accident, choosing the house rather than the gates, doesn't live in a particularly grand home. Neither does my cousin Tony, who chose his two-bedroom flat in a gated development in Wimbledon for the views over the common. After we left the exclusivity of St George's Hill, many of the gated developments I looked at with Simon Ashwell were very ordinary, from starter homes to apartment blocks. Prestige and status is part of the aspiration to an exclusive, luxury lifestyle touted by developers and it does appeal to some people, but it's not enough to explain the spread of gating. It's difficult to get hard evidence, but the far greater popularity of older homes over this type of new housing – new homes built annually are less than 1 per cent of all housing[12] – indicates that only a minority actively seek out this way of life. So, why then has gating and high-security living taken off to such an extent?

Sometimes it takes a fresh perspective from abroad to work out what is going on. Hans Van der Heijden, the award-winning Dutch architect who worked on the Bluecoat Arts Centre in Liverpool, also worked on a number of public-housing projects in Britain and was surprised to see how many social-housing estates are surrounded by walls and CCTV, compared with continental Europe. Van der Heijden first came to Liverpool in 1995 and a year later his architectural practice, BIQ, won an international design competition to redevelop a housing estate in Fazakerley in north Liverpool, a project they worked on for six years.

In a paper about his experiences he writes: 'I remember how surprised and confused we were by the housing estates that were being built at the time and the fact that they always were surrounded by high walls . . . As commuting architects, we were used to continental public spaces that were lined with houses having doors and windows. Places where the public spaces of the squares and streets interact with the private world of the home. Public spaces in Liverpool by contrast seemed surrounded by blank walls, CCTV cameras and nettle beds. Where were the people?'[13] He and his team went on to forge a close relationship with the residents in Fazakerley, who were happy with what the architects were proposing, which was more continental in design. They then came up against a policy called Secured by Design. It is this policy, far more than the stereotypes of exclusivity, which is responsible for the spread of segregated enclaves to include every type of new housing on the market, from starter homes to public housing.

The 'strong advice' Van der Heijden's team received from the Secured by Design policeman working on the project was that the proposed new housing should be surrounded by walls with sharp steel pins or broken glass on top of them, CCTV and only one gate into the estate. Van der Heijden and his team soon discovered that these 'recommendations' could be enforced, because planning permission was likely to be conditional on obtaining a Secured by Design certificate. He describes how he felt that there was 'a gap between what people felt and needed on the ground and what our clients forced on them', and that the consultation with residents was little more than a joke. 'The consultation process was a big book with procedures we had to follow with boxes to tick. An enormous amount of money was spent on it – venues were rented and bus services were provided,' he explained. Yet despite the time and effort put into consulting with residents, their views were not listened to. 'Yes, they were consulted, but that was about it,' he said, echoing the experiences of residents in the market renewal areas of the next chapter.

The upshot was that after six years of working with residents, the Dutch architects were sacked from the project and a local architect built a new scheme. 'It has an enormous, sad wall all around. It has one gate. It looks like a prison and it is not different from any of the other housing schemes we encountered upon our first arrival in Liverpool,' Van der Heijden said.

Defensible Space and Secured by Design

Secured by Design is based on an American design principle called 'defensible space' a term coined by Oscar Newman, an American town planner and architect. He came up with his concept of 'defensible space' when looking at ways of reducing crime in public housing in New York. The starting point for his research was that urban America was witnessing a breakdown in society and that crime was spiralling beyond police control. The only solution, he claimed, was a new form of urban design based on the idea that the design of the environment, rather than social problems, influences behaviour – similar thinking to the Broken Windows theory discussed in Chapter 7 – and that the way to change behaviour was by controlling the environment rather than improving social conditions. In 1973 he published his landmark study, which was entitled *Defensible Space: People and Design in the Violent City*. His conclusions were based on research showing that high-rise living produced higher crime rates than low-rise housing projects.[14]

Researching three deprived neighbourhoods, Newman's main finding was that what he described as 'territoriality' creates space which defends itself. By marking out boundaries clearly, residents would feel a sense of ownership over places, encouraging them to look after their patch and discouraging strangers and opportunistic criminals from entering, so creating a safe environment. This is exactly how today's gated communities and the myriad cul de sac developments which have mushroomed around Britain since the 1970s function, the bottom line being that strangers are a source of danger. The consequence of creating 'defensible' spaces is that any unexpected visitor who wanders in seems dangerous and threatening.

The appeal of 'defensible space' is that it puts forward a straightforward, 'can-do' solution to crime: it holds out the promise that it can simply be 'designed out'. This has made it popular with politicians in both the US and Britain. It is also appealing to developers, who like to build cul de sacs and gated complexes because they can fit more houses on to a plot, making the plot more profitable than if it follows a traditional street pattern. As a result it has been embraced in America and Britain despite a growing body of evidence against it. 'Defensible space' in fact produces isolated, often empty enclaves which promote fear rather than the safety and reassurance which automatically come in busy places, where people are free to wander around and come and go.[15]

Nobody in Britain, outside of a few planning experts, has heard of Oscar Newman, but he bears much of the responsibility for the uniform way we've designed our housing estates since the 1970s, after his conclusions were adopted by Essex County Council's *Design Guide* in 1973.[16] Seen as pioneering at the time, when it came out the *Architect's Journal* compared it with Le Corbusier's *Vers une Architecture*, saying, 'It will definitely influence the environment in the future,'[17] which it has, becoming the template for most local authorities over the following thirty-five years. What seems particularly surprising is that, although Newman's research focused on three deprived public housing projects in New York, his principles have been adopted everywhere in Britain, from suburban cul de sacs all the way to luxury top-of-the-range gated complexes – places which have little in common with poverty-stricken parts of New York.

In Britain, in planning and urban-design circles this is the subject of raging debate, which echoes the uncertainty about whether or not gated communities are safer – American research described later in the chapter finds that they make little difference to crime and may actually increase it. At the centre of the debate about 'defensible space' is the question of whether 'natural surveillance', which deters crime, is created by the 'eyes on the street' of strangers, as argued by Jane Jacobs in her seminal book, *The Death and Life of Great American Cities*,[18] or whether strangers should be seen as dangerous intruders, as Newman believes. Both sides of the argument command influential support. Research from University College London shows that 'defensible space' does not create safer environments, finding that residents of cul de sacs were more likely to be burgled because their isolation means they are targets.[19] Now, bolstered by the growing weight of evidence, even the government has acknowledged the need for change, suggesting in its recent *Manual for Streets* that developers return to the type of street pattern that has characterized the city over centuries.[20]

But no one expects developers to listen because in the other corner is Secured by Design, the influential police-backed design initiative based on Newman's 'defensible space' ideas. Spearheaded by the Association of Chief Police Officers, it began in 1998 as a regional crime-reduction project and was rolled out to cover the country as a whole. Secured by Design is interchangeable with an American initiative called 'Crime Prevention through Environmental Design', or CPTED, which is also written by the police. This leaves us in the strange position of having police officers, rather than architects, responsible for the way places look and feel, which can create bizarre places. In 2005 a new, partially gated development in east London was the proud winner of a Secured by Design national award. As I walked around the complex, I saw that the award-winning housing had small windows, a reinforced steel door with a full-size iron gate in front of it and a grey aluminium roof with a military feel to it. It ticked all the requisite boxes – security grilles, electronic security, anti-climbing paint and perimeter fencing – plus some more besides, but it also looked like a prison. Over the last decade a lot of money has been spent by the government on upgrading public housing estates and many of the improvements, which were not primarily undertaken for reasons of safety,[21] have involved design changes driven by Secured by Design. Other public buildings, in particular schools, have become similar high-security environments, emphasizing gating and CCTV.

Secured by Design is strongly backed by the security and insurance industries. An Association of British Insurers document on security features an illustration of a cul de sac in the shape of a lock and key on its front cover.[22] Because the insurance industry is so strongly in favour, the consequence is, as Hans Van der Heijden found in Fazakerley, that 'defensible space' and high levels of security are built into virtually all new housing to attract lower insurance premiums, creating a virtuous circle for developers, who charge a premium for it. In America commentators describe this virtuous circle as the 'FIRE' economy, an acronym for 'Finance, Insurance and Real Estate', which brings together developers and the insurance and security industries by offering lower insurance premiums for properties with a lot of security. The vested interests of the FIRE economy also contribute to large amounts of high security in the heavily insured private places of the previous section.

The result is that nearly all new developments built in Britain are based on the idea of 'defensible space' and Secured by Design. Whether or not they are newly built suburban cul de sacs or high-security gated complexes is a matter of degree. So, ironically, although the housing market is touted as introducing greater choice, these security-based designs are more down to a lack of choice than to popular demand. The residents in Fazakerley, who were so extensively consulted about their views, were very happy with the freer and more open designs they worked out with the Dutch architects. In a mockery of democratic consultation, they weren't listened to.

No Dogs, No Tulips: Communities of Control

There is something about hanging out the washing which defines the public life and public culture of a city. In Paris I stayed in a flat six floors up and looked outside to see washing lines stretch between the backs of everyone's apartments. When I went to Porto, colourful washing hung over balconies, adding to the appeal of the riverfront, and in Naples or in Venice washing lines slung across narrow streets are emblematic images of these cities. In Britain, the image of a woman hanging out the washing in a back garden is also iconic but belongs to another era, the 1950s' housewife in a headscarf. More recently, newly built gated developments in Britain have started to prohibit people from hanging out the washing altogether.

Just as the private places and business districts of the previous section are controlled by strict rules, residents in gated communities have to sign covenants and leases which mean they have to abide by long lists of regulations, such as never hanging washing outside to dry. And just as businesses in private places or business districts have to pay a management company to run the place for them, residents also pay a company hefty annual service charges which can run into thousands of pounds.

I first became interested in gated communities in 2002, when I wrote a report for the Royal Institution of Chartered Surveyors about the millions of Americans living in them alongside millions trapped in ghettoes of exclusion.[23] Although the emphasis on gates and security is the same, gated communities in America are different to ours, not least because they are so much more enmeshed into American life. Here they have taken off thanks to policies like Secured by Design and the enthusiasm of house builders and insurers, but in America they are built into society in a different way, reflecting the American belief in private property and the dream of creating an ideal community, embedded in the culture since the pilgrims landed.

There are also so many more of them, particularly in Sun Belt states like Florida, California and Arizona, although, here too, it is difficult to get accurate figures. In 1998 it was estimated that 16 million Americans lived behind gates,[24] a figure which is likely to be far higher today. But although there are differences, it is still important to look at what has happened in the US, not only because it highlights a starker version of where we could be headed, but because their gated communities are based on the same system of property law to ours. The consequence is similar trends towards the private governance of the places we live in, mirroring the private government of the Business Improvement Districts of Chapter 3, with the same levels of control over the environment and restrictions on behaviour.

Fortress America, an American book on gated communities by Edward Blakely and Mary Gail Snyder published in 1997, defines gated developments as places which restrict access to residential areas in which normally public spaces, including streets, parks, beaches, rivers and playgrounds are privatized, 'resources that without gates or walls would be open and shared by the locality'.[25] Instead these resources, and services including street cleaning, rubbish collection and security, are paid for by the residents, who also sign up to large numbers of rules and regulations. One particularly draconian lease prohibited dogs over 30 lbs, while according to the rules of another, plants and flowers, not only in front gardens but also in back gardens, have to be approved. 'If I want to plant my tulips, I have to get it approved first by the committee,' a resident in one gated community said.[26] In Hidden Hills, a private gated community in California, which is entirely independent of local government, white picket fences are mandatory.

The long lists of rules are similar in Britain, although some residents fail to realize this, buying their homes without reading the fine print of incredibly long and complex leases. In John's gated development, on the site of the former Victorian poorhouse, all the houses look exactly the same, with the same navy-blue front doors, identical front porches and the same leading on the windows. Signs stipulate 'no ball games' or cycling and no children's activities are allowed on the grass or in any of the open spaces, although most of the houses are obviously for families.

Every agreement in each gated development is different, but the fundamental principles are the same. Residents sign a lease with the developer and the development's management company. A study by the University of Sheffield, looking at a gated community on a former hospital site on the edge of the city, makes clear how these complicated agreements work. The lease states that children's play is forbidden except in designated areas, no use of leisure facilities is permitted except to residents, windows must be cleaned at least once a month, no pots can be placed on exterior window sills, and laundry cannot be hung anywhere outside. It concludes that the covenants 'aim to control the occupiers' behaviour and use of their property in a way which seems at odds with our expectations of the freedoms enjoyed by owner occupiers'.[27] In the Sheffield study only two of the residents questioned were actually aware of what they had signed up to in an incredibly complex twenty-three-page lease, raising questions about how democratic this type of private governance actually is.

There is little evidence that British people are attracted to the 'community' side of living in gated communities, in contrast to the US, where gated living is often based around 'lifestyle' or retirement, with the consequence that so many services and social activities which were once part of everyday public life take place within the walls. Instead, a report commissioned by the UK government into gated communities in 2003 concluded that there is 'no apparent desire to come into contact with the "community" within the gated or walled area' and that 'sense of community is lower in gated "communities"'.[28] Here, a few gated communities do have their own shops and many have a gym, but the experience of living behind gates has little to do with a yearning for community. But although there is little evidence of the 'community' aspect of living behind gates, what all the residents do have in common is that they have to pay privately for the provision of local services, such as rubbish collection and the trimming of hedges.

In America critics point out that this is undermining democracy because residents who are already paying privately for these local services often don't wish to pay local taxes as well, with the consequence that a number of larger gated communities have actually become corporations, entirely separate from local government. Hidden Hills, Rolling Hills, Laguna Woods and Bradbury are private communities in California which have incorporated and opted out of paying local taxes. Canyon Lake, also in California, is rather more than a gated community and, with a population of 14,000 people, is closer to a town. In Florida, Sea Ranch Lakes and in Minnesota North Oaks have also opted out of paying tax and incorporated as gated communities. The idea of opting out of local taxes is far from our experience, but as more people start living in large private places, such as Stratford City, the same issues, of paying twice for local services, are likely to arise.

Just as the privately funded business districts and private places of the previous section undermine the public, democratic nature of city life, creating a different culture and atmosphere in places, the legal structure of gated communities means that residents pay separate charges – which are effectively taxes – and abide by rules – which are effectively laws – that are quite separate from the surrounding environment. These trends apply equally in luxury gated developments and in social-housing estates, where residents may be asked to pay extra for private-security patrols, warden services and maintenance. This is all part of the same withdrawal from locally elected local government, which provides services for the whole of an area and all of its people, in place of private services which are privately paid for and are not open to all. It couldn't be more different to life on an ordinary public street, where services are universal and most behaviour, so long as it's within the law, is allowed.

The Psychology of Gates, Security and Fear

The idea that security will keep people safe sounds so obvious that it should be true. A twelve-foot high iron gate should prevent a criminal from breaking in, in much the same way that capital punishment should lower crime. Yet in the same way that capital punishment does not lead to lower-crime societies, high security does not guarantee safety, and the experiences of people who live like this are far more difficult to unravel, with complex emotional consequences.

In an American study of gated communities around the US, residents said that the gates gave 'a false sense of safety' because the private-security guards 'are not Johnny on the spot' and that 'anybody who wants to jump the gate can jump the gate'.[29] 'There is a perception of safety that may not be real, that could potentially leave one more vulnerable if there was ever an attack,' one said, echoing Monica, who told me that she felt 'any burglar worth his salt' could get over the gates. To emphasize the point, she said she'd climbed over them herself, once when she was wearing a skirt. British research also cited evidence from the US, drawing on a comparative study in California looking at gated communities and non-gated areas which found no difference in crime rates between the gated and non-gated places.[30] In Dallas a police captain went further, claiming that gates actively hinder law enforcement because walls mean criminals are hidden from passers-by and police patrol cars.[31]

Paradoxically, Simon Ashwell feels that despite the obsession with security, fear of crime is not the main reason why his wealthy City buyers want to live behind gates, in what is in any case a very low-crime area. But he does think security is an issue, although not so much as far as crime is concerned. From what his buyers tell him, the appeal is that living behind gates promises a more abstract sense of psychological security, which contrasts favourably with an unstable work environment in the hiring-and-firing culture of the City. 'There's not a great fear of crime, but you do get a sense of security. You drive in and the gates shut behind you and you're in your own little environment,' he said, making me think of how I felt when I drove into a gated community for the first time and heard the gates click satisfyingly shut behind me.

This feeling of relief at arriving back home into one's own safe space is the one clear piece of evidence which runs through all the research into why people want to live in gated communities, in Britain and America. The study into the Bow Quarter in east London highlighted this same paradox, which is that, while very few residents mentioned security as the reason for living there, they also experienced real relief at getting home behind the gates. 'As you walk in the gate you breathe a sigh of relief,' one said. Another described how 'you definitely feel like when you walk through the gates that you're at home'. [32]

But this sense of well-being at being able to retreat into a snug, safe, almost womb-like environment is problematic on a number of levels, practically and emotionally. Practically, although it seems reasonable to expect that a more boundaried environment would offer a greater sense of psychological security, often the opposite happens, as residents get very agitated when territorial boundaries are crossed – which inevitably does happen. 'One of the problems with gates is that they can add to stress because people do it "to get it right" as it were, so if someone is on their property, they can get very angry and agitated. It's about being territorial and drawing a line in the sand and people can get very cross if it's stepped over,' Simon Ashwell said. Importantly this isn't merely anecdotal evidence but is echoed by research by the University of Bristol, which found that living behind gates caused 'increased sensitivity to problems' and 'does not necessarily lead to a reduction in anxiety'.[33]

Similar problems arise when systems don't work, which also happens. On a deeper emotional level, if the appeal of gates and security is to assuage wider anxieties – about work or family or life in general – it means that looking at the real causes of anxiety is avoided; they are projected on to the external environment instead, where they manifest themselves in the unattainable search for more and more security.

One of the most worrying aspects is the emotional impact of so much reliance on technology. This was brought home to me by Monica, who explained what happened when one night her electronically controlled gates went wrong and had to be propped open. As a result she spent the whole night lying awake, far more scared than she had ever been in the twenty years she had lived on an ordinary London street, despite the more-than-adequate locks on the front door. 'For some reason the gates weren't functioning properly and we had to keep them open all night. We went to bed and the gates were wide open and it suddenly struck me that anyone could come in off the street and right up to our front door. I felt much more vulnerable and more at risk, so it doesn't take long to get into that mindset that it's much safer behind the gates,' she said. She wasn't the only one, as she discovered the next morning when her neighbour told her he'd 'felt edgy all night' and couldn't get to sleep either.

As a result Monica thinks that living in a gated community has altered her perception about her own safety and made her feel more fearful. 'It is true that once you get used to being behind the gates, you think about what it would be like without them and you feel very vulnerable. It's what you get used to,' she said. By the same token, it's changed her perception of the ordinary street, with the result that when she visits her son in his terraced house, she is aware that people walking past outside are 'just inches' away from his front room. 'Once you've been living where I'm living, set back, with lots of privacy, you really worry. But they have no sense that they're vulnerable. But would I worry if I didn't live here? Possibly not,' she said. This growing reliance on security is the result of the psychological process of adaptation, described in Chapter 8, which shows how once people become used to a new experience, they require more of it.

When I went to see Monica, I had recently come back from visiting a friend in Italy, and I thought to myself just how different her experience was from the lifestyle I'd seen in the streets of Palermo and Venice, where private lives seep into the public life of the city, with the sound of families having dinner or watching television audible to passers-by, who walk past people sitting in their doorways. Hanging out the washing reflects the same meshing of private and public lives, which is deemed not just offensive but illegal in private communities. { when gates hav issues

But if Monica wasn't sure about her new feelings of vulnerability, she pointed out that there was one very good example of how the gates did offer more security. 'There have been a few points in my life when I've been very glad I live here, and that was when the spate of incidents occurred when someone opened their front door and got murdered on their doorstep. Opening the front door to someone who might do you violent harm – that can't happen to us. We can't protect ourselves from so many things that go on, but this is one thing we can do,' she said.

I think the notion of being attacked by an intruder who bursts into the house is at the centre of our fears in a way it never used to be, even ten years ago. I feel it myself when the doorbell rings unexpectedly. Because I sometimes work at home, this happens from time to time and it always gives me a little jolt, although it's invariably Jehovah's witnesses or a utility company claiming they can offer me a better deal. But these fears of violent attack are not borne out by reality, because despite two highly publicized murders which have occurred in the last few years, police statistics show that this type of crime is down, while burglaries and other intrusions into the home are also significantly lower. What has changed is daily exposure to unexpected events. Friends rarely pop round unannounced these days, because everyone has a mobile phone, which means they can ring if they're in the area. They'll probably even ring first if they happen to be on the street outside. And when they ring, the phone is likely to identify the caller, which means that before answering I know who I'm talking to. So the only people who come round are scheduled to visit, which means that if the doorbell goes unexpectedly, it feels intrusive and possibly threatening, because it's unlikely to be someone I know.

I like my mobile phone and would not be without it, but there is a flip side to the certainty and predictability which has come with the explosion of new technology, which is that tolerance and appreciation of the unexpected recedes, while reliance on that sense of certainty and feeling of control over the environment grows. Living in a high-security gated environment is the most reassuringly hi-tech way of life on offer, but when the technology goes wrong, as it often does, it can suddenly become a frightening experience, as Monica found out.

In his book *The Consequences of Modernity* the sociologist Anthony Giddens says that life is not 'comforting and psychologically snug'.[34] By retreating into safe havens, which substitute physical security and complex technological systems to meet emotional needs, this new way of living is in danger not only of dividing the landscape but of stymieing people's emotional lives in the process, by creating the false illusion that life is 'psychologically snug' and perfectly safe. When forced to venture out of these environments, the danger is that people are far less able to cope with the ordinary risks that are part of healthy life than they were before.

Garnet Street, Derker, Oldham

5

Housing Market Renewal:
The Twenty-First-Century Slum Clearances

Garnet Street in Derker in Oldham is deserted and only one of the houses shows any sign of life, its well-kept window boxes a splash of colour in a terrace of abandoned Victorian homes. Joan, who is seventy-five, has owned this house for forty-five years. She used to have scores of neighbours and knew everybody. Now she has no neighbours and the houses on either side of her are 'tinned up'. Round the corner Kathleen, eighty-three years old, who has owned her home for sixty years, is the only person left living on her street.

Garnet Street is an eerie place to walk. The solid, well-built homes, with plenty of original features, are the kinds of property particularly sought after in London. These aren't houses which are falling down and past their sell-by date, but homes which should be lived in. Instead, the street is silent in the slanting sunlight and the houses lie empty, speaking only of memories. It reminded me of Northern Ireland in the early 1990s, before the peace process, where whole streets in parts of Belfast were home to just one or two residents with the others forced to flee.

Garnet Street is just one of the thousands of Victorian streets – in towns stretching all across the north of England – which have been cleared of their residents and boarded up to await the bulldozers, in the biggest programme of demolition since the slum clearances of the 1950s and 1960s. The easiest way to get to Derker is the local train from Manchester. As I looked out of the train window, I could see that a new feature of the Lancashire landscape, alongside the Victorian chimneys and old warehouses, was row after row of tinned-up terraces. These are part of a government programme called 'Housing Market Renewal Pathfinder', a multi-billion pound programme launched in 2002 with the aim of tackling 'areas of market failure'. Nine 'low-demand' areas, including 850,000 homes, were chosen in places from Stoke-on-Trent in the Midlands, to Liverpool, Salford, Manchester and Oldham in the north west and Middlesbrough and Gateshead in the north east.[1]

When I arrived in Oldham, I was met at the station by Terry, a retired long-distance lorry driver with a soft Lancashire accent. He drove me to his house, where I met his wife Maureen and a group of local residents, who are refusing to leave their homes and are appealing to the High Court to challenge the government's plans to raze their community to the ground. As Terry described to me how he and his wife had saved up to buy their home, which they have lived in for forty-seven years, I noticed that there was something unusual about the way he looked, although I couldn't work out what. Later, sitting in their front room, Maureen told me that large clumps of his hair had recently fallen out, as a result of alopecia caused by stress.

The front room was packed. Kathleen, Dot, Jackie, Winnie and another lady called Joan were neighbours in their sixties, seventies and eighties. Joan said, 'I've lived in the same house for seventy years and now they want to knock it down.' Kathleen, who has been in her home since 1949, said, 'It was a rented house but we saved up to buy it.' Maureen, whose grandchildren were doing their homework upstairs, said, 'It's a parallel with what they did in the sixties. They said they'd learnt a big lesson and it would never happen again, but the same thing has happened again. It's a matter of being scattered to other parts of the borough, to Royton, Chadderton and Shaw. They're splitting families. My daughter lives five minutes away – we're the childminders. We're a family.' In the 1950s and 1960s slum clearance also broke up communities, but many welcomed the improvement in living conditions. Today, the irony is that residents happy with their homes are forced to prove in court that their homes are structurally sound, in the face of council claims that they aren't.[2]

Maureen is one of the founding members of the Derker Community Action Group, set up in 2004. She was one of the first people to hear about the proposed demolition of the area. She heard about it by accident, because, before she retired, she worked for the council and was invited to the consultation accompanying the launch of the plans. 'I got a letter at work asking me to go to a meeting. I was the only resident and I was only invited because of where I worked,' she said. As a result she began to find out about plans to demolish 588 homes in Derker, although the rest of the community was kept in the dark. 'The first these ladies heard about it was when they got packs through the door,' Maureen said. Kathleen cut in, saying, 'There was a map where the houses were colour coded, depending on whether you were going to be demolished.'

Once the proposals were finally out in the open, six months after the 'consultation' that only Maureen was invited to, local opposition to demolition was massive. 'The first meeting was heaving – absolutely packed. There must have been more than 300 of us,' Maureen said. 'We did car-boot sales, table-top sales, social evenings. We asked every resident, if they could afford it, to give us £100. I stood outside in the rain for four to five hours,' Dot added.

Despite the strength of local feeling, compulsory purchase orders (CPOs) were issued for the homes which made up the Derker community. CPOs are legally binding orders which allow the council to purchase people's homes by force. In this case the council had reckoned without the effectiveness of the Community Action Group, which obtained legal aid, successfully challenged the council in the High Court and is now appealing an earlier decision on compulsory purchase. The demolition programme has been stopped in its tracks, until the results of the next court decision, due in mid 2009.[3]

However, although the courts have made it clear local people have a very strong case, since 2004 the community has been virtually destroyed, with only thirty to forty of the original residents left. The legal victory is a hollow one. 'What they've done is made everybody ill and they've ripped us off. Not just the old ones, the young ones as well,' said Winnie, seventy-two. The compulsory purchase price paid to residents for their old properties is far less than the amount required to buy a new home in Derker, which means that these residents are very unlikely to be able to buy another home in the area. Kathleen said, 'Most of us own our own homes, but if we took one of their homes, we'd be in debt – we've never owed anyone in all our lives.'

Now the community has all but broken up and most people have moved away, swayed by the uncertainty or too frightened to stay in their homes as properties on either side are 'tinned up'. 'We've lost hundreds, the majority have had to move outside the area, because there's nothing for them here,' Jackie said. 'A lot of people moved off my street. The old women living on their own were frightened. When they decided to sell, they knocked on my door in tears, saying, "Sorry I've let you down." That's how they've got rid of most people. I'm lucky, I've got my husband and son, but if I was on my own,

I'd have gone.' Pointing to the other way of losing local people, Winnie added, 'Three people have died one after another. They say it's the worry.'

Sitting in Maureen and Terry's front room, and later, seeing row after row of deserted terraces with just one or two families or old people still living there, with their protest posters in the windows exclaiming, 'Vote Labour, never again!', I thought how much courage these residents must have, living in empty streets in order to hang on to their homes and their communities. 'I think we've a right to fight for our homes, don't you?' Kathleen asked me and I agreed, but it also made me sad that at eighty-three this was the way she was spending her life, especially when she told me about the suffering she'd gone through. 'We may look all right but we're not all right,' Kathleen said, showing me two different letters from her GP to the hospital, describing high blood pressure and heart trouble caused by stress.

The council, which claims the programme will drive up the prosperity of the area, takes a rather different view from the Community Action Group. They say the aim of Pathfinder is to plough billions of pounds of investment into the area as part of a 'major fifteen-year programme to transform homes and neighbourhoods', turning places with low house prices and low housing demand into flourishing housing markets, with a wide social mix of residents and housing types.

But for residents like Kathleen, Terry and Maureen, Pathfinder strikes them as a case of the local council wanting to make money from the land by demolishing their existing homes and rebuilding new ones which can be sold at higher prices to wealthier people. 'It has been said, and it's been said more than once, that you'll get a better class of people. It's disgusting. It's social cleansing,' Maureen said.

When I went to see Robert McCracken, the QC representing the Derker Action Group, he described how 'it is very apparent to me that a lot of people in Derker had something they valued in terms of community and place, but the council is promoting this because there's money to be had from central government. It means local people will not be able to buy in the area.' If a phrase like 'social cleansing' sounds melodramatic, Maureen is not the first person to have used it. In 2006 Jane Kennedy MP, a Labour minister since 2001, accused her government of attempting 'social cleansing' in Liverpool, where Pathfinder has also been stopped by a High Court challenge by a local resident.[4] Across the north of England and in the Midlands, many residents, from Derker to Stoke, Middlesbrough to Burnley, and Darwen to Liverpool, are bitterly opposed to having their homes demolished, but the programme has been imposed by force.

Charles Clover, who covered the story as environment correspondent for the *Daily Telegraph*, claims the policy was never announced properly, not allowing public debate. Instead the government's Communities Plan, which included information about Pathfinder, was announced a number of times, alongside plans for the expansion of the Thames Gateway. 'It was never launched as one thing, it was launched as part of a package of measures, to muddy the waters. It meant nobody knew what was happening. This was done furtively,' he said.

'A Classic English Battleaxe'

While the people in Derker and a number of other local action groups have been at the centre of major court battles, the most high-profile case, seen as a key test case for this legislation, rests in the hands of a sixty-one-year-old disabled grandmother who lives in Edge Lane in Kensington, in the north of Liverpool.

Before I met her, I heard Elizabeth Pascoe described as 'a classic English battleaxe in the best possible sense'. Once I found out about the duration and difficulty of her campaign, taking on the battleaxe mantle seemed like an eminently sensible way of dealing with what she has had to face, which includes being firebombed in her home, successfully representing herself in the High Court, and spending tens of thousands of pounds of her own money on the case.

Adderley Street, in Edge Lane, is similar to most of the other condemned streets I've visited; most of the properties are empty but a handful are still clearly occupied. Number 11, where Liz lives, had a particularly strong sense of comings and goings, because she lets rooms out to foreign students. After she'd made me a cup of tea, she showed me into her book-lined front room, where Radio Four was on in the background. A qualified architect, she recently abandoned her PhD to concentrate on the campaign.

The story I heard followed a familiar pattern: local people were not told, let alone consulted, about the proposed changes to their area. 'We didn't

hear about the planned demolition until three or four years into the process,'
she said. Along with many other opponents, she said that the area was not
suffering from housing-market failure and that there was no need to demolish perfectly good homes, a claim which was supported in court by the government's own agency, the Commission for Architecture and the Built
Environment. Instead she believes her community was deliberately run
down, to fit in with the legal requirements of Pathfinder, which state that in
order to clear sites for demolition an area must be 'underused or ineffectively
used'.[5] In 2007 the National Audit Office came to the same conclusion: its
report on Pathfinder confirmed that a number of housing associations in
Merseyside admitted that they kept their properties vacant 'to help speed
clearance'.[6]

Some 400 properties were earmarked for demolition in 2003. By the time
the compulsory purchase orders landed on people's doorsteps a year later,
131 of the properties were already empty. Liz explained that this was because
127 of the houses were owned by housing associations, who paid their tenants to go. That was when her long-drawn-out and draining legal battle
began, when she and the local residents' group objected to the compulsory
purchase orders, triggering a public inquiry. She lost the public inquiry but
took the case to the High Court and eventually won on human-rights grounds,
stalling, for the time being, the plans for Kensington.

As with all things legal, the devil is in the detail. Liz won her case in the
High Court on the basis of a single word. After the public inquiry the inspector had ruled that 'the land was "predominantly" underused', which was not
good enough for the High Court judge, who ruled that this was 'an impermis-
sible watering down of the statutory requirements' and therefore a breach of
the Human Rights Act.

But although Liz won in the High Court, the battle was far from over. The
council, claiming they had lost on a technicality, immediately served her with
another compulsory purchase order and prepared to take her to court all
over again. It was at this point, she says, that the community started to give
up. 'When we got the second compulsory purchase notification, about a hundred people left. Then people did give in. They could see it was going to go
on and on. About thirty of us have died, whether they stayed or gave in,
because it has been very traumatic.' On the day she won her High Court challenge she simultaneously received the next compulsory purchase order and

described her success as a 'pyrrhic victory'. 'It is bittersweet because much of my community has already been destroyed as a result of this initiative. Many of my neighbours who had lived here happily for decades succumbed only recently to various pressures and left,' she said.

When I met her, Liz had given up four years of her life to the campaign and spent £40,000 of her own money, much of which she had to borrow. 'I pay £300 a month in debt, which is why I have the student lodgers,' she said. She has also abandoned her doctorate and there is no doubt that this 'classic English battleaxe', who can be abrasive and most certainly doesn't suffer fools, is very driven. She works 'seventeen hours a day' on the case, which has taken on national significance, not just for her but for the army of lawyers, consultants and developers awaiting the final outcome. 'When I fought the first time, I did it for my community, and since then I've learnt a lot more and I'm doing it for the nation, because if they get away with it, they'll do it again,' Liz said. 'This is about setting a precedent and they hope I die or they grind me down.' Motivated by a mixture of personality and politics and a desire not to be beaten, she has turned this campaign into a personal crusade.

When I left I got a taxi to the other side of the city. I asked the cabbie what he thought about the plans for the area and he was unequivocal about his feelings. 'It's terrible what they're doing. They're knocking down all the houses so someone can make some money out of it. They've broken up neighbourhoods who were perfectly happy in these homes.'

Deliberate Decline and the Value of Land

On the other side of Liverpool I met Jonathan Brown, a town planner who lives near Newsham Park, where a curving sweep of grand nineteenth-century homes, overlooking the Victorian park, is under threat of demolition. Jonathan showed me round the park, pointing out the crumbling Victorian mansions, which still retained some of their splendour amidst the decay. 'This is a quality place, but they're letting it go because of the land values,' Jonathan said, explaining that the many of the buildings are owned by a mix of housing associations and the council. 'Because they're listed, they can't knock them down. The only way properties in a conservation area can be knocked down is if they become a danger to the public.'

Sitting in Jonathan's car, with the park on one side and beautiful, ivy-clad detached houses set in their own grounds on the other, I could see that, done up, this could be one of the most stunning parts of the city. These houses would fetch many millions and I couldn't see what the logic was in demolishing them, but Jonathan said that by assembling a large enough site, the housing associations would have 'first refusal', which means that, working with developers, they could knock down the houses and build flats at a far higher density, generating much bigger profits. These deals, based on speculation and a rising property market, are so profitable because of the difference between the relatively low value of each individual undeveloped parcel of land and the anticipated future value of the entire new development, which is known as the 'marriage value'. From the housing associations' point of view, they say doing up the homes would simply be too expensive. 'Financially it is very difficult to do that given the condition of these properties,' a housing association employee, who didn't want to be identified, told me.

In another part of the city, where a number of housing associations own large numbers of other properties, more grand Victorian townhouses and Victorian terraces are under threat in the famous 'Welsh Streets'. Ringo Starr's old home is here, and around the corner are the late nineteenth-century workers' cottages which gave the area its name, mentioned in Pevsner's *Architectural Guide to Liverpool*; they were built and lived in by the Welsh workers who built much of the city. Ringo himself is an opponent of demolition, calling his latest album *Liverpool 8*, after the area, and rejecting the council's surreal notion of rebuilding his home brick by brick in another part of the city. Explaining the sums, Jonathan said, 'If they pay everyone £30,000–40,000 for their little pocket but then consolidate it into a huge site, they sell each home for £120,000 and the "marriage value" is considerable. And on top of that they get a huge amount of public subsidy.'

Nina Edge is an artist who lives with her young son in a handsome five-bedroom, three-storey townhouse in Kelvin Grove, round the corner from Ringo's home. Now forty-six, she moved to the area more than fifteen years ago, when she became the Henry Moore Sculpture Fellow at the university. She has stayed because there's nowhere she'd rather live. 'It's a very good location. Princes Park is right next door. It takes twenty minutes to walk into town, it's on the main bus route, I've got lots of friends and it's culturally and racially mixed.' To save their homes, she and other residents formed the

Welsh Streets Home Group in 2004. She says the notion that there is no housing market in the area is totally wrong and that the home next door to hers, which is owned by Liverpool Housing Trust, is empty because the Trust refused to sell it. 'We know there's a market – lots of people have tried to buy homes, but they've been knocked back.' To prove it, Nina put an ad in the free property magazine *You Move*, advertising an 1880s' home in the area, with five bedrooms and two reception rooms, complete with a picture of her house. More than 100 people replied. 'They were really angry,' she said, referring to the council and New Heartlands, the Pathfinder organization. 'It freaked them out that loads of young professionals and creatives were living here already.' Instead Nina emphasizes that it is precisely because the area is attractive that it has been targeted. 'The demolition zone is around the corner from the main boulevard into town and we have an amazing amenity in Joseph Paxton's Princes Park, which is next to Sefton Park,' she said.

The story of a market cycle, where Pathfinder deliberately runs places down by leaving properties empty and allowing them to fall into dereliction, is heard again and again across all the Pathfinder areas. 'A lot of these sites are chosen on the basis of where there's a lot of public ownership,' Jonathan explained, which means that where properties are owned by housing associations or the council, it's down to them whether they are left vacant or not. 'It's a blight imposed by the city council,' he said. In the Welsh Streets, although owners like Nina have formed a very active campaign group, more than 70 per cent of the properties are in council or housing-association hands, which means that there is huge scope for leaving properties empty.

As well as pointing out how areas are deliberately run down, critics also point to the decline which residents have to put up with, often for years, while they wait for these large-scale programmes to begin. Jonathan showed me around Anfield, which is also in Liverpool's Pathfinder area, where once again street after street of handsome Victorian homes were characterized by 'tinned up' properties, although the original community was still very much in evidence. 'These won't be demolished for another ten years – this part of the programme is in the "third phase",' he said, with the consequence that residents have no choice but to live in an area earmarked for decline and demolition for the next decade. Driving round the condemned streets, we passed the entrance to Anfield football stadium, which was knee-deep in flowers and wreaths commemorating the anniversary of the Hillsborough disaster. The football club is moving too, to another part of the city. The wreaths were a fitting symbol for a community brought to its knees.

For Nina, the saddest thing is that she feels the demolitions are repeating the painful memories of the 1960s, which are still imprinted in the minds of so many Liverpudlians following the slum clearances which moved thousands out to New Towns. 'It's such a big thing in Liverpool's folk memory that people were moved out to Skelmersdale, Widnes and Runcorn,' she said. Jonathan put it even more strongly: 'With the destruction of the sixties at least they had the excuse they were building the new Jerusalem. Now it's all about land deals.' It's not just local people who are drawing these parallels. In 2005 the House of Commons Select Committee warned that Pathfinder must not become 'a major demolition programme, which will repeat the mistakes of previous clearance programmes that destroyed the heritage of areas and failed to replace it with neighbourhoods of lasting value'.[7]

The massive post-war slum clearance programmes demolished two million homes in towns and cities all over Britain, destroying close-knit communities of terraced houses, though it hoped to improve standards of living. As Jonathan says, then at least demolition was in the name of improved living standards, while today perfectly good homes are being pulled down. The post-war aspiration was that the new 'flats in the sky', with their bathrooms and fitted kitchens, would replace the slums of old, with their overcrowding and outside toilets. The reality was that all too often poor-quality high-rise accommodation, which has itself been demolished, was provided by the industrial building systems used at the time. In 1968 Ronan Point in the east of London collapsed, killing four people, and in Newcastle the grandiose vision of council leader T. Dan Smith, to create a 'Brasilia of the North', ended in corruption, with the resignation of Home Secretary Reginald Maudling and prison terms for Smith and architect John Poulson. The failure of these grand schemes appeared to have led to a complete rejection of the large-scale, centralized approach – until the Pathfinder programme and 'Housing Market Renewal'. It is very difficult to get figures on the amount of demolition proposed by Pathfinder, but early discussions talked of pulling down 400,000 Victorian properties and so far 57,000 demolitions have been scheduled.[8] Launched in 2002, the intention was that the programme will run for ten to fifteen years, with many market-renewal areas continuing until 2015.

Today's goals are very different from the 1950s and 1960s. Advocates of Pathfinder claim that the programme aims to introduce a wider social mix of people into areas and raise land values, improving prosperity in places. Inevitably this means bringing many new people in, but those working in market renewal areas claim that homes for a small percentage of the original community are also planned. Local people repeatedly say this is not what happens, with families who have lived in areas often for generations forced to leave, breaking up communities across the north of England and the Midlands and echoing the experience of the post-war years of working-class communities. For opponents, it means social cleansing or social engineering. In its Memorandum to the House of Commons Select Committee, the Derker Community Action Group said, 'We feel that Pathfinder is social engineering at its most ludicrous and unjust.'[9]

Compulsory Purchase, Eminent Domain and the Fifth Amendment

Across the Atlantic new laws, similar to British changes in legislation, are also forcing people to give up their properties to make way for economic development. Legislative changes have taken place almost simultaneously in the UK and the US, but in America compulsory purchase is called eminent domain and is enshrined in the US constitution under the Fifth Amendment.

In America the right to individual private property is central to national culture, and this aspect of the Fifth Amendment was drafted in the hope of making individual property rights more secure. To achieve this, it introduced the requirements of 'just compensation' and development for 'public use' as preconditions for condemning land and providing compensation. However, in 2005 Kelo v. London, a landmark Supreme Court case, broadened the definition of 'public use' to give far more emphasis to economic development when deciding if property can be seized.[10] Because the Supreme Court Judgement was interpreted by many as undermining private-property rights, national outrage was sparked at what was seen as a direct attack on the constitution.

In the UK the entirely obscure Compulsory Purchase Act 2004 similarly allowed, for the first time in history, that the 'economic well-being' alone of an area would be sufficient to justify the use of compulsory purchase, a point confirmed by legal experts. The Act received little attention. The difference between Britain and the US lies not in the law but in reactions to the law. In America these changes provoked national demonstrations, blanket coverage across the media, and even saw protestors camping on the lawn of one of the Supreme Court judges. The outcry was such that former President George W. Bush issued an Executive Order limiting the scope of the new law, and several states are considering legislation of their own to restrict it.

In Britain, although eminent QCs such as Robert McCracken, who represented the Derker Action Group, believe that the UK's 2004 Act has 'undoubtedly watered down the test' for approving compulsory purchase, and that it 'was much harder to satisfy in the past', nobody else seems to have noticed. The result is that compulsory purchase is likely to become ever more widely used. Just as with the private areas of the city discussed in Chapter 2, this country is pursuing the extreme market agenda towards place, which comes at the expense of individual property rights, far more vehemently than in the US.

Pathfinder is about the human stories of desperate individuals trying to save their homes and the complex legal details of the court battles which have ensued, all at the behest of a highly centralized government programme. Nobody is better placed to give a verdict on it than Paul Stinchcombe, a former MP who voted for the legislation when he was in parliament but has acted as a barrister for Liz Pascoe and other protestors since losing his seat in 2005.

'I am horribly conflicted because I passed the legislation,' he admitted to me. 'I was familiar with the legislation but when I came to the litigation a few years later, I saw some of the unintended consequences. It was intended to be part of the regeneration process, but, as with all grand intentions, it had unforeseen consequences on the ground, the first of which was riding roughshod over the community, and the second is that as soon as you start getting investors in, they're interested in the bottom line and not necessarily in regeneration. The trouble is that as soon as you start exerting powers of compulsion, you run the very grave risk of not putting communities there that people want and need, because the place is now behoven to private investors and the bottom line. You end up with the wrong results and the wrong development.'

How It All Began

As our homes become, above all, places of investment, so do our cities. In the late 1990s articles began to appear about houses changing hands for as little as 50 pence in northern towns and cities. Suddenly we were hearing of huge areas of 'low demand' and 'abandonment' in the north, resulting in the kind of 'market collapse' which meant that properties had lost almost all their value and were virtually worthless.

In 2002 I was commissioned by a housing magazine to write a piece on the fledgling Pathfinder programme. This gave me a chance to begin to understand the stories I had read a couple of years earlier. As part of the piece, I interviewed Brendan Nevin, a housing academic and the architect of the Pathfinder policy. Working at the Centre for Urban and Regional Studies at the University of Birmingham, Nevin had produced a series of research papers on areas of low demand in the Midlands and the north, which looked at the 'inner core' of cities, areas just outside but near the city centre, perhaps fifteen or twenty minutes walk away, often potentially desirable parts of town, near parks or rivers. The research pointed out that these were among the places which had, by the late 1990s, been hit by collapsing house prices. Nevin and his colleagues put forward a solution to the problem, which they said would fuel housing markets in these well-located places: by demolishing the outdated homes and replacing them with new ones, the areas would become attractive to higher-income people who traditionally leapfrogged the 'inner core' in favour of the suburbs.

Though some original communities would face upheaval, the greater goal was to create a new economic strategy for the old industrial cities of the north, changing the social and economic population mix of these well-placed parts of the city, boosting the property markets and development in the area, and reinvigorating city centres in the process. Vast swathes of Victorian housing would be demolished and hundreds of thousands of new homes built for sale. In Nevin's view, which holds that the old terraces are now obsolete and should be replaced with the type of new-build suburban housing popular with professional office workers, boosting the regional economy is paramount. This was a perspective which chimed with the Treasury under Gordon Brown, who was then Chancellor.

Wainman Street, Salford

Nevin, who swiftly got the ear of the Treasury, told me the aim was to 'restructure housing provision in some older industrial cities'. The rationale, as he explained, was that these places were emptying out and were no longer popular, leading to market failure. 'Increasing abandonment is at the heart of it,' he emphasized.

There were a number of major problems with his thesis, however, which quickly became apparent to many residents. Existing communities were, for the most part, not abandoned and quite happy with their architecturally valuable homes, despite the well-documented problems of 'low demand' in certain specific areas. With the majority of the communities targeted by Pathfinder in no mood to be 'restructured', the stage was set for conflict. In a memorandum to the House of Commons Select Committee in 2001, which paved the way for the policy, the Centre for Urban and Regional Studies did acknowledge that local people would lose out, stating, 'The process of renewal of markets will in some cases cause considerable disruption and have major adverse consequences for some residents.'[11]

At the same time, from the sheer number of homes targeted, it became clear that the nine initial Pathfinder areas selected by the government covered far larger swathes of the country than the small pockets of abandoned homes which had hit the headlines back in the late 1990s. Nevin's research estimated that 1.5 million homes were at risk of market failure, of which 850,000 went on to be included in the Pathfinder areas; the memorandum to the select committee talked of the 're-design of major areas of older towns and cities', which would entail 'significant demolition'.[12] While low demand had certainly been a problem in some limited areas, it was now used as an excuse to roll out a mass demolition programme, on a scale not seen since the 1950s and 1960s. The second problem was that soon after Nevin's research was published, the issue of market failure ceased to be a problem as the markets in these areas picked up. While this made a joke out of the economic rationale for the policy, the policy didn't go away.

As the fate of hundreds of communities hung in the balance, in London a battle was raging. Many policy experts and officials were becoming uncomfortable about the introduction of a policy which they feared would herald the return of the post-war slum clearances that destroyed so many communities, only this time without the excuse that these architecturally sound properties were overcrowded, unsanitary and needed to be pulled down. Behind the scenes a power struggle ensued between the Treasury and the Office of the Deputy Prime Minister, the department responsible for communities, under John Prescott. Needless to say, the Treasury won, determined to promote a property strategy which would fuel housing markets and the regional economy. So what was the evidence that persuaded the government, at the behest of the Treasury, to plough billions of pounds of taxpayers' money into a mass demolition programme that was proving so contentious before it had even started? The irony is that communities were being broken up when the aim of the policy was to improve the quality of life in places by increasing prosperity.

A Precursor to Pathfinder

Pathfinder is not the first time this type of policy had been tried. In 2000 an enormously unpopular council policy called Going for Growth, introduced by Labour-led Newcastle city council, saw thousands of people protesting against plans to demolish their homes in the West End and East End of Newcastle. A microcosm of what was later rolled out with Pathfinder across the north, Going for Growth was Newcastle city council's twenty-year strategy to reverse population loss by demolishing thousands of homes and 'remodelling' parts of the city – the 'inner core', which also happened to have stunning riverside views – into 'urban villages', which would attract the middle-income people leaving the city for the suburbs and the green belt. Today there are huge swathes of green areas where hundreds of homes once were, with new plans for Scotswood, in the West End, stalled. The controversial proposals were hit when the Labour council failed to be re-elected in 2004 and were dealt a further blow by the credit crunch.

In an echo of the conversations I later had in Derker and in Liverpool, Rose McCourt, from Save our Scotswood, the local campaign protesting against Going for Growth, had described to me how there had been no consultation with residents about the plans to demolish their homes. 'We first heard about Going for Growth with a phone call from the *Newcastle Journal*, when the reporter told us street by street which homes were earmarked for demolition.' In the pack which later went to residents – uncannily similar to the pack Derker residents found on their doormats – the 6,600 homes to be demolished were coloured red, which indicated they were 'unviable'. The result was an unprecedented community campaign.[13] 'Seven hundred people turned up to the first meeting. We couldn't fit everyone into the church and we had to have another meeting the following night. After that we had to hold meetings at the Scotswood social club, it was the only place big enough. People were literally emptying their purses into the bucket – on a Thursday,' Rose said.[14]

When I met Rose in 2003, Going for Growth had already run into serious trouble, with the architect Richard Rogers resigning from the project. Talking about Scotswood at the time he said, 'When I walked through the beautiful streets of Scotswood and thought about how it was to be demolished, my heart filled with questions.' He went on to say, 'In this kind of situation it's a matter of life or death. In the 1950s and 1960s we took the wrong road.'[15]

But despite Rogers' high-profile outburst and massive local opposition, the policy remained in full swing until 2004, with residents leaving and more and more homes boarded up in preparation for demolition. In another upsetting echo of what I would hear again five years later, Rose said she believed that the stress of moving after a lifetime in the same home had resulted in the death of her neighbour. Eventually, in 2004 the Labour administration lost the council elections after thirty-one years in power, a defeat which was widely seen as the result of the unpopularity of Going for Growth. When the incoming Liberal Democrats vowed to scrap the plans, the announcement was heralded in the *Newcastle Journal* with the headline 'Lib Dems in pledge to halt the bulldozers'.

By anyone's reckoning the policy had been a failure, demolishing hundreds of homes and arousing huge local protest, only to put nothing in its place. So it is astonishing to find Going for Growth described as 'a precursor of the market renewal Pathfinders'.[16] Meanwhile, Nevin's research, which was outdated almost before it was published, was considered sound enough evidence to convince the government to go ahead with the mass demolitions, allocating an initial £500 million and establishing nine Pathfinder areas in 2002. At the time the *Guardian* wrote: 'It is rare that the ideas of academics are taken up wholesale by government, but it happened to Nevin. The new £500m housing market renewal project to rescue areas with a mixture of demolition and redevelopment – in the hope of pushing up private prices – is based entirely on his concept. Nevin gave up academia to take charge of implementing the plan in Stoke and help coordinate the initiative nationwide.'[17]

Acre Lane, Derker, Oldham

If the policy had been controversial to start off with, things were only going to get worse with the report from the House of Commons Select Committee warning that Pathfinder must not 'repeat the mistakes of previous clearance programmes'. The response of the government was to allocate further funding in 2005, bringing the total up to £1.2 billion, and to announce the creation of three additional Pathfinders areas, making twelve in all. A further £1 billion has been allocated between 2008 and 2011, although in the light of the recession the future of the entire programme is in doubt.

Since Pathfinder began, it has been mired in controversy with damning reports from a slew of public and heritage bodies, not to mention MPs, ministers and the House of Commons Select Committee. Following the critical House of Commons Select Committee report, there has also been a damning report from the Audit Commission, while the court cases, invoking human rights, show no signs of abating. Sylvia Nelson, who is the chair of Homes Under Threat, the national umbrella group of activist groups against the programme, said, 'It is not up to the government to decide on a whim where we have to live, all because of a paper exercise that's based on old figures and misinformation.'[18]

Perhaps most disturbing of all is the market renewal programme's approach to criticism and accountability; the independent evaluation of the programme commissioned by the government was undertaken by Nevin Leather Associates, a consultancy co-founded by Brendan Nevin – the architect of Pathfinder himself.

Who Benefits?

The evidence so far is that Pathfinder displaces local people and builds very little. Who are the beneficiaries? A look at the fine print of the contracts between property developers and local authorities shows just how attractive these deals are for developers who are given the status of 'preferred bidder' and for councils who receive billions in government funding.

In Liverpool the 'Overarching Agreement' reached between the council and the developers has carved the Pathfinder parts of the city up into four 'zones of opportunity', with a single developer in charge of each. So, Liz Pascoe's zone comes under house builder Bellway, David Wilson Homes is the developer for City Centre North, Gleesons has City Centre South, and the Stanley Park, Anfield area belongs to Keepmoat. According to the confidential agreement, which is not available for public scrutiny, the council undertakes not to do any deals with other developers. When it comes to public subsidy, it promises to do everything in its power to pull in the maximum amount, stating that 'the council will use all reasonable endeavours to request and actively pursue as much grant funding as possible in connection with the development'. And as far as compulsory purchase is concerned, it pledges to have it confirmed 'as soon as possible'.[19] A damning report by SAVE, the heritage organization, raises the conflict of interest this creates, stating: 'There is a great danger here that local authorities and Pathfinder bodies will simply act in the interests of the commercial developers choosing areas, rather than in the interests of the public they serve and to whom they should be accountable.'[20]

Town planner Jonathan Brown describes Liverpool's 'Overarching Agreement' as a 'monopoly agreement' and agrees with SAVE that it commits the council to do everything in its power to act in the interests of developers, maximizing the grant funding available to the 'zones of opportunity' and using its compulsory purchase powers to the hilt. 'It gives developers a lot of influence over public money,' he said. Pathfinder funding will reach a possible £2.2 billion by 2011, with the New Heartlands agency requiring £800 million in grant funding over a fifteen-year period, according to its business plan for 2008–11.[21] The other Pathfinders run along similar lines. Developers claim that the leverage effect of government funding would be quadrupled by private investment, but it is impossible to ascertain how much private money has gone in.[22] What is known is that the financial collapse has brought much private investment to a halt.

Given the vast sums, Jonathan believes the programme in Liverpool, and elsewhere, was 'never about market renewal' but about making money. 'As the market recovered, why didn't they say, "We don't need to assemble that site any more"? Because the deal had been signed and it will make the developers a hell of a lot of money.' Reflecting this, Bellway's Annual Report stated: 'Bellway's growing involvement in the government's Pathfinder projects in Birmingham, Liverpool and Newcastle will secure a new source of land which will include a high proportion of housing association and first-time-buyer sales, helping to underpin the Group's growth plans and provide a solid foundation for the future.'[23]

But a policy which is underpinned by the market will rise and fall with the market and that report was written before the economic downturn. Now the future is uncertain, particularly for the companies who are the supposed winners, because a boom-based policy which relies solely on creating a strong housing market is unable to adapt to a changing economic climate. The result is that the strange landscape created by Pathfinder is not only one of boarded-up streets but also of large empty plots where construction has stalled, because the worry is that no one will want to buy the houses once they've gone up. Looking at the grassed-over plots in Liverpool or in Salford, in neatly preserved rows where streets once stood, I had the same feeling as I'd had in Derker of a ghostly place left with only memories hanging in the air.

Pathfinder started as a response to a market phenomenon of low prices and continued despite the improved markets which came with boom times. With the economic downturn, the programme is now being scaled back, showing that it's not the policy which has had the impact on the market but the market which calls the tune. The problem with a policy which displays an excessive reliance on the market is not only that it disregards people's lives but that when the market is down, it all but grinds to a halt.

Gaskell Street, St Helen's

6

Housing: The Untold Story

'They're Doing This for Greed, Not for Need'

Betty McVay has lived in West Pilton in Edinburgh all her life. Just five minutes' drive but a world away from sought-after Stockbridge and the Georgian elegance of the New Town, West Pilton has suffered serious deprivation for decades. In 1981 Greater Pilton, which includes Muirhouse, West Pilton, Royston, Granton and Drylaw, was part of the European Poverty Programme, and today it remains among the most deprived parts of Scotland.[1] Despite this, West Pilton is a strong community. Betty, who is now seventy-five, has fostered twenty-three children, alongside her six children and twelve grandchildren. There are many like her.

The other day a friend of Betty's got a strange phone call from a man who said he was 'speaking on behalf of Chinese George'. 'You know him – he's well-known in the area,' the man said. Betty's friend had no idea what he was talking about and put the phone down, but when her husband insisted on calling back, it turned out that the call came from a lawyer's office phoning on behalf of a private landlord who wanted to buy her house. 'She sold to them – they know when to strike,' Betty said. As to 'Chinese George', she said, 'I've never seen him, nobody has, but this lawyer phones people up offering to take properties off their hands.' She thinks it's one of the property companies operating across the area, which have mushroomed as the shortage of social housing has become particularly acute. With the shortage of social housing, which means public housing, it is common practice for private landlords, often operating through property companies, to rent out properties to tenants on benefit – at the so-called 'bottom end' of the market.

Betty knows more than most about private landlords at the 'bottom end'.

She was one of the leaders of a campaign against the privatization of a large part of the council housing in West Pilton in the 1980s. That privatization paved the way for today's concentration of private landlords, which is even more pronounced here than in other parts of the UK, as large amounts of housing were sold en masse. After an unusually cold winter in the early 1980s, there was a thaw, boilers burst and floods damaged hundreds of badly built council homes. The then Conservative council decided the only alternative was to sell more than 700 of the homes affected to a consortium of private house builders, who did them up for sale. 'They were done up, but they should have been demolished. They started to deteriorate quite fast and the people who bought them found them hard to sell, so they sold for lower prices to private landlords,' she said. The result is that around 70 per cent of those properties were bought by investors and property companies, rather than by people wanting to live there, and they are now rented out to tenants on housing benefit.

It's easy to tell which they are from their overgrown front gardens and communal areas of neglected, weed-strewn open space, because private landlords, unlike the council, have no obligation to keep them looking nice. Walking around the streets of West Pilton, it seemed incongruous to me that the only estate agents' placards I saw were planted in waist-high unkempt grass. Although the rest of the housing market had slumped by 2008, this part of it was still relatively buoyant. I phoned one of the agents and found out how much the properties were going for. The two-bedroom property I was enquiring about was on the market for £99,500 and was suitable for 'a first-time buyer or an investor'. When I asked more questions about investing, the agent suggested I phone 'a renting company', which manages properties for investors and where I could get more information about the profits I could make.

This was my second visit to West Pilton. The last time I had come was with Shelter in 2004, when I had been commissioned to write up an inquiry the housing charity held into the impact of poor housing conditions on a million children in Britain.[2] At that time the worst housing conditions were also in private rented housing, but concentrated among homeless families. When I went back, the problems were different, but the private landlords had not gone away. Instead they'd moved into the mainstream, no longer just providing accommodation for homeless families, but for a growing proportion of the community who would once have been in social housing. As the amount of social housing continues to shrink, the property companies entrench their hold over the area.

In a policy paper by Shelter published in 2008 called 'Private Renting for Public Good', the housing charity describes the impact of introducing the market into housing for the poorest in society. 'As demand grows there is a race to the bottom,' writes Adam Sampson, director of Shelter, describing how those who suffer most are those least able to compete financially, who are 'in no position to exercise choice in the market, which leaves them open to exploitation and to living in the worst conditions'.[3]

In Edinburgh I heard what this meant when a support worker at the West Pilton Child and Families Centre told me that some landlords fail to provide even basic furniture like beds. 'I've got one family where there is just one bed for the family. It's one mum and two kids and they sleep in the double bed together.' Gilly Hainsworth, who also works in Pilton and is the director of the Haven children's centre, talked of similar experiences. 'I was visiting a woman who sleeps on her settee. I know another family with a similar arrangement. She's got a disability, so it's not very comfortable.' Her words echoed what I'd heard before when the head teacher at the local primary school told the Shelter inquiry, 'There was one family where the wee one came in absolutely delighted because he'd just got a bed. He told everybody, he was so proud. He didn't realize everybody else had a bed.'[4]

At the local primary school and at the local child-and-family centre the Shelter panel also heard of the incidence of 'buggy babies' – babies who are left in their buggy twenty-four hours a day because of overcrowding and poor conditions such as damp and mould. Simon Toyne, who was then the deputy unit manager at the West Pilton child-and-family centre, said: 'If the place is cluttered and there's nowhere for the child to sit or lie or play, you get "buggy children". We get a lot of young babies that end up in their buggies for hours on end. Their heads get straightened because they've spent so much time lying down. In a baby, the skull is soft so it misshapes their head. The skull sets and they're left with life-long damage. It's such a huge stigma for something that could have been avoided. There's a huge amount of guilt in parents who later realize it's too late to do anything.' We were also told of the huge number of mental health problems, with children as young as eight talking of suicide. When I returned in 2008, I heard how the 'buggy babies' were still there.

The property companies targeting West Pilton are active not only in Edinburgh but in every town and city all over Britain, from Newquay to Hartlepool and from London to Blackpool. This is one part of the housing market which remains fairly strong, in spite of the recession, as public housing becomes a thing of the past and policies such as Pathfinder limit the amount of available housing even further. A report commissioned by the government in 2008 describes this part of the private rented market as the 'slum' rental market 'at the very bottom end' of the sector.[5] These areas tend to cluster, creating ghettoes of exclusion and sharpening the picture of polarization and segregation that characterizes British cities. They are transient places. In a vicious cycle, they offer the worst conditions and house the most 'vulnerable' tenants – a euphemism which covers those who need the most help and those who cause the most trouble.

Social-housing landlords are, like any others, not keen to house difficult tenants and place great store by what are known as 'allocations policies', which is a little like selection in schools, allowing housing associations to pick the good tenants. They also have a range of legal tools at their disposal, including the power to remove people from the housing register and to evict them. The result is that those who are known to cause trouble are excluded from social housing and left to the slums of the private rented sector, which are fast turning into ghettoes, in contrast to the high-security environments of public housing, fortified by Secured by Design policies. A parenting officer told me how 'enforcement-led evictions' were making things worse. 'It's been led by housing and it increases ghettoization, creating enclaves of poor-quality private rented housing, which means that things become even more polarized,' he said, a comment which reflects crime figures looked at in the next section, which shows that crime is highest in areas of private rented housing.

There is no security. Tenants who complain about poor conditions face the risk of eviction, a catch-22 the Citizens Advice Bureau revealed in its report of 2007: *The Tenants' Dilemma: Warning, Your Home is at Risk if You Dare Complain*. [6] Many are what's known as 'HMOs' – Houses in Multiple Occupation – which are bedsits with high concentrations of economic migrants, who may be forced to share mattresses in shifts. Often they clash with the poor, mainly white population, who are increasingly turning to the BNP. There are enclaves of streets like this in every town and city, very often just around the corner from high-security gated developments.

A major problem for tenants is that they can get kicked out at any time, not only for complaining about repairs but because they often can't pay the rent. One of the main problems for people who rent private properties paid for by housing benefit is that the benefit they receive is normally quite a lot less than the rent. This isn't anecdotal evidence: it was confirmed by the government's own independent review of social housing in 2007, which found that the majority of tenants on benefit faced a shortfall of £24 a week for rent.[7] Finding that amount extra from income support of £60.60 a week is a considerable hit, leaving barely more than £5 a day to live on. The system is changing now, adding another layer of confusion, with Local Housing Allowance replacing housing benefit, but there is little evidence that it will improve, with the changes already subject to legal challenges and accusations from tenants and council housing departments that the government slipped new legislation through the backdoor without proper consultation. Under Local Housing Allowance new, much larger market areas have been drawn up, which means that tenants living in more expensive parts of the city are likely to find their benefit pooled with cheaper areas, bringing benefit levels down. Shelter warns this 'may force claimants to cluster in particular areas' and 'worsen the effects of marginalization', which means that the pattern of ghettoization will increase.[8]

Local Housing Allowance was introduced in 2008 and at the time of writing it is too early to tell what its effects will be, but the early signs are not encouraging; figures obtained from the Department of Work and Pensions suggest that more than 63,000 people across England could be priced out of their homes.[9] Equally disturbing are the accusations that the government is riding roughshod over the legal system after the House of Lords found in favour of a test case by Sheffield tenant Daniel Heffernan, who argued that his benefit had been unfairly reduced and that the Sheffield-wide market area was too large. Rather than alter the proposals, the government pushed through an amendment enabling it to overturn the Lords' judgement after only a week's consultation, which was quietly tabled on the first day back after the Christmas recess.[10] The British Property Federation claimed the 'backdoor' change made a 'mockery' of the consultation process.[11]

One organization which works with tenants in trouble all around the country and can give a national snapshot of what is going on for those forced to rent from private landlords is the Citizens Advice Bureau. Jim McKenzie, manager of the Citizens Advice Bureau in Truro in Cornwall, said: 'It should be accommodation which is affordable but very often it isn't and those checks aren't made. I think it's going to get worse.' In Hartlepool I was told, 'It could be the case that the landlord comes in with a rent of £90 but the rent officer says the maximum benefit that can be paid is £60. We have three to four enquiries a week from tenants who can't meet the shortfall. It is becoming more frequent as rent levels rise. If they can't meet the shortfall, it is very difficult; we get a lot of clients who present themselves as homeless.'

In Blackpool I heard from CAB's Julia Hannaford what conditions can be like. 'In our inner wards in the most deprived parts of the city, private renting is up to 50 per cent. It's very, very run-down, poor-quality accommodation. It's very poor when people move in and the repairs are never done. A lot of our clients move from poor-quality housing every few months. It means children moving around the area, sometimes having to change schools – there's no stability.' Yet despite all the evidence, because of the acute shortage of housing the government is determined that far more public housing should be provided through the private rented market. At a recent government seminar it was described as the 'new game in town'. Comments were invited from the audience of housing professionals about what they were doing to grow private renting in their areas. One response was that rather than trying to expand it, housing managers were 'proactively trying to suppress it' because conditions were so bad. Another said, 'We have 60 per cent of our housing in the private rented sector and we don't need any more.' Yet another added that the correlation between private renting and deprivation was recognized at his council.

For John Sim, manager of private-sector housing at St Helen's Council in 2009, one of the main problems is that private landlords are so poorly regulated. He carried out an investigation into conditions in a part of the city which was causing concern and found that 82 per cent of private rented properties did not meet the minimum standards set out in the Housing Act of 2004, with 71 per cent revealing hazards which included insulation, overcrowding, damp and mould growth. 'The growth of the private rented sector has, unfortunately, been at the bottom end – the unprofessional landlords who aren't interested in management of the property, just capital appreciation of assets. It's really the housing of last resort and you end up in some of the worst properties,' he said.

Lord Richard Best, who has worked in housing for more than thirty years, as former head of the Joseph Rowntree Foundation and the National Housing Federation, agrees. In a recent paper he wrote: 'It seems astonishing that the private rented sector – a multi-million pound industry that profoundly affects the lives of millions of consumers – has no regulator, no ombudsman and no redress scheme. Following the buy-to-let boom, there are now hundreds of thousands of landlords who have not had to pass any tests of competence, demonstrate any knowledge of landlord and tenant law, or prove their honesty, financial probity or absence from criminal convictions, let alone have any experience of property management. Any drug dealer can set up overnight as a landlord, or indeed as a letting agent.'[12] And yet this is the government's preferred mechanism for housing poor people.

West Pilton is an area with serious problems yet the community is strong. But what is happening incenses community leaders like Betty McVay. 'It's all about money. Politicians used to think homes were for people but now the private landlords are running riot. It's become a greedy market. Politicians should be standing up and saying that what is happening in our society is that people are doing this for greed and not for need. It's awful for communities like this who have tried so hard,' she said.

Why Poverty is Hidden

In Truro in Cornwall the shortage of housing is forcing people to live in trailers, in caravan parks leased by landlords, where conditions can be even worse. 'We have a much higher proportion of people than you would believe living in mobile homes and they have even fewer rights. These are potentially the new enclaves of deprivation,' CAB's Jim McKenzie said.

The trailer parks in Truro and the 'buggy babies' in Edinburgh are the worst examples of the housing conditions that I came across, but more and more British towns and cities have areas of third-world conditions, particularly in the north west and north east, London and parts of Glasgow. Edinburgh boasts a more well-heeled and affluent image than Glasgow, but as Gilly Hainsworth drove me from Pilton to the centre of the city, we passed an area which she said was known as 'Bosnia'. 'It's strange where the boundaries are,' she said. 'Edinburgh is a good place to live and there's a good quality

Ascot Walk, Salford

of life, but it's complete apartheid. It's the same for every city in Britain – there's 20 per cent of the population who have a completely different life and that percentage is growing all the time.' According to figures from the Joseph Rowntree Foundation, 13 million people – 22 per cent of the population – live below what is defined as the 'low income threshold',[13] while the number of people on very low incomes reached an all-time high of 5.5 million in 2006/7.[14]

Poverty is often described as 'hidden'. Although those who live nearby will be dimly aware of these enclaves, fast turning into ghettoes, they avoid them at all costs and live a life as separate from these places as the 'different planets' of Disraeli's Sybil. The places and the conditions also remain hidden from the media, not only because we all prefer to look away but also because local authorities are not keen to publicize their problems. Today the relationship between every local council and the press is controlled by the 'press office', which aims to present the local authority in the best possible light. This inevitably means sweeping these problems under the carpet, sometimes aggressively so.

When I visited places with hardly any shops or buses, let alone a pub or a bank, I saw the kind of poverty I had never seen before in Britain. Walking round areas of run-down housing, with patches of wasteland and no amenities bar numerous CCTV cameras, the perception of rising affluence that characterized the Blair era was light years away. More working-age adults live in poverty than when Labour came to power[15] and the reality is that since 1979 the poor have got much poorer. The UK has a higher proportion of the population in relative poverty than nearly every other EU country, almost double the Netherlands' and one and a half times that in France.[16] Even less well known than the facts about poverty are the housing policies that have, in large part, caused it. This is the great untold story. Housing, by which we invariably mean 'poor housing', is not a sexy subject. It's rarely covered by the media and so press offices and local-authority marketing departments collude in presenting a rosy picture of housing, with stories which focus on the building of aspirational new apartment blocks rather than the growth of slums. Once every one of the broadsheets had a housing and planning correspondent, now none of them do. 'Property', on the other hand, has spawned supplements filled to bursting and countless television programmes.

The other key reason why such a significant social change remains so obscure is because it is mired in unprecedented amounts of jargon and complex policy detail, which is confusing even for those who take an active interest. Stock transfer, ALMOs, RSLs, Choice-Based Lettings, Local Housing Allowance and Broad Market Rental Areas are just a few of the terms which keep an understanding of the subject at a distance from ordinary people and from the emotional reality of these policy changes on people's lives. The impact of introducing the market into housing – and into many other aspects of public policy – is to breed jargon at every turn, creating a cloak of incomprehensibility, confusing people who might voice louder criticisms if they only knew what was going on.

The press and the public have missed a radical change in housing. The process of introducing market forces into the part of the public sector which was once housing policy began with Mrs Thatcher and was stepped up by Labour. While the debate over health and education is fairly robust, there has been no debate over the future of housing. The result is effectively the end of social housing in Britain, a national housing crisis and the creation of new slums.

How Public Housing was Killed off

In 1978, the last year before Mrs Thatcher came to power, the government built more than 100,000 council homes and the private sector built 150,000.[17] Since then the figures for private-sector house building have remained roughly stable – although that fell with the downturn – but the government builds hardly any, which is the simple reason why there is such a shortage of housing, not merely for people on low incomes but for many professionals. When the government talks about the shortage of affordable housing, they never mention their role in this, instead emphasizing that the market must be encouraged to build the amount of homes we need. But the point is that private house builders have never met all Britain's housing needs and they never will, because legislation states that housing must be provided for those in genuine need[18] regardless of the ability to pay for it.

From the end of the First World War until Mrs Thatcher came to power, public housing, which was once simply called council housing, provided housing for a wide range of people, more than a third of whom were on above-average incomes. That's in sharp contrast to today where, like the public housing 'projects' of the US, public housing is seen as housing of last resort, places where two thirds of tenants are unemployed and on benefit.

When the Conservatives came to power, they not only stopped building, they also famously introduced new legislation giving council-house tenants the 'right to buy' their homes, with the help of discounts on the market value of the property of up to 50 per cent. The BBC reported at the time: 'The government believes the bill will transform the social structure of Britain for good.' It went on to say, 'Shelter, the organization for homeless people, has said the move will increase the number of homeless people and decrease the number of homes available to accommodate them.'[19] More than 1.5 million people did buy their homes and the policy, which was very popular with those who could afford to buy, became one of the emblems of the Thatcher government, continuing once Labour came to power. So did the housing shortages predicted by Shelter, which have affected millions more than those officially defined as homeless, fuelling the housing crisis in the process. There are currently more than 1.67 million households on the waiting list for social housing in England, a staggering figure which reflects a 64 per cent increase since 1997. More than 600,000 of these households are homeless, living in overcrowded, temporary or other unsuitable accommodation.[20]

'Right to buy' was a justifiably popular policy. It transferred wealth to the less well-off, though it also created clusters of poverty in places where the majority of tenants were unable to buy their homes. Yet its most significant legacy, which has so much bearing on today's housing crisis, was not the selling off of council properties, but the Tory decision to forbid councils to re-invest the money they made from the sales to build more council housing. According to research from Cambridge University, 242,000 new homes need to be built annually to meet demand to 2026[21] – a not dissimilar figure to the number built in 1980. In keeping with these targets, since 1997 similar numbers of private-sector homes – around 150,000 – have been turned out every year, increasing briefly during the housing boom only to fall back sharply. But the amount of social housing built has plummeted, and is even less than when New Labour came to power, averaging 11 per cent of all new homes since 2002, compared to 46 per cent in 1980 and 15 per cent in 1989, when Thatcherism was at its height.[22] Right to buy killed off councils' ability to build more public housing and from this point on, first under the Conservatives and then more aggressively under successive Labour governments, the market began to enter every aspect of housing policy, each policy change bringing with it its own impenetrable jargon. First off was the introduction in 1986 of 'stock transfer', which oversaw the 'transfer' of millions of council homes from local authorities to voluntary-sector housing associations, also known as 'Registered Social Landlords', or RSLs. This is when council housing underwent its first major linguistic change and confusingly started to be called 'social housing'.

Ironically, given the increasingly market-orientated nature of today's Registered Social Landlords, this part of the voluntary sector was once described as the 'housing association movement' and was characterized by its radicalism and progressive nature. It had emerged from the charitable and voluntary sector of the early twentieth century, embodied by organizations such as the philanthropic Peabody Trust, founded with a bequest from a banker in the mid nineteenth century, but it also included the type of housing cooperatives popular in the 1960s and 1970s, which often emerged from the squatting movement. During the 1970s housing associations attracted activists and campaigners involved in left-wing politics and in the 1980s the housing association movement was strongly allied with anti-Thatcherism and Labour in opposition. As New Labour got ready for power, there was huge hope that a change of government would push housing up the political agenda. By the end of the 1990s, when it was clear which way the political wind towards housing was blowing, the image of the sector had totally changed, as housing associations with many billions of pounds in reserves merged with each other and underwent expensive branding exercises. Today, many have the turnover of a multinational company and resemble private developers, paying their chief executives commensurate salaries.

They have also been tarnished by the 'stock transfer' process itself, which has proved very controversial for many councils and housing associations. 'Stock transfer' was supposed to reflect 'tenants' choice', with tenants voting in a secret ballot about whether or not they wanted a housing association rather than their local council as their landlord. But many of these allegedly free and fair elections seem to have had more in common with elections in tinpot dictatorships, with repeated accusations of ballot rigging,[23] while in some areas, such as Birmingham, tenants voted 'no', leaving the policy and the local-authority housing department in disarray.[24]

When the Tories started to introduce the market into housing, they didn't plan to do away with building public housing completely; the idea was that in place of the council-house building programmes of the post-war period – many of which resulted in the disastrous system-building of tower blocks which had to be knocked down – 'social housing' would be built by housing associations working with private-sector developers. Under this system, which came in with an obscure change to planning law in 1990 known as 'Section 106', house builders had to work with local authorities to negotiate a percentage of public housing in all new developments. Over the last twenty years some housing has been built under Section 106, but nowhere near what's needed. That is not to say that many housing associations do not provide decent homes at below market rents. The criticism is that this approach has failed to build the amount of housing Britain needs, resulting in no more than the 11 per cent or so built over the last few years, a figure which is falling further as the recession bites. The government continually pledges to increase the amount of social housing built and has announced that councils will finally be allowed to build again, but given the current figures and the sheer amount lost, this is unlikely to make a significant difference.

The other market policy which was facilitated by the Tories but really came into its own under New Labour was the provision of public housing through the private rented market. In 1988 the Conservatives deregulated all lettings and ended nearly seventy years of rent control. In the mid 1990s a new form of mortgage finance, the 'buy-to-let' mortgage, was introduced. This was aimed specifically at investors who wanted to buy properties for the purpose of renting them out. The result today is that 'buy-to-let' makes up nearly a third of the private rented sector. In a typical blurring of terms, when the government talks of the private rented sector, they rarely distinguish between homes let to young professionals in their twenties, whose lifestyles are well suited to short-term renting, and the phenomenon of providing public housing through this market, which has come about because of the lack of social housing. It is left to the housing experts who actually work at the sharp end, like Lord Best and John Sim at St Helen's, to point out that the people who are profiting the most from these changes are the landlords.

As the shortage of housing becomes more acute, the government is relying more on the private rented sector to provide public housing for the poorest, while the hope has been that a historically unprecedented policy of maximum housing growth by the private sector will cater to everyone else, with the aim of bringing down house prices by flooding the market with new homes for sale. When Gordon Brown came to power, one of his first initiatives was to emphasize that he would be ramping up this growth strategy, which had been spearheaded by the Treasury throughout his time as Chancellor, announcing plans for ten new 'eco towns' and pledging to build a colossal three million homes by 2020. As the government pinned its housing policy almost entirely on the profits and growth of the private sector, the language of housing changed once again, with the use of the term 'affordable housing' replacing social housing. Except that much of affordable housing isn't public housing at all, it's market housing which the government hoped to make affordable by encouraging developers to build it in such large numbers.

That was when the housing market was still booming, but even then the growth policy had no chance of success, because it was based on the fallacy that the private sector could meet the demand created by the death of public housing. What perplexed the Treasury while Brown was Chancellor was why supply and demand was out of synch with the economists' rulebook, with the private sector failing to respond to the demand for more homes. The reason was very simple: house builders have greater guarantees of profits if they limit supply and so keep prices high. House builders are not at fault in this respect, as they are private companies whose first priority is to deliver maximum returns for their shareholders. But the supply of housing is a public good which cannot be met by house builders alone, who inevitably put the market first.

Trying to find an answer to this conundrum, in 2003 the government commissioned Kate Barker, previously chief European economist at Ford Europe, to carry out a review into housing supply. To her credit, this was also the conclusion she reached in her interim report and, to be fair to the Treasury, the suspicion that house builders were deliberately constraining supply was an issue they had long been grappling with. In her interim report Barker found that to maximize their profits, house builders control production rates and 'trickle out' no more than 100–200 houses a year from a large development. 'This may not be desirable from society's point of view,' she wrote.[25]

But by the time the final review came out six months later, the role of house builders in limiting supply had been airbrushed out by the Treasury. Instead, the clear recommendation was that the only solution to the shortage of housing was to remove restrictions on the planning system, to encourage house builders to build such a large number of new homes that prices would come down. When Gordon Brown appointed Yvette Cooper secretary of state for communities and local government, she was interviewed by the architectural journalist Rowan Moore for the magazine *Prospect*. When Moore put to her that the decline in house building over the last thirty to forty years was almost entirely due to the end of council-house building, Cooper responded, 'We effectively have a market failure,' because 'the private sector has not responded to rising demand for private housing'. Rather than acknowledging the true nature of this market failure – which is that housing is unable to operate as a pure market because it has to cater for those on low incomes – the government decided the only option was to create even more favourable market conditions. They did this because they felt they had no option: developers clearly had no market incentive to build what was required and the government was ideologically opposed to public house building.

Now the boom has turned to bust, it is clear that the private house builders were right and the government was wrong. Thousands of newly built homes for sale in city centres and market renewal areas lie empty and unsold. The consequence is that house building has crashed to its lowest level since 1945. It might seem reasonable to expect that as prices come down, the affordability crisis will ease, but because housing relies on mortgage finance, it doesn't work like that. The economic downturn has led to falling house prices, but it has been nowhere near the level needed to allow people on lower incomes on to the housing ladder, particularly because the credit crunch means mortgages are much harder to obtain, leading to the lowest number of first-time buyers since records began.

At the same time there have been bizarre and unexpected impacts on other parts of the housing market, the downturn colliding with the Pathfinder policy and the extreme shortage of housing. In hindsight, although no one predicted it, it seems obvious that homelessness and overcrowding would be the result of the demolition of so many thousands of homes, with the result that homelessness and waiting lists for housing have soared across the Pathfinder areas. Policies like this, combined with the slow death of public housing, have ironically creating an entirely different type of market for housing, flourishing at what is euphemistically described as 'the bottom end' of the market.

How the Homeless Moved into Yuppie Flats

The view from the 'executive apartments' at Rushgrove Gate swept down across the river to the steel and glass towers of Canary Wharf. Round the corner the Docklands Light Railway sped commuters to the office in minutes. Yet the spanking new apartment blocks didn't feel quite as the brochure promised, and not only because of the brutalist 1960s deck-access block visible through the window. Rather than housing the Docklands professionals the flats had been built for, all their residents were homeless.

Rushgrove Gate was built in 2005. The development attracted media interest because it was owned by investor Imagine Homes, which was run until the downturn by Grant Bovey, husband of TV presenter Anthea Turner. Located in Woolwich, one of the more deprived parts of London, Bovey's announcement that he had sold all the flats off-plan, before they had even been built, drew the attention of the *Financial Times*. The paper investigated and found that he had sold the entire block to an investment company called Veritas, which, it emerged, he owned himself. The *FT* reported: 'He has struck a deal to fill the "exciting new-look property" with council tenants, raising questions over how much private-sector demand exists for such flats. Imagine Homes marketed the Woolwich property for six weeks, during which time it failed to turn up a single buyer.'[26] Instead, there were was plenty of demand for the properties from another source – homeless families.

Bovey's wasn't an isolated case: it was starting to happen in developments all over Docklands. In this bizarre new market cycle, when new blocks failed to sell to individuals, they were bought by buy-to-let investors, who then leased the flats back to local councils. As councils are legally obliged to provide emergency temporary accommodation for people who become 'unintentionally' homeless, these flats ended up as temporary accommodation. Fuelled by the severe shortage of social housing, this was common practice by 2005, creating a very lucrative business opportunity for investors, who were paid hundreds of pounds a week by councils to house homeless people at market rents.

The unexpected cycle began in boom times but with the arrival of the downturn, it has become a lot more serious. The need to house homeless families in a time of severe housing shortage has suddenly created a new market opportunity, at a very considerable cost to the taxpayer. Karen Buck, who is the Labour MP for Regent's Park and Kensington North, explained to me how the 'crazy' system works, with Westminster Council, for example, paying an astronomical £435 a week of taxpayers' money to private landlords, through housing benefit, to house each homeless family. The most extreme example to hit the headlines revealed how a homeless family was paid £12,000 in benefit a month to live in a £1 million home in west London.[27] However, much more common than anomalies like this is the growing tendency for councils to move homeless families out to 'cheaper' places like Woolwich or Barking. Councils receive the same amount of subsidy from central government for homeless families, but because they have no legal requirement to house them within their own boroughs, moving them to cheaper areas means there are profits to be made. 'They make a profit on it, quite a lot of local authorities do. Of course, it's crazy,' Buck said.

'Homelessness' is another of those words that is not as easy to understand as it sounds. The assumption is that being without a home means sleeping on the streets. More than 75,000 of the households who are officially registered 'homeless' are not sleeping on the streets but neither do they have a home. They may have been evicted for not paying the rent or they may be living in dreadfully overcrowded accommodation in 'concealed households' which they neither own or rent. Or they may be 'sofa surfers', who move around sleeping on friends' sofas. If they can convince the council that they really are 'unintentionally' homeless, the local authority has a legal duty to house them.

The result is that they are placed in emergency temporary accommodation, perhaps in executive apartments like the ones in Rushgrove Gate, or at 'the bottom end', in the kind of slum housing John Sim encounters daily in his job as private-sector housing manager at St Helen's Council. Bizarrely, in some places families may find themselves in the more exclusive parts of town, subsidized by benefit payments to the tune of hundreds of pounds a week, although that is not as good as it sounds because they end up in a benefit trap, unable to work because the rent is so astronomically high. Housing homeless people in the private rented sector has created a hugely profitable business for property companies like Orchard & Shipman, which describes itself as the 'leading provider' of what is known as 'private-sector leasing'.[28] As the bottom falls out of the rest of the property market, buy-to-let investors are being encouraged to let their properties to homeless families through companies like Orchard & Shipman. According to its website, the company guarantees rental income to private landlords for a minimum of five years and 'has extensive experience of the provision and management of temporary accommodation for homeless families'. They are not exceptional in any way, with research from Shelter revealing that nearly 42,000 homeless families are now housed by 'private-sector leasing' schemes.

Alongside markets, that other bedfellow of New Labour policy, targets, has overtaken homelessness. The government has promised to halve the number of homeless households by 2010. Reducing homelessness is obviously a good thing, but the allegation repeatedly made across the country is that councils are meeting targets but not solving the problem. In Cornwall Jim McKenzie told me, 'The government is putting pressure on local authorities not to accept people as homeless – one way to reduce your targets is not to accept people. Then they just become homeless, but not statutorily. I attended a housing conference and was told homelessness had been cut by a third but then I heard they'd rejected two thirds. The whole of homelessness is driven by targets.' So what happens to people who are homeless but not officially recognized as such? Another housing manager at a council in the north said: 'I don't know. I suspect they share houses. We haven't done any research into people we can't re-house, because we don't have that type of resource.'

The result is that this market- and target-driven homelessness policy is either placing homeless people in the benefit trap or failing to provide housing for them at all. Simultaneously, with the housing market failing to meet demand by oversupplying the kind of expensive apartments families don't want and can't afford, entire blocks like the ones in Docklands are filled with homeless families. In Parr, a deprived part of St Helen's, more 'executive apartments' have been bought by private landlords and investors, who have allowed the area to deteriorate. 'There was no money coming in so they dropped the rent to the point where the only people who were prepared to pay were pretty frightful. It's brothels and crack houses and it's on its way to becoming a slum,' David Ireland, the director of the Empty Homes Agency, said. Now another block of 300 or so apartments is under construction in another part of St Helen's, with the first phase already bought by investors. John Sim said, 'We have concerns about what's going to happen with that too.' He added that colleagues in other parts of the country have told him they are also experiencing similar problems.

I was told by one house builder that allowing private investors to house the homeless was a good way of letting the market deal with the chronic shortage of housing, but from Docklands to St Helen's that seems less like a policy and more like a powerless response in the face of the unpredictable vagaries of the market. Neither is it a straightforward case that the shortage of housing will be met by the thousands of apartments lying empty in city centres, because that is not how this distorted market works. Instead, just like the new phenomenon of 'slum rental', in many places it is creating the ghettoes of tomorrow, as homeless families are clustered into new housing built for sale in 'cheaper' areas.

State Socialism Versus Private Enterprise – Is There an Alternative?

Barking and Dagenham, the borough to the east of London's Docklands, on the border with Essex, is one of these cheaper areas, often referred to as 'cold spots' by estate agents. Because property prices are a little lower, private landlords have moved in renting accommodation to large numbers of people needing social housing, including concentrations of economic migrants and asylum seekers. Alongside poor conditions and overcrowding, the kind of racism which exists in other 'cold' areas, often in old industrial towns, is resulting in growing support for the far-right British National Party among the poor white working-class community. Woolwich, another 'cold' area, which borders the well-heeled affluence of Greenwich, is similar, with 'white' pubs emblazoned with flags of St George next door to HMOs housing north African families. This patchwork of segregation between 'cold' and 'hot' areas is the same all across London, from Haringey and Highgate in the north to Peckham and Dulwich in the south. It's also the opposite of the government's frequently stated aim to create 'mixed communities' and break up concentrations of deprivation.

It is no coincidence that Jon Cruddas, Labour MP for Dagenham, put housing right at the top of his bid to become deputy leader of the Labour Party in 2008. In Barking and Dagenham the BNP won twelve of the fourteen council seats they contested in the local elections, and Cruddas claims that BNP leader Nick Griffin is considering standing against him at the general election. From where Cruddas is standing, it's the acute shortage of social housing, creating the conditions he sees every day, which is feeding support for the far right. Cruddas's answer is two-fold: to allow councils to build housing again, and to stop developers from holding on to land but failing to build on it.

Following a successful showing in the deputy-leadership campaign, it was reported that Gordon Brown wished to appoint Cruddas housing minister, an offer which stalled as it became clear that the Cruddas agenda for housing would not be sanctioned by New Labour. At the time a source close to Cruddas said, 'In the conversations he had with the powers that be, it was clear that there would not be a significant policy shift towards greater public social housing.'[29] The recession and a reassessment of the role of the private sector has led to a shift in attitudes and a growing role for councils, but given the huge weight of demand, it is unlikely to make a significant difference. Despite the financial crisis, the two main parties remain pledged to extending home ownership, continuing the social revolution Margaret Thatcher began with 'right to buy'. As the market is unable to meet demand, particularly in the current climate, the consequence is a stalemate.

In Britain, housing is organized quite differently compared to the rest of Europe, where there is a wider range of tenures to choose from. With more than two thirds owning their own homes, we have one of the largest owner-occupied sectors, exceeded only by Ireland, Spain and Greece, where social structures relating to landholdings are quite different. Although severely depleted, the size of the public housing sector also remains relatively large, leaving housing polarized between two monolithic blocks. In continental Europe, on the other hand, there are many options, including private renting and cooperative housing, in addition to home ownership and public housing. But in Britain other options were squeezed out, in particular the continental model of choosing to rent rather than to own, with rent controls introduced during the First World War decimating the apartment lifestyle so popular in Europe. It is this more than anything which has perpetuated the myth that an Englishman's home is his castle and that the English prefer houses to flats.

However, what differentiates Britain from the continent is not how much of the population owns or rents, but ideology. Housing policy was driven by public-sector state socialism in the post-war period until market-based policies took over from 1979, which is the ideology that still prevails, while in the rest of Europe a more mixed housing economy is the norm. Closely related to this is the cultural aspiration or stigma which became associated with different types of housing, with home ownership the desired state, in contrast to the 1960s and 1970s, when public housing housed a wide section of society. On the continent, whether somebody lives in cooperative housing in Sweden, a housing association flat in Holland or a rented apartment in Paris has far less bearing, both on the quality of their home and their social standing.

This cultural issue is at least as important as the question of how the new homes Britain needs will be provided. We must move beyond the idea that the only possible foundation for housing policy is the expansion of home ownership. The best way of doing this would be to open up other alternatives, including public housing and cooperative housing, to everybody suffering from the housing crisis, from teachers and nurses to young professionals, as well as those on low incomes. It goes without saying that people on low incomes would remain the majority in public housing, but bringing in a broad range of others would do a lot to improve its social standing. It is likely that much of the new housing lying empty, particularly in regeneration areas in the north, will be bought by housing associations, bringing new opportunities to increase the amount of social housing.

Then there's the cooperative movement, which began in Britain, its historical roots stretching back to the Chartists and the Rochdale pioneers, and spread out to flourish in other parts of Europe, particularly in Holland and in Scandinavia. In Sweden 18 per cent of all homes are provided by cooperatives, but in Britain the amount is tiny. David Ireland, the director of the Empty Homes Agency, feels this is the big missed opportunity, contrasting the Dutch approach with our own; in Holland legislation has encouraged housing cooperatives to take over empty properties. In Britain there are currently 830,000 empty properties, which amounts to 3.5 per cent of the country's housing, compared to the Netherlands, where only 1.5 per cent are empty. 'There are plenty of properties which could potentially be used,' he explained, if only the political will was there. The reason it isn't is because the UK's cooperative movement, which began to thrive in the 1970s, fed into what was then the 'housing association movement' but has now been subsumed by the commercialism of housing associations. Now, with the financial crisis, he feels there's a place for cooperatives again.

One of the main aims of housing policy, frequently repeated by ministers, is to create mixed communities. The use of the private rented sector to house those on low incomes at the 'bottom end' is creating slum conditions and enclaves of poverty and deprivation which run totally counter to this. Britain would benefit from more renting, but it should follow the European model of providing a high-quality alternative which people can afford to pay for, rather than funnelling large amounts of public money into a strange market cycle which is creating ghettoes. One of the best ways of creating mixed communities happened almost by accident at the behest of the buying policies of the early housing associations, which purchased properties in Victorian terraces, mingling privately owned properties with their own, and creating the mixed nature of desirable parts of London such as Islington. More recently, in keeping with its market emphasis, the government has sought to mix communities by introducing homes for sale into areas of predominantly public housing, but reversing the approach would mix areas far more effectively.

This is the way to create properly mixed communities, but it is the opposite of the current government policy of selling off land, property and 'local-authority assets'. Instead, mirroring the civic achievements of the Victorians, it would rely on ring-fencing land, property and housing for the public good. This could be done by creating trusts in local areas, supported by a planning system which laid out a blueprint for a certain amount of subsidized housing in every locality. Genuinely mixed communities, with diverse populations and a more balanced local economy, also mean more distinctive and exciting places, rather than the sterile sameness of new places today, driven by the importance of rising property values over and above any other consideration.

These are all initiatives that policy makers free of ideological baggage could employ, and the financial crisis and property crash provide a desperately needed opportunity by challenging the political mindset towards housing established by Margaret Thatcher and continued so enthusiastically by New Labour. In European countries which are not shackled by the terms of Britain's housing debate – state socialism versus private enterprise – alternative ways of doing things, such as providing the same level of subsidy across all tenures, as in Sweden, creates a much more balanced housing economy.

The urgent demands of the housing crisis make all-encompassing solutions tempting, closer to the grand visions which characterized post-war house building and more recently the market renewal Pathfinder programme, but history shows that these grandiose schemes rarely provide long-term solutions. Instead, an open-minded approach, prepared to look at a range of options, could make the most of unexpected opportunities. There is public money available for housing and with the Pathfinder programme in doubt, this could potentially run into billions. If this could be channelled through a range of alternatives, including councils, trusts, cooperatives and housing associations closer to their founding spirit, a more mixed economy – and society – will be the result.

It is the opposite to the policies pursued since 1979, which have emphasized the importance of owning one's own home above all else, while running down every other type of housing, in particular social housing. Introducing the market into every aspect of housing has not worked, fuelling a national housing shortage and the creation of ghettoes of poverty. There are alternatives and the collapse in the property market provides an unexpected chance to look at other ways of doing things.

PART THREE: CIVIL SOCIETY

Fenced-in housing and open space: Collyhurst, Manchester

7

Fear of Crime, 'Respect', Trust and Happiness

The last decade has seen the creation of a security-conscious environment quite familiar in Docklands but new to the rest of Britain's cities. 'Defensible space' determines the look and feel of privatized streets and plazas, and homes are built according to strict Secured by Design principles. Side by side with privately owned places devoted to shopping and city-centre apartment living are enclaves of poverty, giving the lie to the promise of 'trickle-down' economics. The really appalling pockets of poverty are in the minority. What are far more common are the social housing estates of relative deprivation which are also designed with fear and security just as much in mind. The aim of all this security is to make people feel safer, but fear of crime is soaring.

Are these the cities we want to live in? We fear being attacked and believe that crime, and in particular violent crime, is rising when it is falling. Yet fear of crime is not linked to actual crime – fear of crime comes with distrust of strangers. Denmark has a similar crime rate to the UK, yet is a less fearful nation and it is also happier and more equal.[1] In Britain unhappiness and depression are double the rates in continental Europe.[2] Are the decisions we're making about how to design our cities making us less happy and more fearful as a result?

Fear of Crime

The Smiths are an average British family. When confronted with the statistics that show crime has been falling sharply, they simply don't believe them. Although none of them has been a victim of crime, they point to the knifings and shootings around the country as evidence that their fears about crime, especially violent crime, are well founded.

Mr Smith was an accountant until he was made redundant and Mrs Smith works part time as a secretary. They live in an affluent suburb and go into the centre of town to shop, but there are many parts of the city they never go to. Down in London, their older son, Jack, works in insurance and is anxious that his job may not survive the financial crisis, leaving him unable to pay the large mortgage on his apartment, which is in a gated complex in Docklands. Their younger daughter, Elaine, is a teacher, also living in London in nearby Hackney, and although she hasn't been able to get on to the housing ladder, she is at least fairly certain that her job is secure. Their granny, who is in her late eighties, lives on her own in a bungalow and rarely goes out, keeping up with the outside world through the telly which is on *Sky News* or *News 24* most of the time.

Twenty years ago the Smiths were burgled while they were on holiday but, fortunately, none of them has been the victim of crime since then. Even so, each member of the family, apart from Elaine, is one of the 80 per cent of Britons who think that crime is rising, although it has been falling steadily since 1995.[3] But while most of them believe that crime, and in particular violent crime, is getting worse, some members of the family, especially Granny and Jack, seem more preoccupied with crime than the others. Recently Jack has also become quite depressed and started a course of cognitive behaviour therapy, offered by his local NHS hospital. As for Elaine, although she lives in a statistically far higher crime area than the rest of her family, she is the least worried and is quite happy to walk home on her own at night.

The Smiths are, of course, a fictitious family which I invented to illustrate the point that fear of crime does not have a causal relationship with actual crime. If it did, Elaine, who lives in the most dangerous part of town, should be far more fearful than Jack in his secure gated complex.

But she isn't, because fear of crime arises from a multitude of complex reasons, underpinned by the emotional state of the individual. This chapter will outline some of the main factors which affect our emotional state and show how the attempts to meet internal needs with an emphasis on external safety – security of all kinds and a highly controlled environment, all considered in this book – is undermining trust between people and, as we trust people less, so we fear crime more.

What are the real reasons behind the soaring fear of crime? This is a problem which affects Britain in particular, where worry about crime is a far greater concern than in other major European countries and even than in the US.[4] It is true that while crime has been declining steadily since 1995, it is far higher throughout Europe and America than it was in the 1950s and 1960s, when Granny was young and Mr and Mrs Smith were children. It is also true that the UK has high crime levels compared to the rest of Europe, topping the European Crime and Safety and Survey, alongside Ireland, Estonia and Denmark.

But rather than confirming that there is a causal link between crime and fear of crime and that Britons should have something to fear because crime in the UK is among the highest in Europe, international comparisons do exactly the opposite. Denmark, for example, which has similar crime levels to the UK, has high levels of happiness, which correlate with low levels of fear. The European Crime and Safety Survey found that a binge-drinking culture, urbanization and large numbers of young people are closely related to violent crime, which are features the UK and Denmark have in common,[5] but Britain and Denmark differ when it comes to fear and happiness, with Denmark emerging as the happiest country in the world, according to the data from the World Values Survey.[6]

Jack Smith, my young insurance executive in his gated complex, is someone who has become far more worried about crime and feels intimidated even looking out of the window at the nearby estates on the Isle of Dogs. As a result he has bought lots of security products to make him feel safer, but the problem is that the more he has, the more he wants. Mr and Mrs Smith also feel more fearful than they used to and they trust people less, worried by immigrants and beggars on the streets. Only Elaine is relatively relaxed and actually quite affronted by all the CCTV on the streets. As for Granny, the specific way stories about crime are reported on television has given her a completely skewed perception of the dangers of the world out there.

But before a look at the real reasons behind fear of crime is possible, the facts about actual crime need to be established, incontrovertibly, because the most common response to news of falling crime figures is that they are simply not true.

Lies, Damn Lies and Statistics:
The Facts about Violent Crime

When I was last in Liverpool, the taxi driver driving me from one interview to another told me crime was a terrible problem in the city. When I quoted him the official figures which show that Liverpool has a low crime rate compared to similar-size cities like Manchester or Leeds, he said he just didn't believe it. He isn't the only one. Leading opinion makers and newspapers don't believe it either, often stating that while overall crime may be falling, violent crime is rising. This is how the *Daily Mail* commented on recent crime figures:

A few nights ago, as an eighteen-year-old stab victim lay in a pool of blood awaiting his statistical turn to become the twenty-first teenager to die violently on the streets of London this year, we learned that crime statistics are dropping dramatically. All is well. Home Secretary Jacqui Smith, while concerned that 'knives are still being used', is best pleased. As well she might be, for the figures are the creation of none other than the British Crime Survey, itself a creation of Jacqui's Home Office. If the British Crime Survey sounds like a vast analytical laboratory stuffed with academics in some ivy-clad university city, that is the whole idea.[7]

So what are the true facts about crime and can they be established, or is it another case of 'lies, damn lies and statistics'?

There are two ways of recording crime: the British Crime Survey (BCS), which is based on interviews with victims and is published by the Home Office, and crimes recorded by the police, known as 'Police Recorded Crime'. It's the British Crime Survey, which was established in 1982 and is an annual survey, which receives the most coverage in the press and is frequently cited as showing sharp falls in crime. It also comes in for the most criticism, with reports claiming it obscures violent crime.

The BCS records increases in crime throughout the 1980s, reaching a peak of 19 million crimes in 1995. Since then crime has steadily decreased, down to 10.1 million crimes in 2007/8, which is less than when the survey began. According to the police, the explanation is that crime falls when the economy is doing well, and the expectation is that there will be some rises in crime and in particular property theft and burglary as a result of the recession.

Back in 1981, Police Recorded Crime stood at a far lower 3 million crimes, and the BCS was introduced and designed to address that gap – described at the time as the 'dark figure' of crime – by including less serious crimes in particular. The BCS interviews a sample of the population to gauge how prevalent less violent crime is across the population. So the claim that the BCS fails to report violent crimes is something of a red herring, because from the start its aim was not to report the most violent crimes. It doesn't even include murder, which is termed a 'victimless' crime, because the victim cannot be interviewed. As for other types of serious violent crime, the Home Office report on the survey states that while the BCS is able to provide a measure of the general experience of violence, the relatively rare occurrence of the most serious violence means that Police Recorded Crime statistics are more reliable.

To get an overview of the amount of overall violent crime, criminologist Mike Hough suggests the most reliable method is to look at both sources together. But, when it comes to the most serious violent crime, if Police Recorded Crime is the best indicator for that, what do those figures show? Given the reams of articles and authoritative statements about rising violent crime, I was surprised to find that murder, attempted murder and serious wounding have all declined steadily every year since 2004, and that the Police Recorded Crime figures for 2007/8 show that violence against the person is down again by 8 per cent and most serious violence is down 12 per cent.[8] The one category of crime which showed a significant increase was drugs offences, up 18 per cent. Hough, who is the director of the Institute for Criminal Policy Research at King's College London, said that rise reflects the growth of on-the-street cannabis warnings. But it is the issue of violent crime which is the most controversial, with the majority of media reports stating that it is rising.

Some of these reports do fall into the 'lies, damn lies and statistics' category, by failing to compare like with like or not putting figures into context. One particularly contentious area is weapons offences. For example, in 2007/8 overall gun crime rose by 2 per cent, because although deaths and serious injuries involving guns showed falls, slight injuries increased. This followed a 13 per cent decline in overall gun crime the previous year, but, despite the context, the figures were widely reported as showing a rise in gun crime.[9] Knife crime is the other type of crime much in the news, although the statistics are difficult to compare because it wasn't recorded by police as a specific category of violent crime until 2007. According to the Metropolitan Police, twenty-two teenagers were stabbed to death in London in 2008, compared to sixteen in 2007, a significant rise of six. But the increase is offset by the fact that there were six fewer fatal teenage shootings than in 2007. And again, as the context for both gun crime and knife crime is a steady fall in the figures for murder, attempted murder and serious violence, it seems clear that violent crime is going down.

But with every media outlet claiming rises in violent crime, I went to see Hough to make double sure my analysis was correct. 'The big story is that things got worse in the 1980s and then they got better, for property crime and for violent crime. The subsidiary story is that there is something going on in the poorest inner-city areas with gang crime and the crimes of socially excluded young men. It's getting worse in the poorest areas, where there's the greatest legacy of Thatcherism and de-industrialization. But the overall picture is quite a reassuring one,' he said.

These are the facts, but although the government, academics and the police – not groups which are often in agreement – all support the figures, most people do not believe them. The deeper underlying reasons, which relate to the physical environment around us, are complex and counter-intuitive, but before looking at those, the role of the media has to be understood.

Fear of Crime and the Media

It is impossible to talk about fear of crime without mentioning the reporting of crime, especially violent crime, in newspapers, on television and online. The BBC, which is far from the worst offender, has been publicly reprimanded after a complaint by a media watchdog about misleading reporting of crime rises was upheld.[10] The same watchdog found that all of the BBC *News Online* headlines over a three-year period systemically cherry-picked rises in crime, while ignoring falls. It's a similar story from the tabloids to the broadsheets and political magazines across the spectrum. When I queried figures from the highbrow magazine *Prospect*, which quoted a 40 per cent increase in violent crime, I received an apologetic reply from one of their editors, which conceded that the statistic was 'misleading' and was based on data 'which shouldn't really have been compared'.[11]

The reporting on crime is directly related to fear of crime, according to the public itself. *Closing the Gaps*, a study into crime and public perceptions by Ipsos MORI, found that when people who thought crime was rising were asked why they thought so, 60 per cent said because of what they saw on television and 46 per cent said because of what they read in the newspapers. Personal experience and reports of crime from friends and acquaintances, on the other hand, were far less likely to be cited.[12]

When Nick Ross, the presenter of the BBC's *Crimewatch*, publicly declared that 'the media have long been peddling a big lie about crime', he was greeted with outrage. Speaking on the *Today* programme, Ross said, 'The most common forms of crime have plunged. Burglary is down 58 per cent, car crime down 61 per cent, violence by 48 per cent. Yes, we do get the wrong impression, yes, it isn't healthy and yes, the media are in part to blame, hunting in packs and hungry for the narrative, regardless of the underlying truth.' In response the *Daily Mail* stuck the knife in by implying he had only spoken out because the BBC had not renewed his contract.[13]

When Ross referred to 'the narrative', he was talking about the way crime is reported. In his book *The Culture of Fear*,[14] the American writer Barry Glassner describes how the media's promotion of fear is down to the way stories are told, with stories about crime focusing on the horrifying story of an individual, rather than placing events in a context which addresses failures in public policy. Adding to the horror, stories about crime focus on the most violent angle, in line with the old adage 'if it bleeds, it leads'. Taking knife crime as an example, the *Evening Standard* reported a fatal stabbing with the moving headline 'Another Knife Victim: Stabbed 16-Year-Old Dies after Begging for His Mother.'[15] The alternative would have been an even-handed piece pointing out that this tragic murder was in the context of a rise in knife crime accompanied by an equally significant fall in gun crime. It goes without saying which story newspaper editors believe is likely to move readers to buy the paper.

The term 'narrative' wasn't a familiar part of the political discussion until New Labour introduced it during the 1990s, although storytelling and narrative techniques have long been used in marketing and advertising. In 1994 the New Labour thinkers Geoff Mulgan and Charles Leadbetter wrote, 'Politics . . . is about constructing narratives that make sense to people: stories that encompass their identities, aspirations and fears and the policies that reflect them.'[16]

Since then 'narratives' that deliver a simple message have moved to the centre of politics, with the 'Respect' campaign and the 'clean and safe' mantra of Business Improvement Districts perfect examples. Keeping places 'clean and safe' and ensuring people behave with 'respect' towards one and another sound like excellent ideas with which few people would disagree. These narratives provide a way into the issues and make difficult topics apparently straightforward, pulling the reader in and grabbing their attention. I constructed a narrative of my own in the introduction of this chapter, to make a complicated subject easier to understand. But reinforcing a simple narrative can obscure the complex reality, in exactly the same way that stories of individuals often fail to place policy issues in their proper context.

When it comes to crime and violence, the tendency is for the media to fall back on a stock narrative, which is that violent crime, especially crime involving guns and knives, is consistently rising. The surge in media coverage of knife crime in London in 2008 followed this to the letter, focusing on the story of individuals rather than the context, with front-page stories of yet another teenage stabbing occurring on an almost daily basis at one period. For an elderly person like the Smith's granny, who rarely leaves the house and relies on lurid TV news, to imagine that kids were killing kids on every London street would be understandable. A proper look at the statistics during the glut of coverage on knife crime, however, shows a more complex picture: deaths involving knives were at a historically low level, but there had been an increase in stabbings among young people, while deaths involving guns had declined. When a story takes off and becomes a media storm, as knife crime did then, it gathers its own momentum; news values change and context and analysis go out the window. This happens for a mix of reasons, underpinned by the fact that 'fear sells' and the reality that teenage murder is a 'good story', invoking human interest, tragedy, revenge and calls that 'something must be done'. Linked to this is the viral effect of a story gathering speed, which transforms the newsworthiness of similar stories, propelling anything relevant to the top of the agenda, where before it may not even have made the back page.

In turn politicians are loath to speak out too loudly to the contrary and have their own set of tough narratives which play well in the media. 'Because of the way the media interacts with politicians, New Labour make very little play about the fall in crime, because they feel they won't be believed. It sets up a spiral of political statements, fuelled by the media, who like the narrative that crime is out of control,' Mike Hough explained.

Given the attachment of media and politicians to the idea that crime, and especially violent crime, is rising, it is hardly surprising so many people fear it's true.

The Paradox of Security: Fear Breeds Fear

The media has an important role to play in ramping up fear of crime, but the deeper, more complex and at times counter-intuitive reasons are rooted in the physical environment.

Stark divisions in cities, stamped on to the psyche of places by security-conscious architecture, are a key factor behind rising fear of crime. In Liverpool my taxi driver assured me the city was one of the highest-crime places in the country. Yet the truth is that Merseyside has the second-lowest crime rate in the north-west region, and crime in the city itself is significantly lower than in Leeds and Manchester, which are of comparable size.[17] It is a classic example of a place where fear of crime rather than crime itself is the problem. Although it is not a high-crime city, it is also one of the most heavily policed and security-conscious places in the country.

To prove just how well defended the region is, the chief constable of Merseyside police was happy to boast that he had sufficient equipment to invade a small country. 'I tell my people on briefing parades, when they start complaining about lack of resources, that with 6,000 people in the organization and all the equipment and assets we have at our disposal, we could invade a small South American country. Although we're not going to . . . not tonight,' he said.[18]

It is also the poorest city in Britain, ranking as the most deprived city in the UK, according to the government's Index of Multiple Deprivation.[19] In outlying areas drones – the unmanned spy planes used in Iraq – patrol the skies over the most deprived parts of Liverpool. The contrast with the centre, with its new high-end shopping centre, could not be greater, except for the level of security, which is similarly high, with Liverpool One employing uniformed private guards to police thirty-four private streets. The security guards enforce restrictive policies on who may or may not enter the area and what they can and cannot do there, following the 'clean and safe' mantra discussed in Chapter 2 to the letter.

The link between security and segregation is most pronounced at the extremes of the social spectrum, in very wealthy or very deprived areas. But all around the country security is becoming an ever increasing part of the physical environment, fuelled by property, insurance and risk, and the role of the police in urban design, through the Secured by Design approach described in Chapter 4. It goes without saying that this is a process boosted by the climate surrounding the 'War on Terror' and the London bombings in 2005.

Take Elaine Smith, who recently moved house. What surprised her most about her new home was the sheer amount of security already there – from CCTV to numerous locks and double locks on the doors and windows and multiple, highly complex alarm systems. Because it reminded her of the security at her brother Jack's gated complex, which made her feel uncomfortable, she decided to get the majority of her hi-tech security features removed. But that was easier said than done. When she finally managed to find builders to take the locks away, they were amazed at what she wanted and told her they rarely found themselves on that sort of job.

There is now a growing body of research into the relationship between security and fear, in the US and the UK, which shows that taking more precautions against crime and strengthening security can increase levels of fear and social isolation.[20] In the UK research commissioned by the Joseph Rowntree Foundation, which looked at extra security in a relatively low-crime neighbourhood, concluded that an 'unintended consequence' of extra security, including intruder alarms and other security measures, was 'to raise concerns over security and safety',[21] while a study on a social housing estate found that security brings an innate contradiction with it, because 'symbols of security can remind us our insecurities'.[22]

The paradox of security is that the better it works, the less it should be necessary. Yet the need for security can become addictive, with people finding that however much they have, it can never be enough, and that, rather like an addictive drug, once they have got used to it, they can't do without it. The economist Richard Layard provides one explanation for this in his book *Happiness*, where he describes the psychological process of adaptation as a kind of treadmill: once people become used to a new experience, they require more of it to sustain their happiness. The example he gives is clearly related to rising standards of living, of growing up without central heating and, despite the cold, feeling fine, in contrast to the present day where, because he has become used to heating, he would feel miserable without it. The various technological innovations many have come to take for granted, from email to satellite navigation systems, have a similar effect, leaving people bereft when they go wrong.

The impact of security hits so hard because the need for physical security and safety is intertwined with the need for emotional security and safety. But just as there is no causal relationship between actual crime and fear of crime, there is no causal relationship between the presence of security and feelings of safety, because feeling safe is an emotional state based on internal feelings rather than external realities, which people quickly adapt to in any case, reverting to their initial state of mind. So Elaine, who feels secure in herself and in her job, is happy to walk through the relatively dangerous streets of Hackney, while Jack, who is anxious about losing his job and fearful of the estates on the Isle of Dogs, is far more scared of crime, even though he lives in a secure gated complex.

To a greater or lesser degree the emotional state of an individual and whether or not they feel safe in the world determines the health of their approach to most things, whether it be work, relationships or where they live. But when it comes to fear of crime, because this is inevitably connected to people's perceptions of their actual physical safety, it is very difficult to separate emotions from realities and internal well-being from external threats.

American studies which show that more security increases fear also reveal a link between fear and a person's sense of self and mastery over the environment. Monica's example, in Chapter 4, showed that her sense of mastery, or personal control, over her environment was diminished by her growing reliance on her security gates, and that this mastery did not return when she needed it, when the security broke down. The spread of security guards and the massive growth of CCTV has the same effect of substituting external controls for personal responsibility for the environment. But rather than reassess such a growing reliance on more and more security in place of personal responsibility, few people question it and fear continues to spiral, fuelled by a security industry which needs fear to prosper.

Because it is visible division and segregation which is making people feel less safe, more security is not going to address the fear that Pat, the hairdresser on the Isle of Dogs, feels about going shopping in the Canary Wharf complex, or Jack's anxiety when he leaves his gated campus for an unfamiliar part of town. This segregation of the physical environment is a relatively new phenomenon, only really taking off in the last decade – the period which coincides with soaring fear of crime. Fear of crime doesn't correlate with actual crime but research shows it does correlate with fear of strangers and fear of difference. Creating such a segregated environment is entrenching this fear of difference and fear of strangers.

Stranger Danger or 'Eyes on the Street'?

Whether strangers are dangerous or essential to healthy city life is the question which has been at the heart of debates about cities for the last fifty years. Jane Jacobs' classic text, *The Death and Life of Great American Cities*, published in 1961,[23] and Richard Sennett's *The Fall of Public Man*, which came out in 1977, argue that the presence of strangers in cities is the essence of civility and safety. Sennett describes the city as the place 'where strangers are most likely to meet' and defines 'civility' as 'treating others as strangers and forging a social bond on that distance'.[24] Jacobs bases her case on 'natural surveillance', which is built around the informal social controls of strangers.

She argues that streets, which are the vitals organs of the city, are kept safe by the 'natural surveillance' of people who do not know each other. 'Peace is not kept by the police but by the intricate, almost unconscious network of voluntary controls enforced by people themselves. In areas where public order is left to the police and special guards, they become jungles,' she writes. More specifically, she adds that the street 'which makes an asset out of the presence of strangers' must have continuous users to add to the effective 'eyes on the street'. We all know how, when walking home late at night, it's places that are quiet and empty which feel the most dangerous, while the continuous presence of people around creates a greater feeling of safety.

Jacobs' work in particular is continually praised by politicians, who pepper speeches with references to her emphasis on diversity in cities. But the irony is that while Jacobs' and Sennett's works are revered as classics, policy has consistently followed the route laid down by another American thinker, architect and town planner, Oscar Newman, author of *Defensible Space*.[25]

He made the case for strangers as dangerous intruders. The role of strangers in places is central because, as Jacobs identified, it is what determines levels of trust in places. 'The unconscious assumption is that the eyes on the street provide general support when the chips are down. The short word for this assumption of support is trust. The trust of a city street is formed over time from many, many little public sidewalk contacts,' she wrote. These little contacts included an exchange with the news-stand man, talking to the grocer, nodding at an acquaintance, admiring new babies and eying the girls. 'Most of it is ostensibly trivial but the sum is not trivial at all. The sum of such casual, public contact at a local level . . . is a feeling for the public identity of people, a web of public respect and trust,' she continued, concluding, 'the absence of this trust is a disaster to a city street. Its cultivation cannot be institutionalized.' This is the trust between strangers which occurs naturally in healthy places and is still part of daily life to a far greater degree in countries like Denmark.

Since Jacobs was writing, levels of trust between people in the US and in Britain have plummeted and the high street she describes has changed, with fewer smaller shops and news-stands where personal exchanges might take place. At the same time the issue of trust has begun to receive large amounts of attention, as trust is found to correlate not only with fear of crime but also with happiness in society. But rather than follow her suggestions on 'natural surveillance' and encourage 'casual, public contact', city life in Britain is moving in the opposite direction. Today, the type of defensible architecture promoted by Newman, which discourages strangers and diversity, has become the template for all new development, dovetailing with the new private places and the Secured by Design approach. Instead, as levels of trust in the UK continue to drop, policymakers are ignoring Jacobs' warning that 'its cultivation cannot be institutionalized' and are trying to do just that.

'Respect'

So fear of crime is soaring while actual crime has been falling steadily since the mid 1990s. New Labour's attempt to answer what Jack Straw labelled the 'evil of fear' in 1999 has been a driving force in New Labour's domestic policy agenda of the past ten years. When Straw was home secretary, he announced that fear of crime was a contemporary evil on a par with the 'five great evils' of want, disease, ignorance, squalor and idleness, which the founder of the welfare state, William Beveridge, vowed to tackle after the Second World War.[26] Having designed fear into our cities through their property and design policies, Labour responded to the problem of fear with an attempt to institutionalize the cultivation of trust, rather than nurturing a climate of natural trust between people in cities. Their plan was laid out in their Anti-Social Behaviour White Paper of 2003. In it they outlined their belief that fear of crime is in fact caused by antisocial behaviour. This very vaguely defined phrase, which barely existed before New Labour came to power, translates as low-level disorder which causes a nuisance but isn't actually criminal, for example litter, graffiti or 'hanging around'. The White Paper, called *Respect and Responsibility*, stated: 'Antisocial behaviour gives rise to fear of crime.' It went on to say that while overall crime continued its downward trend, dropping by a quarter since 1997, 'the fear of crime has not fallen to the same extent . . . Whilst the media coverage of disturbing crimes can fuel the fear of crime, the real experience of behaviour and disorder makes many even more afraid of crime.'[27]

This belief that low-level disorder is behind the rising fear of crime has created a whole new agenda and body of law towards antisocial behaviour, which spans a huge range of domestic policy issues, from minor disorder to serious criminal activity involving the closure of crack dens. Extreme problem families and noisy neighbours are at the serious end of antisocial behaviour, but 'hanging around', taking photographs and handing out political leaflets can equally qualify. A feature of the legislation is that a disproportionate number of antisocial-behaviour orders have been handed out to people with mental health problems which result in unusual behaviours, such as autism or Tourette's syndrome.[28] When antisocial-behaviour orders are breached, which they are in the majority of cases, the consequences can be up to five years in prison.[29]

So what is antisocial behaviour and where has it come from? 'The morals of the children are ten times worse than formerly,' Lord Ashley told the House of Commons in 1823, showing that moral panics about the behaviour of young people are nothing new.[30] According to the legislation, antisocial behaviour is defined as behaviour which can cause 'harassment, alarm or distress to one or more persons not of the same household [as the perpetrator]'.

But while the definition is broad enough to cover just about anything, the antisocial-behaviour agenda, which is also branded the 'Respect' agenda, has introduced specific legislation, including parenting orders, curfews, evictions, antisocial-behaviour orders and dispersal orders. The growing use of stop-and-search powers without reasonable suspicion in many parts of the country[31] is seen by young people as another aspect of the 'Respect' agenda, and they certainly overlap. Stop-and-search is used particularly enthusiastically in designated 'Respect Action Areas' around the country.

This raft of policies is mainly used to control behaviour in poor areas, partly because it is in poor areas that people are most concerned about the range of problems which come under the antisocial-behaviour umbrella and partly because many of these initiatives are easier to enforce in places which suffer deprivation, because they come linked with fines and sanctions which can affect access to housing and benefits. But antisocial behaviour is not just targeted in poor places: these policies also aid the work of private-security firms in the private places and privately governed areas of the first part of the book.

The problems connected with antisocial behaviour are real, but what is ironic is that, despite the government's emphasis, most people are not that concerned by it; only 16 per cent told the British Crime Survey that antisocial behaviour was a 'fairly big' or 'big' problem in their area.[32] That is a very small percentage compared with the whopping 80 per cent of Britons who fear that crime is going up when it isn't. So why has so much time and energy been spent creating policies on antisocial behaviour in an attempt to tackle the rising fear of crime? Like so many of the policy ideas in this book, the agenda was imported from America and comes down to a theory of crime called the Broken Windows theory.

'Broken Windows'

First outlined by James Q. Wilson and George Kelling in a famous article in *Atlantic Monthly* in 1982, Broken Windows is a zero-tolerance approach to policing. The article argued that tolerating minor routine incivilities, such as window breaking, begging and drunkenness, increases 'respectable fears' and encourages a spiral of community decline. 'One unrepaired broken window is a signal that no one cares, and so breaking more windows costs nothing,' they wrote, implying that the presence of broken windows will encourage people to break more windows and lead to more serious crime.[33]

Mirroring the same language more than twenty years later, the Anti-Social Behaviour White Paper said: 'If a window is broken or a wall is covered in graffiti it can contribute to an environment in which crime takes hold, particularly if intervention is not prompt and effective. Environmental decline, antisocial behaviour and crime go hand in hand and create a sense of helplessness that nothing can be done.'[34]

Broken Windows policing emerged in the 1980s and 1990s and swept through the American criminal justice system like wildfire,[35] before coming to Britain. The most high-profile place to embrace it was New York, under Mayor Rudy Giuliani, who was elected in 1993 on a platform of crime, disorder and 'quality of life', another new political catchphrase. Giuliani's election was accompanied by the appointment of William J. Bratton as police chief. Together they targeted minor offences, cleaning up graffiti and cracking down on turnstile jumping, squeegee cleaning, begging and homelessness. Although Giuliani sacked Bratton after two years, he continued his policing approach and his eight years in office coincided with a dramatic drop in crime in the city. The clean-up of New York was attributed to Bratton and Giuliani's use of the 'broken windows' approach, though this has been challenged since, not least by Steven Levitt in *Freakonomics*.[36]

Recent studies show that Broken Windows was not responsible for the clean-up of New York and no evidence has been put forward to show that this approach to policing cuts crime. Instead researchers point out that crime began falling in most major US cities from the early 1990s and fell more sharply in places like San Diego, which didn't crackdown on small offences. The conclusion from a number of studies is that the fall in crime in New York, and in other cities, was down to the reduction of the crack epidemic.[37] During the same period researchers found that complaints against police misconduct, for surveillance policies such as stop-and-search and dispersal, rose by 37 per cent, lowering trust between the police and community.[38] In the UK, according to figures from the Independent Police Complaints Commission, a record number of allegations against police were made for 2007/8, more than since records began in 1985, with a rise of nearly 25 per cent relating to the use of stop-and-search.[39] Although few questions have been asked here, in the US even the pioneers of Broken Windows no longer agree with each other. James Q. Wilson admitted, 'I still to this day do not know if improving order will or will not reduce crime.' In another interview he said, 'God knows what the truth is.'[40]

Reflecting the widespread view among legal experts that Broken Windows policies do not cut crime, the authors of an expert legal guide to the new legislation in Britain write: 'It is surprising that the government has developed so many new national policies and measures to deal with anti-social behaviour and disorder when it is not at all related to crime or crime reduction.'[41] In fact the most vocal defenders of Broken Windows in the US are William Bratton, writer of *Turnaround: How America's Top Cop Reversed the Crime Epidemic*, who clearly has a vested interest, and George Kelling, the other author of the 1982 article which introduced the concept. But while graffiti and 'hanging around' are being excised, fear of crime has not gone down. Instead it has increased significantly, reflecting the lack of a causal link between a reduction in disorder and fear of crime. An Ipsos MORI survey revealed that in 1997, when Labour came to power, over two thirds of people believed the government could reduce crime, but a decade on the proportion had plummeted to 27 per cent by 2007, compared to 57 per cent in Germany and 48 per cent in Italy,[42] countries which do not favour the Broken Windows approach. Instead European countries, in particular Germany and Scandinavia, focus on the provision of youth services for young people, discussed in the next chapter. Broken Windows was very popular with politicians and police forces: it offered a straightforward and logical explanation of how to tackle crime relatively cheaply, and was accompanied by a very visible fall in the crime figures in New York, which had been a famously dangerous city. Politicians the world over thought they'd found the answers to their crime problems and in 1998 representatives from 200 police departments, 150 from abroad, descended on the NYPD for lessons on 'New York style policing'. Bratton wrote his book, *Turnaround*, and by 2000 another 285 departments had visited the NYPD, 85 per cent from abroad.[43]

Of all the overseas delegations, Britain was among the most enthusiastic. Jack Straw arranged a visit to meet Giuliani soon after he was appointed shadow home secretary. When Straw went over in 1995, the mayor and Bratton had just introduced a police strategy aimed at 'reclaiming the public spaces of New York', identifying the homeless, beggars, prostitutes, squeegee cleaners, squatters, graffiti artists, reckless bicyclists and unruly youths as enemies of public order[44] whose activities would not be tolerated.

The moment Straw got back to Britain he lifted Giuliani's rhetoric virtually word for word, promising that if Labour won the election they too would 'reclaim the streets' for the law-abiding citizen from the begging of winos, addicts and those same famous 'squeegee merchants'. From then on the American rhetoric of 'reclaiming the public realm' and 'quality of life' has been at the heart of the antisocial-behaviour and 'Respect' agenda, which is the British branding given to this very American way of doing things.

Communitarianism – with a British Twist

Around the same time as Straw's visit to New York, Tony Blair's Labour Party in opposition was becoming interested in a set of policies heavily influenced by another American idea known as 'Communitarianism', a strain of thinking credited with influencing Bill Clinton when he was at the White House, based on the work of the sociologist Amitai Etzioni, professor at George Washington University. Etzioni is the author of a book called *The Spirit of Community*, which came out in 1993. Since then Barack Obama and David Cameron have also allied themselves with many of his ideas.

Etzioni wrote that 'rights and responsibilities are two sides of the same coin'[45] and his thinking is shot through with an emphasis on the language of rights and responsibilities, in particular parenting responsibilities and moral obligations, as a means of creating communities of shared values, appealing to right-minded people to act together to control disorder.[46] The same rhetoric defines New Labour's ideas about community, welfare reform and antisocial behaviour and was laid out in Tony Blair's first speech in 1997, which he made when he visited the Aylesbury Estate, one of the most deprived housing estates in Britain. Addressing tenants on the estate, he promised: 'There will be no forgotten people in the Britain I want to build.'[47] Explaining his vision for society, Blair continued, 'The basis of this modern civic society is an ethic of mutual responsibility or duty, something for something, a society where we play by the rules. You only take out if you put in.'[48]

Making sure no one is forgotten is a fine goal, but critics of Blair's brand of Communitarianism claim that it reduced community to no more than a contractual relationship,[49] and that because rights are conditional on responsibilities, there is a danger of authoritarianism, since the question of who decides what the 'shared values' of a community should be is not straightforward.[50] In *The Third Way to a Good Society*, published by the leading Labour think tank, Demos, in 2000, Etzioni himself makes it clear that he is not in agreement with aspects of Labour's take on Communitarianism and is very critical of 'the rush to legislate good behaviour'.[51]

What he is referring to is the antisocial-behaviour legislation introduced by Labour with the aim of improving people's behaviour – particularly that of young people, noisy neighbours and bad parents – and punishing them if they don't respond. The enthusiasm for sanctions for low-level offences which are not actually criminal can all be traced back to New Labour thinking in the mid 1990s. Particularly appealing to politicians was the fact that this was a problem which seemed to chime strongly with New Labour's heartlands, which include many poor areas where fear of crime is much higher and is often attributed to a small number of problem families[52] – places like Jack Straw's own constituency in Blackburn.

Straw's childhood on the council estate he grew up on also gave him a personal take on the subject, after a dispute with their next-door neighbour ended up in court, with his mother and the neighbour, Mrs Swindell, accusing each other of assault. Thirteen-year-old Jack gave evidence for his mother and the case against her – that she hit one of Mrs Swindell's sons – was dismissed, while Mrs Swindell was fined and bound over to keep the peace for a year.[53] Straw's claim to a personal understanding of the experiences of working-class families, in contrast to 'woolly-minded Hampstead liberals' was continued vehemently by his successor at the Home Office, David Blunkett, who frequently dismissed opponents as 'airy-fairy libertarians' or even 'the Liberati'.[54]

Years later, Straw referred to his childhood experience with Mrs Swindell and was very sympathetic to an influential group of housing associations who were in close touch with him and who were keen to see tougher powers to act against troublemakers and bad neighbours on their estates.[55] Consequently in 1995 the Labour Party published *A Quiet Life: Tough Action on Criminal Neighbours*, a policy paper which said that the criminal courts were unable to help the victims of nuisance neighbours and proposed new 'community safety orders' which would have criminal consequences if they were breached, paving the way for what were later to become ASBOs.[56]

The other key figures behind the introduction of the new legislation are former Home Secretary David Blunkett and Frank Field, the controversial former Labour minister and admirer of Mrs Thatcher, who is MP for Birkenhead, which also includes areas of deprivation in Labour's heartlands. Field is an important New Labour thinker who had been tasked with coming up with new ideas for the Labour Party on 'youth nuisance'. In his book *Neighbours from Hell: The Politics of Behaviour*, Field, who was famously told by Tony Blair to 'think the unthinkable', placed great emphasis on problem families and poor parenting, going as far as to suggest that the police should be brought in to act as 'surrogate parents'.[57]

Out of this mix of American ideas of zero tolerance and Communitarianism, and New Labour's desire to 'legislate for good behaviour', came the antisocial-behaviour and 'Respect' agenda. When David Blunkett succeeded Jack Straw at the Home Office in 2001, he pursued it even more vigorously than his predecessor, overseeing the passage of the Anti-Social Behaviour Act and making sure this new body of law became an entrenched part of British life, blurring the boundaries between civil and criminal law. An ASBO is applied for by a local authority, Registered Social Landlord or the police and is a civil matter, imposed by a magistrate's court. If the orders are breached, as they are in the majority of cases, then offenders can face more than five years in prison, for an offence which wasn't criminal in the first place.

How Antisocial Behaviour Changed the Criminal Justice System

Controversial from the start, orders have been issued for activities such as preaching in the street. Phil Howard, a well-known local character was banned from London's Oxford Circus for proclaiming his message of 'Don't be a sinner, be a winner' after Westminster Council requested that magistrates impose an ASBO on him, on the grounds that he was acting in an antisocial manner, likely to cause harassment, alarm or distress. The legion of notorious bans on behaviour includes an eighty-seven-year-old man ordered not to make sarcastic remarks to his neighbours, two teenage brothers forbidden to say the word 'grass', and a suicidal woman banned from going near bridges. According to the British Institute for Brain Injured Children, more than 30 per cent of under-seventeens with an antisocial-behaviour order have a diagnosed mental health disorder.[58] *← Public health issue*

Targeting people with mental health problems, prone to unusual behaviour, raises disturbing questions which show that the legislation is as much about penalizing difference as anything else. But most important of all for criminologists is the fact that the legislation marks a fundamental change in the criminal justice system, because it has altered the principle of universal deterrence, which has been in place for centuries and rests on the premise that we are all subject to the same criminal laws. The difference now is that the conditions attached to ASBOs, established through civil law proceedings, create tailor-made criminal laws for certain individuals. Explaining the opaque changes to me, Mike Hough outlined how if he were to receive an ASBO which included the condition that he could not feed the pigeons in London parks for two years and if he breached those conditions, he would have committed a criminal offence. 'If I ignore this condition, I have then committed a criminal offence and can be sent to prison for five years. So a special criminal law that applies only to me has, in effect, been created,' he said.

In a highly critical report into human rights in the UK, the European Commissioner for Human Rights, Alvaro Gil-Robles, said, 'Such orders look rather like personalized penal codes, where non-criminal behaviour becomes criminal for individuals who have incurred the wrath of the community.' He questioned whether 'loudly hanging around street corners' should be a 'two-stop criminal offence' and warned that ASBOs are more likely to exacerbate antisocial behaviour by alienating and stigmatizing young people. The report was especially critical of the 'naming and shaming' of people on ASBOs and 'the distribution of leaflets containing photos of the ASBO subject', expressing concern 'over such a transfer of policing duties to local residents'.[59]

By 2009, well over 10,000 ASBOs had been given out, although Gordon Brown had indicated he would take a critical look at the policy when he became prime minister – not least because the overwhelming evidence is that ASBOs don't work. In Manchester, which has earned itself the dubious title of 'ASBO capital of Britain', more than 90 per cent of orders have been breached.[60] In 2005 the council imposed a record 554 ASBOs, the most handed out anywhere in the UK; Cityco, the company running the business district in Manchester city centre, was particularly enthusiastic. Councils, Registered Social Landlords and the police are allowed to apply for ASBOs, but companies like Cityco, which orchestrated the removal of anti-war protestors described in Chapter 3, are instrumental in encouraging councils to impose more of them. Even so, despite their efforts, by 2007 the number of ASBOs in Manchester had slumped to 165.[61]

Chief Inspector Neil Wain, the Commander of Stockport, has written a book about antisocial behaviour, based on his personal experience in Greater Manchester. In the introduction to *The ASBO: Wrong Turning, Dead End*, he writes, 'As a serving police officer I had considerable experience of the use of ASBOs, and what struck me was not only did they get breached on a regular basis, they did not appear to be controlling the behaviour of those subject to them.'[62] Leafing through his book on my way to meet him, on yet another Virgin train to the north-west plagued by engineering works, I was struck again by the astonishing lack of evidence to support this policy – just as there is little evidence to support 'Pathfinder' or the roll-out of CCTV. The lack of evaluation has been criticized by the Home Affairs Select Committee and the National Audit Office, which specifically mentioned the 'absence of formal evaluation by the Home Office' in its report on antisocial behaviour.[63]

When we met in his office in the utilitarian surroundings of Stockport Police Station I asked Chief Inspector Wain if his views were typical among the police. 'A lot of people have come along to me and said, "You've said what we've all been thinking" – especially frontline officers. Colleagues at the same rank have also been very supportive,' he said. Contrary to the stereotype that the police would welcome a more punitive approach, he explained that there has been 'unease at some of this legislation which has started to creep through'. Like doctors and teachers, it seems the police are starting to resemble another disaffected public-sector body, angered that evidence and expertise are being overlooked.

Like Jack Straw, Neil Wain also grew up on a council estate and his experiences have influenced his attitude to minor nuisance, although in the opposite direction to Straw's. 'I always say to people that if I was growing up in the way I did, and did the things I did then, I could be on the way to an ASBO. I distinctly recall hanging about on street corners and playing football in the street. If we really wanted to play a game, we had to climb over the fence into the school yard. Now young people are excluded from more and more places where they used to play and schools are covered in CCTV, so that would be subject to sanction,' he said.

One of the most shocking sections of his book, which is based on interviews with more than twenty people who have had ASBOs imposed on them, is the following transcript from an interview with 'Sean', which is not his real name. He was serving a sentence of three months' youth custody as a result of breaching his ASBO, and at twenty had been subject to two ASBOs already, the longest of which was imposed on him when he was sixteen for five years. One order was imposed for criminal matters, for allowing himself to be carried in stolen vehicles, and the other for antisocial behaviour, which he said was playing football in the street. Under the conditions imposed, he had been excluded from the estate where his father lived and the housing estate where his mother lived and he had grown up. He had breached his order several times, on each occasion not for committing a crime but just for visiting his parents.

The ASBO got enforced around my mum's area, so my mates weren't allowed on there. They didn't even, they've got no reason to go there, cause they don't live there, so they got barred from round there but they barred me as well, so I wasn't allowed at my mum's. So it's just been a bit hard . . .

I've been staying, you know, at different houses through all the years I've been on it and it's just, I don't know (pause). I've got nowhere to stay. I've not been feeding myself or nothing and it's just stress but I've got no one to speak to about it, nothing. I don't think they know how serious it is for me.

It's my mum, when she gets ill she phones me and asks if I can help her. So I have to get a taxi round there, you know, so I don't get seen. But people, I don't know, they must see me and tell (the police), but I ain't doing nothing wrong. Not like I'm acting in an antisocial manner. I'm just helping my family.

I'm not seeing my family grow up, my little brothers (pause), just it's been hard. They don't (pause), there's not even no one that you can speak to about it.[64]

The prohibitions placed on Sean seem both unjust and unrealistic. He is bound to need to visit his family at some point. That is not to say that he and many others on ASBOs are not either involved in or on the fringes of serious trouble, and I can see the point of view of a victim support officer who said, 'You have to do a lot to get an ASBO.' But ASBOs are not working. The numbers of young people in custody – the highest in Europe – are rising in parallel with the rates of breach for ASBOs, which means we are setting up a generation of young people to fail.

The failure of ASBOs has led to the drop in the numbers handed out and, although the system is too entrenched in legislation – and too politically popular – to be reversed, its use is likely to come under continued scrutiny. But if ASBOs themselves are being questioned by local police and even the government, the rest of the policies which make up the 'Respect' agenda are still firmly in place. While much of the 'Respect' terminology has also come in for criticism, all that has happened is that Respect Action Areas have been 'rebadged', as one council official put it. ASBOs may be declining, but all the other legislation, including Acceptable Behaviour Contracts, parenting orders and Dispersal Orders, is in frequent use, with more than 1,000 areas in England and Wales designated dispersal zones.[65] In plain English dispersal zones are areas where the police or Community Support Officers may disperse groups of just two or more where their presence is likely to result in a member of the public being 'harassed, intimidated, alarmed or distressed'. In reality, a report from the social-policy research and development charity the Joseph Rowntree Foundation found that the powers simply mean young people are approached by police and told to go home. A young person interviewed for the study said: 'Since the dispersal, lots of special police people have been going around and saying, "It's getting late now, you should go home." They said it's coming up to the dispersal time, you're going to have to split up or go home.'[66]

Just as ASBOs have created nonsensical situations, so have dispersal zones, even targeting young children playing in the street. Describing the effects of dispersal orders, Rachel Morrison, who lives in Salford, said:

My kids can't go out to play. Since they've brought dispersal orders to my area, my seven-year-old son has been told off by a Community Police Officer for being on the street – at 4 pm. And my daughter went into a shop to get a kebab and the real police walked in and gave her a warning – if she can't go into a kebab shop, what can she do? If they see kids on the street, they get a police caution, and if you get two cautions, a letter goes out to the parents. I think it's their way of trying to protect us from youths, but I don't need protection.[67]

All of this is stigmatizing young people. Condemning the dispersal policy, the Joseph Rowntree Foundation report concluded that 'circumscribing

FEAR OF CRIME, 'RESPECT', TRUST AND HAPPINESS

their ability to congregate in public spaces seemed to them eminently unfair and unwarranted'. 'For many, meeting friends and peers in local public spaces constitutes a fundamental aspect of developing their sense of identity and control, as well as providing space in which to forge their independent capacity to manage risk and danger,' the authors wrote, echoing the criticisms about private-security firms in town centres which actively remove young people from their areas.[68]

As for stop-and-search and the issuing of fixed-penalty notices for minor offences, all the signs are that this type of zero-tolerance clampdown is set to continue and is likely to ramp up as private security starts to play a bigger role in policing, with both of the main parties competing to sound tougher than the other. These policies may not grab the kind of headlines that ASBOs have done, but they are just as much a part of the antisocial-behaviour and 'Respect' agenda. The irony is that they do nothing to encourage a climate of mutual respect and responsibility. Instead, punitive solutions undermine the sense of responsibility among young people, replacing it with punishment and control.

How 'Respect' Works on the Ground

When Jack Straw introduced the antisocial-behaviour legislation for the first time in 1997, he warmed to his theme that he understood what working-class communities wanted, dismissing those who criticized the proposals on human-rights grounds and telling the House of Commons that 'the bill represents a triumph of community politics over detached metropolitan élites'.[69] Expanding on this in an article in the *Times*, he said that what pleased him most about the bill was that it reflected the views of 'local communities across the country' rather than those whose 'comfortable notions of human behaviour were matched only by their comfortable distance away from its worst excesses'.[70] New Labour knew what communities wanted. 'In the period before last year's general election, my colleagues and I spent much of our time talking to those at the sharp end of the problems of crime and disorder – victims, the police, magistrates, local councils,' he said.

To find out how, more than a decade later, local communities have been affected by these policies, I went up to Salford, one of forty places in the

Graham and the kids, Whit Lane, Salford

country designated a 'Respect Action Area', and the constituency of Hazel Blears, a particularly strong champion of the policy. Graham Cooper, a local youth worker, suggested I come and spend some time with him and the young people he works with, many of whom have been christened 'NEETs' by policymakers, which is an acronym for young people between sixteen and twenty-five who are 'Not Engaged in Education or Training'. Recent figures estimate their number at over 1.3 million nationally, a statistic which, like those on sickness benefit, is not included in official unemployment figures. Of course, these are more likely to be the troublesome kids the 'Respect' policies aim to pull into line, rather than those they are designed to protect, but I also spoke to council workers, youth workers, employees of government regeneration schemes, the police and local people.

No one could accuse Graham of belonging to a 'metropolitan élite'. He's now in his early forties, but as a teenager he'd have probably been put on an ASBO himself. Instead, he went into care, borstal and finally prison, and is always on the alert. He says what changed him was his mother's terminal illness and caring for her until she died. He is now married with two sons and owns a fruit and veg business, which he runs, when he is not working with the young people, from a psychedelic graffiti-covered van. Graham is tough and charismatic, he's been through it and the kids know it and genuinely respect him.

By the time I went to Salford in 2008, there was some confusion about the official future of the 'Respect' agenda, but as the area had been a 'Respect Action Area' and all the policies continued to be in place, it didn't make much difference to the people on the ground. I went up to stay a few times, once for a festival organized by Graham and the young people called 'Party in the Park', and again on a cold, dark Friday in February.

'Party in the Park'

I could hear the party before I got to it, the sound of calypso music contrasting with the shuttered parade of shops and large billboards declaring the area part of the government's New Deal for Communities programme. Turning the corner, I saw a large stage at the end of a park, which backed on to a rundown housing estate. 'Party in the Park' has become an annual event, which started after the community came together when a thirteen-year-old local girl called Amber was run over by a car and killed in 2005, while playing in the street. The event is very much the brainchild of Amber's mother, Dionne, and of Graham Cooper.

At one end bands took the stage, while at the other a project called 'Pants and Top' was collecting the views of young people asking what they thought was good about the area – 'top' – and what they didn't – 'pants'. Council workers, youth workers and a lot of young people were milling about, making a collage of everyone's views. I asked 'Jim', who works for the council and didn't want to give me his real name, what he thought about the 'Respect' polices. He said, 'The "Respect area" – that's a bit of a joke. It's pure spin. There are fewer youth workers and sports development workers. When they do spend more money, it's around enforcement. The council spends around £750,000 on youth services and twice as much on ASBOs. For young people there's obviously a lot of stigmatization. That's why we're doing this today – asking young people what they think.'

Most young people thought the 'people' and the 'parks' were 'top' but 'pants' was the lack of things to do. 'There are very few structured activities here,' Ameen, a development worker, said. Wandering around the park, I was repeatedly told, 'This kind of event doesn't normally happen round here.' I walked past a block of housing on the other side of the park, opposite a bouncy castle. The houses, which opened on to the park, were dilapidated, although they weren't more than twenty years old. A few families, couples and men and women stood outside with their front doors open, swigging tinnies and talking.

Wandering back, I met Beth, who is Salford's education, children and young people's manager for the government's New Deal programme. She believes one of the biggest problems with the Respect agenda is that 'it implies disrespect by young people – and they react to that'. Instead, she prefers to bring groups of old and young people together, breaking down the intergenerational barriers, which she says are made worse by antisocial-behaviour policies. 'We're trying to bring young people and older people together – when they know each other, they don't feel threatened by groups of young people – young people always hang around in groups,' she said.

The single thing which has made her incandescent with rage is the introduction of a security device called the Mosquito, created especially to tackle antisocial behaviour, which emits a high-pitched whine at a frequency designed to make young people – who have more sensitive hearing than adults – feel ill, with the aim of keeping them away from certain places. She told me that 'Our community safety manager went out and bought one without asking anyone. He was going to put it up by the bus stop and shop – it would also be difficult for young children, a baby in its pram, unable to move, would be in agony. We tested it in our office – people in their thirties were experiencing pain and sickness. Luckily I created such a fuss and told people like Graham, so he backed down and had to put it on an old lady's wall. It's obviously totally against human rights. Imagine putting something up that pierced the ears of black or disabled people.'

The human-rights organization Liberty agrees with Beth that the Mosquito, invented in Wales in 2005, is likely to violate the European Convention on Human Rights and the UK's Human Rights Act. Belgium has banned it, its legality has been tested in France, and in Ireland it has been found to constitute assault. But in Britain Compound Security Services, the security firm behind the device, has been so successful that demand has outstripped supply, to the extent that it has brought in an American company with global ambitions to take over production.[71]

But the one thing every teenage boy I spoke to in Salford complained about was stop-and-search. Curtis and Scott who are both seventeen get stopped and searched at least once a week. 'We walked out the gym last week and were stopped. It's like they're belittling you. They just take the mick, rib you to death, make you feel this big. You start getting rude. They radio and start checking up on you,' Scott said. 'They make you stand with your arms up, they start checking the bands round your boxer shorts. How come it's just us? It's not people in their twenties and thirties. It depends on where you live – they don't do it in the posh areas – it makes you paranoid,' Curtis added.

As the afternoon drew to an end, everyone gravitated towards the stage and the headline band of the day, which was a local UB40 tribute band, playing eighties' reggae classics. Amber's mother took the mike and told the crowd: 'You can police us but you don't need to police us. Look at what we can do. One thirteen-year-old girl made us realize we are a community.' She handed the mike to Graham, who said, 'Once again we've shown them we're not a load of animals. They didn't want us drinking beer this year. There's been no trouble. Let's give ourselves a round of applause.'

Later I went for a drink with Graham. Walking into the pub, I was surprised at the large sign on the door which said that no one under the age of twenty-five was allowed entry. When I asked Graham what young people over eighteen do if they can't go to the pub, he said this was one of the biggest problems in the area. 'Young people don't know how to drink, they're not brought into the pub at sixteen by their dad like I was. We've had our pubs taken off us bit by bit in this area – this pub is the only one – for 2,000 people, and even then young people aren't allowed in.'

Talking about his work with the NEETs, he explained: 'You step in where their fathers are. When I go on holiday they say, "What am I going to do?" They know I can have a good fight. I've done five years in prison and I was in borstal at fifteen and a half. But it's not that they look up to me. They know I care and that means a lot.' But when it came to the 'Respect' policies, he said, 'There's a really negative side to this and it could drown you. But I'm going to be positive. If you could see what we do with these people classed as NEETs.'

Friday Night in Salford

Six months later, I went back to Salford on a drizzly February evening. Graham picked me up from the station in the minibus he uses to take groups of young people camping and fishing, and we set off to see what really happens on a Friday night in Salford.

The answer is not much. The few pubs we passed as we made our way to Langworthy, Kersal and Broughton had signs outside barring anybody under twenty-five. On the evening I visited, the Beacon Centre, a £3 million facility for young people, was shut and the owner was locking up at Oliver's Gym. Most young people like to go out with friends at the weekend, but Graham told me there is nothing to do here. 'Five or six years ago the pubs in Salford stopped letting eighteen-year-olds in. Friday night in a city like Salford and there's nothing for them to do. They have to go into the bushes with a six pack and then they go out on to the streets because they feel strangled. The city centre would be all right, but they don't go because they don't have the money for that kind of night out.' The result is that 'the intoxication is a bit different, because they're running in and out the bushes with the police behind them,' he said.

Our first stop was Lower Broughton, where we stopped to talk to a group of young lads on a street corner. What were they doing? 'Larking about, looking for something to do. There's nothing for us to do.' So what do they do? 'We mooch about, move from one place to another.' I asked them, if they could choose to have anything, what would they like? 'Respect' and 'being treated like adults' they said, but not the kind of 'Respect' the government talks about, all of them agreeing that the 'worst thing' was being 'stopped by the police for no reason'.

Along with the lack of facilities, Graham believes stop-and-search is one of the biggest problems the area faces, humiliating and alienating teenage boys in particular, because it's nearly always boys rather than girls who are searched. 'When this became a Respect Area the police went mad on it. Because of the way they dress, with their trousers down to their knees, they search inside the waistband of their pants, around the groin. It's like an intimate body search – if they were girls, it would be considered assault,' he said. So why are young men stopped? Graham said there was no specific reason: 'It's just a matter of routine – a fact of life.'

I asked the police the same question and was told by a spokesperson that 'feedback from independent advisory groups shows that people appreciate its use and find it reassuring'. I also asked what the police were searching for, with figures for knife and gun crime comparatively low in Salford. I expected the answer to be drugs, but in fact there was no specific information available for Salford. Figures from Greater Manchester Police revealed that 73 per cent of stop-and-searches did not result in any outcome.[72]

Next we came across a big group of lads. Graham pulled over and explained I was writing a book and wanted to talk to them. Fifteen or so testosterone-fuelled teenagers piled into the back of the van. Most of them were excluded from school or in part-time education, but they all knew Graham. I asked the same questions. What would they do that evening? 'Get pissed and do fuck all.' Everyone complained about stop-and-search. 'They stop us because we wear hoods – it's an excuse to pull you.' They asked Graham to drop them outside Kashmir Slice, an Indian takeaway, and seemed elated at getting a ride in the van. 'They're excited – it's Friday night, but they can't get into the pub,' Graham explained. Later we came across many of the same group and when I asked what the best part of the evening had been, they said, 'Getting in the van.'

During the course of the evening I felt threatened once when we stopped outside Bargain Booze and a lad on a motorbike said to his mate, 'That's the grass bus'. Graham didn't know either of them and we moved on. So far I'd only met boys, but the next group we met, on the edge of an estate, were mainly teenage girls. 'Lads get a harder time because they wear black and have their hoods up. They get pulled all the time. Only lads get stopped and searched, girls never do.' But it was the same story of nothing to do. 'Where can you go on a Friday night? Nowhere. You can sit in the bus shelter or walk about the streets.' When I asked what they thought of Salford, though, they said they loved it. 'We're bored a lot, but even though there's nothing to do, we have a laugh. We make jokes.'

We also drove to the university area, because Graham wanted to show me the contrast between the facilities provided for similar-age students and locals. 'This is a very large area which was public land but, because the university has taken it over, there are by-laws in place which restrict access. This is Peel Park, which is lit up like a Christmas tree, but the parks in our communities are pitch black. It shows you where the priorities are,' he said. 'In some respects the economic benefits of the university are massive, but do local people feel them? Not a chance. They're even barred from using the gym,' he added, as we drove past the gated campus area. He believes the aim of stop-and-search is to 'target white teenage lads because they wear black and have hoods. Students who wear jeans and hair gel are all right, and lads round here have noticed that,' he said.

Graham is no apologist for young people who intimidate their neighbours. He believes that there are severe issues which come under the very loosely defined 'Respect' agenda, which include neighbourhood harassment. But as far as the young people he works with are concerned, he believes the Respect initiatives are misplaced and are making the problem worse. He's particularly proud that none of the young people he works with are on an ASBO and says that's simply because 'we do things with them'. But the lack of facilities, the ban on drinking in pubs and the roll-out of stop-and-search makes his work an uphill struggle.

Problem Families

If the behaviour of young people is one plank of the antisocial-behaviour agenda, the responsibility of their parents is the other, reflected in legislation which punishes parents for the bad behaviour of their children, such as the mother who was sent to prison because her daughter was truanting from school.[73]

That case hit the headlines because it was unusual, but far more common is the introduction of parenting courses which are run by local authorities around the country. When I contacted Salford city council to find out more about the 'Respect' agenda, their community safety officer said he was concerned that I did not know of all the good work that was going on, particularly when it came to parenting. So, I met with 'Dave', a parenting officer who gave me a candid view of his work. Dave, who didn't want to give me his real name so he could speak more freely, said that he didn't like the antisocial-behaviour legislation, but that the agenda had given him the opportunity to get in touch with families who need help. 'I personally think it's wrong. It's not ethical to criminalize non-criminal behaviour, but I've crafted something within this,' he said.

Over the last six months he has worked with fifty families, running an eight-week course, which involves watching videos, role play and doing homework on tasks. In the majority of cases he feels they achieve real results, telling me about a family he worked with recently where a fourteen-year-old boy who had been bullying was referred by the behavioural and educational support team. 'The mother was at her wits' end. He was out of control. I met her and suggested a course. In her particular case, learning to give praise was especially important. The words wouldn't come for her, it was such an alien concept. She went home with the homework, "praise your teenager". She came back and said it turned things around. It works like that,' he said.

Of the fifty families he's seen, the majority are there voluntarily but 20 per cent are on parenting orders. These function in a very similar way to ASBOs, where breach can be punishable by prison. Most of the parents who have to attend are unhappy with the enforcement aspect and some refuse to cooperate. 'I have had people with parenting orders on the courses who've virtually sat facing the other way,' he said. On the whole he manages to 'persuade and cajole' people, but doesn't think they should be forced to attend. However, he is keen to point out that is a tiny minority, 'only 1 per cent' of all the families he works with.

Although he is proud of the work he does, Dave feels the scale of the problem has been exaggerated and that the legislation itself is the problem. 'The existence of the legislation fuels the paranoia. Problem families are nothing new – it was there thirty years ago,' he said. This chimes exactly with my memories of growing up and of a particular family at my school who became notorious locally, while a friend of mine, who is now a poet and artist, described to me how his family were seen as 'scum'. The number of problem families remains a tiny minority. Even so, Dave believes 'they are becoming another group'.

A few years ago, at a panel debate in 2002 which accompanied the launch of a report I had written on gated communities and ghettoes, Frank Field was asked what he thought should happen to extreme problem families. He replied that they should be put in a concrete bunker underneath the Westway, the flyover through London, and left there. Most people in the audience thought his comment was a joke and didn't take it seriously. Joking apart, Frank Field has always been something of a soothsayer for New Labour; his thinking in the mid 1990s was instrumental in kick-starting the whole approach towards antisocial behaviour. Field's comments about concrete bunkers and his suggestions for the police to act as 'surrogate parents' reveal the extent to which these policies are underpinned by a philosophy of control and exclusion. The consequence of excluding problem families from social housing is the creation of ghettoes of terrible conditions described in the last chapter.

Is Behaviour Worse?

As Lord Ashley's comments about young people in 1823 revealed, every generation believes that behaviour, of its young people in particular, is not what it was. The term 'moral panic' was coined in the 1960s after the shock which greeted the clashes between mods and rockers. In the 1970s punk, with its Mohican haircuts and safety pins, terrified the older generation. Punk gave way to skinheads and football hooligans. Later in the 1980s a more overtly racist narrative linked young black men to inner-city crime. The early 1990s saw the horror of the James Bulger case, when Jon Venables and Robert Thompson, aged ten, murdered the two-year-old toddler, and in subsequent years we heard a lot about feral children with names like 'ratboy' and 'spider-boy'.[74] Since 1997 we have had the all-encompassing phenomenon of 'antisocial behaviour'.

There are no quantitative studies showing whether behaviour in Brighton in 1964 was worse than in parts of London in the 1980s or in deprived parts of Britain today. When I asked Neil Wain if antisocial behaviour had got worse, he said the answer was complex, not least because of the failure to define what antisocial behaviour actually is. One element he identified was a 'real intolerance of young people in many areas', alongside the failure to back up Care in the Community with the necessary support.

When it comes to the kind of window breaking and vandalism that the antisocial-behaviour legislation is based on, the general consensus is that there has been little change over the years, although the perception is that, like crime, it has got much worse.

Because of the changes to mental health policy, there has been an increase in some of the wide range of social problems associated with antisocial behaviour, in particular homelessness and mental health problems, which often go together. These problems make people uncomfortable, leading to support for the policies to 'reclaim the public realm' which underpin the Business Improvement Districts and the private places of the first part of the book. The impact of changing policies towards mental health during the 1980s has been enormously significant, with the closure of the long-stay mental hospitals like Holloway Sanatorium, which have been replaced by Care in the Community. This was in many ways a far-sighted policy, but with lack of funding it has seen many people with mental health problems slip through the net and into life on the streets. In his Dimbleby Lecture, Sir Ian Blair, the former head of the Metropolitan Police, said the closure of long-stay psychiatric institutions was one of the major social trends contributing to antisocial behaviour. The raft of antisocial-behaviour measures is an attempt to use legal means to address social problems, but inevitably the failure to address root causes means these are little more than sticking-plaster solutions to long-term social issues.

Bernard Hare, the writer, has described the emergence of a new social group, 'this bottom 2 per cent, this underclass', a subsection of the 20 per cent who are worse off today than they were a generation ago. In an article in the *Guardian* he wrote: 'My own feeling is that addicts of all denominations, mentally ill people, physically disabled people, older people, refugees, asylum seekers, migrant workers, sex slaves, the homeless and the unemployed ought to get a mention somewhere as being among the bottom 2 per cent per cent of the population.' But, he continued, instead the government seems to be pointing the finger mainly at white working-class families.[75]

The behaviour of this wide range of people, but in particular of young, mainly white working-class men and the problem families of the previous section, is the target of much of the 'Respect' agenda. While extreme problem families are a very small minority, on the basis of anecdotal evidence there are more of them than there were, with the cocktail of third-generation unemployment and drugs propelling a small number of families, particularly in old industrial areas with little employment, off the rails and into a chaotic existence.

Changing trends in behaviour across the social and economic spectrum are also witnessing changes, with a report from the Mental Health Foundation finding that 64 per cent believe people are getting angrier, as the idea of 'rage' is linked to more everyday occurrences.[76] Shopping rage, trolley rage, call-centre rage, PC rage, pavement rage and, of course, road rage all reflect a mix of increasing individualism and a growing sense of entitlement and frustration in a busy world where time is at a premium, bringing with it a reduced tolerance when things go wrong. When it comes to young people, their sense of entitlement and sensitivity to status and issues of 'respect' create a combustible mix. On the one hand a teenager playing loud music from their mobile phone on the bus happens more often than it used to, while on the other, the 'respect' culture among young people themselves means teenagers are more likely to respond aggressively when challenged. But the report found that young people's interest in status and respect is nothing new. At the same time, while young people's petty infractions might be annoying, there is no link with any rise in crime or the potential to commit crime. Bernard Harcourt, professor of law and political science at the University of Chicago and a vehement critic of zero tolerance and Broken Windows, describes how this approach turns those responsible for minor disorder into criminals.[77]

What has changed in Britain is the role of the police and the loss of the authority figures of old, who we have replaced with 'enforcement agents'. As the full weight of the government's target culture is brought to bear on the police, they have been pushed into an enforcement role which leaves little room for the old 'Dixon of Dock Green' role as keeper of the peace. Chief Inspector Wain explained that the drive towards what is known as 'sanction detection' has taken away police discretion almost completely. The need to fulfil targets for the detection of crimes has removed the flexibility the police used to use when deciding whether or not to prosecute minor offences.

Now, because of pressure to secure detections, small incidents which could have been settled amicably by the police, enhancing their role in the community in the process, are forced into the court system. Giving me a typical example of how the system has changed, Wain described how previously 'Mrs Smith would have come to us and said, "My Johnny's been in a fight on the way home from school."' If there were no injuries, the officer would judge it was basically a school fight and would have used his discretion, visited the parents and recorded it in the notes, but there would have been no sanction. In today's culture, however, the introduction of targets for performance means 'Johnny's fight is a relatively easy detection which will lead to a caution, a charge, a penalty notice or a final warning,' Wain said.

What worries Wain is that 'sanction detection' is leading to the unnecessary criminalization of young people, which will lead to more, rather than less, crime in the process. 'The more people come into contact with the criminal justice system, the more they will have a negative view of it, and all the research shows the earlier a person enters the system, the later they come out. People say this is soft on crime, but potentially what we are doing is driving more young people into crime and keeping them there for longer,' he said. In turn, as young people feel criminalized, they respond with assertive defences of their 'rights', stereotypically responding to perceived challenges by attempting litigious statements such as, 'I know my rights,' and 'Don't touch me.'

Policies like 'sanction detection' mean that the police have been forced to abandon discretion, which is mirrored by the rise of an increasingly litigious rights culture. The more we legislate for good behaviour, the less likely we are to find it occurring naturally. Wain pointed out that the authority figures who characterized my childhood, such as bus conductors, caretakers and park keepers, were there to do a job and as a sideline they undertook a public guardianship role. Their removal by Mrs Thatcher, for commercial reasons, left a void, and they are now being replaced by private security, but the difference is, unlike the conductors who were doing a job which had value in itself, these people are employed directly as 'enforcement agents', as Wain describes them.

'One wonders whether the old park keepers had more respect because of the job they did, compared to the new local-authority ranger with his book of fixed-penalty notices. It means the interaction between people and their relationship is different,' he said. Although a warden or a private guard is not quite the same as the 'eye in the sky' of a CCTV camera, it made me think that the impact of CCTV on buses creates an atmosphere similar to that of places dominated by guards who only have authority by virtue of their uniform and are there to watch out for trouble. They have replaced the more 'natural surveillance' of figures who gain respect because of the richer nature of their job.

The Impact of CCTV

CCTV on buses is one small part of the British trend of replacing 'natural surveillance' with enforcement and technology. CCTV is a phenomenon in Britain, which has an estimated 4.2 million cameras, more than in the whole of Europe put together. Since the early 1990s and the murder of Jamie Bulger, iconically captured on CCTV just before his death, Britain has become the CCTV capital of the world, spending one fifth of the global total on the technology. Although there is no evidence that CCTV reduces crime, British cities are vigorously expanding their camera networks and introducing ever more sophisticated surveillance technology. The Home Office spent 78 per cent of its crime-prevention budget on CCTV over the last decade,[78] based on the argument that it makes people feel safer.

Research does show that, when asked, most people like the idea of CCTV and agree that its introduction would make them feel safer. It holds out the seductive promise of greater control over the most dangerous threats we face. Yet a slew of studies, including research commissioned by the government, shows that CCTV has no impact on crime figures and in some cases may actually increase it. One of the most important studies is by criminologist Jason Ditton, who carried out a study for the Scottish Office of CCTV in Glasgow, which found that recorded crime actually increased after CCTV had been installed. Confirming the popularity of CCTV, the study found that the majority of people supported its introduction and believed that it would make them feel safer, but the findings after CCTV was put in showed that there was no improvement in feelings of safety. Ditton concluded that the 'unequivocal message' is that CCTV did not make people feel safer in the centre of Glasgow.[79]

That is a significant finding, but what I found even more interesting is the impact that the 'electronic eye on the street' has on 'natural surveillance'. The consequence of the introduction of CCTV is a retreat from 'collective and individual responsibility to self-interest and a culture of fear'.[80] The counter-intuitive result is that, as people feel they need no longer be responsible for what happens around them, crime goes up. So, given the evidence, why did the government not respond? As with the raft of measures which come under the 'Respect' banner, expert evidence has made little impact on the government, particularly when, as is the case with CCTV, the policy is popular and gives the impression that something is being done.

Giving up responsibility for personal safety is one aspect of the abdication of control over surroundings that comes with CCTV. The other is the removal of the collective responsibility people unconsciously feel for each other in a healthy environment, echoing the disturbing findings by the Conservative think tank Reform, which found that Britons were far more likely to walk on by if they witnessed a minor incident than their European counterparts.[81] In Britain we can leave the problem to a CCTV operator or a security guard. In the rest of continental Europe, where the culture of CCTV and security is less developed, people are more likely to look out for each other. CCTV is one aspect of the security-conscious architecture which is taking over Britain's towns and cities. Every gated community and privately owned shopping complex is covered in CCTV, and so are the social-housing estates and public spaces in deprived parts of the country, with the spread of cameras a key plank of the 'Respect' agenda. Like 'community', 'respect' in society is something we all want but fear that we have lost, so the government decided to institutionalize its creation. Yet in other European countries, which do not rely on policies to force good behaviour, civic-minded behaviour occurs more naturally and fear of crime is lower. They also have far less CCTV. Denmark, the happiest country in the world, has no open street CCTV system at all.

[handwritten annotation: Not 100% guaranteed to keep community safe so Respect Trust is vital amongst community]

'Respect' and 'Disrespect'

'Respect' is not about respecting the perpetrators but about respecting and protecting the majority in the community, and the measures are often very popular. The question is, do they work?

So far, while taking into account the fact that these policies were not designed primarily for those targeted by the legislation, the evidence about their impact is damning. Uncomfortably echoing the 'Pathfinder' policy and the roll-out of CCTV, these are policies with no evidence base, which have made huge changes to the way people live their lives. Louise Casey, the former head of both the antisocial-behaviour unit at the Home Office and the Respect Task Force, has little truck with evidence and famously told police in a leaked after-dinner speech, 'If Number 10 says bloody "evidence-based policy" to me more once more, I'll deck them.'[82] Another policeman, who preferred not to be identified, described how Casey was convinced she was 'on a mission' when it came to the 'Respect' agenda. 'There was a lack of tolerance. She was on the far side of Genghis Khan. It was almost like, "If you don't have enough ASBOs the Respect Task Force will come and see you."' More recently Casey's review of crime and community, commissioned by Gordon Brown, suggested that people on community service, renamed 'community payback', should wear American-style orange bibs, which swiftly became the case. The review also recommended that the probation service should contract out 'community payback' to private companies more likely to enforce tough sanctions.[83]

There is plenty of evidence, particularly from the US, that the 'disrespect' the policy implies towards those it targets is damaging and counterproductive. Research by American psychiatrist James Gilligan concluded that disrespect, shame and humiliation is the basic psychological motivation for violence. In thirty-five years of working with violent criminals and asking what had driven them to violence, Gilligan heard the same answer. 'Time after time, they would reply, "Because he disrespected me."' He added, 'They used that phrase so often that they abbreviated it into the slang phrase, "He dis'ed me,'"[84] coining the American slang term to 'diss' someone. Now an everyday part of speech to the extent that 'Are you disrespecting me?' is one of the most popular catchphrases from the comedy the *Catherine Tate Show*, the irony is that the 'Respect' agenda, introduced in order to strengthen civil society, is seen (by young people in particular) as a joke and a provocation. In place of mutual respect between people, the emphasis on policies like stop-and-search are perceived as bringing humiliation and disrespect for young people, with the role of 'respect' and 'disrespect' also closely tied to fear and unhappiness.

Like capital punishment, which the majority would support if it was re-introduced, populist, punitive policies go down well and give the impression that something is being done by politicians who are listening to people's concerns. The 'Respect' and antisocial-behaviour agenda has been an attempt by New Labour to address in a meaningful way the problems of social exclusion caused by rapid economic change, but without making any fundamental changes to the new economic order.[85] The consequence is that the policies have not had any impact on cohesion in communities and fear of crime, which are a result of social problems and not the environment. Instead, fear of crime has continued to soar, as the gulf between the groups targeted and the rest of the community widens and fractures are entrenched by the very policies designed to address them. Rather than reassuring communities, this approach feeds into the cycle of fear and is alienating and stigmatizing a generation of young people in particular, for whom 'Respect' means 'disrespect'. These policies are damaging already low levels of trust between people and increasing the lack of trust in government and politicians, who, despite the tough-talking rhetoric, are unable to address rising fear of crime. That is because their solutions are part of the problem.

Trust

Thirty years after Newman identified strangers as dangerous intruders, another American thinker took centre stage in the debate on declining trust – and therefore fear of crime – in society. Robert Putnam is the political scientist whose landmark study *Bowling Alone: The Collapse and Revival of American Community* introduced the concept of 'social capital', which is another new phrase that has joined the political lexicon and has become interchangeable with the idea of communities which work well, where there are strong social bonds between people.

His core argument is based on the idea that social networks in communities and participation in civic associations and societies – the bowling leagues of the title – promote civic trust, and that as participation in these organizations has declined, so has trust. More specifically he defined 'social capital' as 'connections among individuals – social networks and the norms of reciprocity and trustworthiness that arise from them'.[86]

Putnam, who was invited to Camp David by Bill Clinton, soon made the familiar journey across the Atlantic. He was embraced by New Labour, becoming a frequent visitor to Downing Street, and cropping up in Republican and Conservative speeches. But although his ideas found receptive audiences across the political spectrum, Putnam is far more controversial among academics. His thesis that greater participation in civic societies strengthens societies has been criticized as representing an idyllic vision of the past, which was rather more repressive and less positive than depicted, with some organizations responsible for the suppression of civil rights, while the collapse of participation in certain organizations is seen as representing change rather than decline.[87] Some types of participation have declined in the US, but others, such as attending sporting events and even volunteering, have increased.[88] Sociologist Claude Fischer argues that the concept of 'social capital' itself is flawed, based on uncertain empirical evidence. He claims it is replacing simpler terms such as membership, family, sociability and trust, and that a discussion about growing individualism and privatism would be more useful.[89] Instead, 'social capital' is, like the 'Respect' agenda, an attempt to institutionalize the cultivation of trust, which Jane Jacobs warned against.

But although the concept is much criticized among the academic community, it is very popular with politicians. It offers a relatively straightforward solution to fractures in society, which is to increase civic participation. Political scientist Barbara Arneil claims that this overlooks the fact that lack of cohesion is driven not so much by a decline in civic participation as by the enormous gap in levels of trust between privileged and deprived groups, and within deprived groups, which is why fear of crime is so much higher in the poorest parts of the country, where living conditions are hardest. In more affluent areas the networks described by Putnam tend to arise spontaneously, from organic-vegetable boxes and car clubs to local protest groups of NIMBY residents opposed to a road widening or new superstore.

The idea that increasing participation in civic societies in deprived parts of Liverpool or in Docklands would increase trust between finance executives and residents on the Isle of Dogs seems fanciful, because it is unlikely that both Jack and Pat would turn up to the same kind of singing group advocated by Putnam. It is far more likely that networks of social capital will only benefit those who already know each other, which means that segregation will persist. This is the biggest flaw with the concept of social capital – the role of people who do not know each other – and it is this question of trust between strangers that Jane Jacobs was so concerned with. Putnam calls this 'bridging capital' and he claims that more 'bonding capital', the trust between groups who are similar, will strengthen 'bridging capital', but there is no evidence of this.

Researchers looking at trust ask the same question, about trust between strangers. The standard question used by the World Values Survey is, 'Would you say that most people can be trusted – or would you say that you can't be too careful in dealing with people?' In 1959 56 per cent of Britons said yes, most people can be trusted, but by 1999 the figure had fallen to 30 per cent.[90] The US showed a similar drop, from 56 per cent in the mid 1960s to 33 per cent. Norway, on the other hand, registers levels of trust of 64 per cent, in keeping with Scandinavian neighbours like Denmark, where trust and happiness are amongst the highest in the world. Stark, visible differences between social groups are also among the lowest.

Ironically, given that the social-capital argument is based on increasing trust between people, it is more likely to be doing the opposite, by encouraging networks of like-minded people rather than creating places which promote the diversity of strangers. Think of a middle-class classical-music recital where everyone trusts everyone else not to nick their drinks and nobody does. But if there was someone there who looked visibly out of place and a minor indiscretion occurred, it goes without saying where the finger of blame would be pointed. More recent work by Robert Putnam on diversity has confirmed this virtually self-evident view, that similar groups are more likely to trust each other, with his research showing that the more diverse a community is, the less likely its inhabitants are to trust anyone. 'In the presence of diversity, we hunker down. We act like turtles. The effect of diversity is worse than had been imagined,' Putnam said, describing research which found that trust was lowest in Los Angeles, 'the most diverse human habitation in human history'.[91]

Revealing in what direction his political compass really lies, Putnam, who has been hailed as a progressive thinker, points out that there are two organizations in the US which show how well diversity can work – the US army and the evangelical church.[92] As for Los Angeles, his analysis places far less emphasis on the fact that, as well as being ethnically diverse, it is also famously one of the most socially divided cities in the US in terms of income, divisions which are entrenched by the kind of high-security living Mike Davis described in his book *City of Quartz*.[93] It is a natural human tendency for similar groups, especially wealthier ones, to seek each other out, but to increase trust and cohesion in cities, we need to challenge the urge to 'hunker down' and retreat, because that only entrenches difference and increases fear and distrust, as is the case in LA. Strangers, especially those who are visibly different, do increase fear, and that needs to be acknowledged, particularly in the debate on immigration. But it is only by creating environments where we become used to visible difference and allow ourselves to rely on strangers to keep us safe that greater cohesion will follow.

It is very likely that the Canary Wharf executive who ventures out of his comfort zone into the Isle of Dogs will feel intimidated, and he will be stared at for looking out of place. Similarly Pat is too intimidated to go shopping at Canary Wharf, feeling she doesn't belong there. This feeling of belonging in certain places also helps to explain another gap in perception which consistently emerges from the crime figures, which is that while most people think that crime is rising, they believe that the problem is far worse across the country but not as bad where they actually live.

The statistics are quite clear on this, with 41 per cent polled not very confident about crime in the country as a whole compared with 27 per cent not confident about crime where they lived.[94] The same perception of safety close to home, compared to the world out there, was also reflected in what my taxi driver in Liverpool said when I asked him why he thought the city had such a big problem with crime even though neither he nor his mates had been victims of crime. 'It's because I don't go out of my area, where I know people,' he told me.

Because it makes them feel safe, many people welcome the rise of an increasingly segregated city. Richard Sennett has written about how 'the search for a place in the world', where jobs for life have gone and trust in institutions has been corroded, leads people to seek out places which are 'defensive refuges against a hostile world'.[95] But just as the desire for security and safety only feeds an addiction for even more security, Sennett also describes how the 'fraternity by exclusion of outsiders never ends'. The most extreme example of this I came across was the phenomenon of 'double gating' within gated communities, where each home within the gated community is a high-security gated development in its own right.

What is happening more commonly in every town and city is the development of the 'defensible', often empty, private places of Chapter 2, where strangers are seen as intruders to be monitored by CCTV and security guards, rather than as part of the hustle and bustle of city life, spontaneously bringing natural surveillance and safety to places where strangers unconsciously trust each other and look out for each other. Instead, the lack of trust is reaching epidemic proportions, particularly when it comes to society's attitude to children. I recently attended a lecture by Rabbi Julia Neuberger on Britain's 'unkind, risk-averse and untrusting' society, where she described the tragic case of two-year-old Abigail Rae, who drowned in a pond after she escaped from her nursery school. The inquest into her death heard that Clive Peachy, a bricklayer, had passed the toddler as she wandered down the road alone, but failed to stop and help her because he was afraid that people would think he was trying to abduct her.[96]

All of this is disastrously the wrong way round, with Barry Glassner arguing in *The Culture of Fear* that from a psychological point of view the extreme fear and outrage expressed in the panic over violence against children is a projection which obscures the failure to provide for children's needs adequately, in terms of housing, education and nutrition. In fact, although the victims of child murders and abduction have become household names – Sarah Payne, Holly Wells and Jessica Chapman and Madeleine McCann – Home Office research concludes that the annual number of child murders is extremely low and has changed little over the last thirty years,[97] although, like Clive Peachy, few people believe it and behave accordingly. Neuberger concludes that suspicion of their motives has forced some people, particularly men, to restrain themselves from showing ordinary common decency. But if trust between people is to grow, that very small element of risk has to be accepted. Life is no fun if it is perfectly safe, which is what city managers and developers wrestle with when they try to artificially create a 'buzz' in places. More importantly, when life becomes too safe, paradoxically we become more fearful and less trusting, as the natural human bonds which occur spontaneously between people are stifled. Allowing those bonds between strangers to unconsciously flourish is far more likely to happen in environments which are genuinely for everyone than in places which entrench the architecture of difference. This is what happens in the genuinely open squares and public places of continental Europe, where it is more common for all generations, regardless of income and social class, to mix more freely.

The Politics of Happiness

When Labour came to power, their rallying call was the rousing song, 'Things Can Only Get Better'. Well over a decade on, when asked by pollsters whether life in general is getting better or worse, 71 per cent said life was getting worse, up from 60 per cent in 2007 and only 40 per cent in 1998.[98]

This feeling that things are getting worse, which was right at the top of the political agenda before the recession began, is reflected by the attention focused on 'happiness' and trust by writers, broadcasters, columnists, policy wonks and government departments. Rather like the paradox that crime is falling but fear of crime is rising, the conundrum that growing economic prosperity was accompanied by increasing unhappiness and mental illness was confounding politicians and policymakers. Two books brought the debate to prominence, economist Richard Layard's *Happiness: Lessons from a New Science*[99] and *Affluenza*, by psychologist Oliver James.[100]

The idea that politicians were concerned about people's happiness rather than merely focused on questions of GDP seemed quite new and rather refreshing when it hit the political scene. In fact it is not new at all, but is very well rehearsed in the United States, where it is called 'well-being', another term which has crossed the Atlantic. In 1976 Tibor Scitovsky published his classic, *The Joyless Economy*,[101] which dealt with the apparent paradox that increased income does not increase happiness. More recently the American psychologist Martin Seligman, responsible for popularizing the term 'well-being', is credited with founding the 'positive psychology' movement. Seligman, who has met UK policy advisors and ministers, is a key influence on New Labour's interest in teaching happiness in schools and in promoting cognitive behaviour therapy, based on techniques widely used in the US.

'Well-being' might appear a new area of interest, but questions of happiness, mental health and trust have long preoccupied sociologists and politicians. Writing about social policy during the Second World War, sociologist Richard Titmuss found that the war coincided with improved mental health, to the great surprise of the nation's psychiatrists, who were anticipating widespread problems as a result of bombing. He concluded that this could not be simply put down to the cohesive effect of facing a common enemy, although that undoubtedly played a part. Instead, he pointed to the impact of universal services which became available during the war, from free school milk to pensions. These had the consequence of creating 'less social disparagement', which led to better mental health.[102]

Richard Titmuss pointed out the link between 'less social disparagement', better mental health and happiness nearly sixty years ago. 'Less social disparagement' is interchangeable with 'respect' and shows that the way to strengthen civil society is by creating a climate of interaction and trust between different social groups, rather than by falling back on institutional solutions where behaviour is controlled, through the design of the environment, the imposition of antisocial-behaviour measures and now, most recently, the teaching of happiness. Research also consistently shows that depression and mental health issues are connected to social isolation and levels of inequality, yet instead of focusing on causes like this, the teaching of happiness techniques is being promoted. In terms of social isolation, the impact on older people of the closure of small shops and post offices which can be a lifeline barely makes it into discussions, while the creation of large parts of the city which provide few facilities for older people goes unremarked. When it comes to inequality, rather than facing difficult issues and attempting to emulate the social model of other European countries, where rates of depression are half those in Britain and the US, we are eagerly following the American approach to mental health.

So many of today's fractures in civil society have come about as a result of the single-minded approach to extracting the maximum profit from the places we live in, through policies on property. The government is aware of the problem of rising fear, but the irony is that not only have they failed to look at the true causes, the solutions put forward are making the problem worse. Policies on housing and the private places mushrooming in cities are creating a physical environment which reflects the stark divisions of the city, creating homogenous enclaves which undermine trust between people, heightening fear. This is compounded by the raft of policies attempting to legislate for good behaviour and the security-conscious approach to crime and design. The consequence is a growing distrust of strangers who are the essence of civility and the undermining of 'natural surveillance' which enhances greater collective trust. The next chapter will look at ways of increasing collective trust that are much more common in continental Europe than in Britain, which has consistently copied policies from America towards crime and fear of crime.

8

Moving Forwards

Shared Space

Much of this book has been about the spread of highly controlled 'defensible' environments, monitored by technology and designed in ways which prevent certain kinds of behaviour and encourage others, and which encourage certain kinds of people and discourage others. This is the template for British towns and cities today, with the aim of creating environments which make a profit and which feel safe. I have argued that, counter-intuitively, we are making the city a far more fearful place, handing over our collective and personal responsibility for our safety to private companies which run many of the places we live in, and drifting towards a more authoritarian and less democratic city.

So, going to meet a friend who was staying in Kensington in London, I was surprised to find a place which contradicted my thinking. Walking down the high street, I felt something seemed different but I couldn't put my finger on what. It felt somehow lighter, freer and more open, which it was – all the barriers, railings and crossings have been taken away, encouraging people to cross wherever they like. I was more surprised when I found out that the changes had been inspired by a man walking backwards, with his arms folded, into traffic.[1]

The ideas man was Hans Monderman, a Dutch engineer who died in 2008. His insight was that barriers, railings, kerbs and even traffic lights – all the signs intended to keep pedestrians and motorists apart – actually discourage both groups from engaging with each other, making life more dangerous. In Kensington, the result of removing the barriers was that, rather than making the road more dangerous by allowing people to walk into the traffic,

Grey's Monument, Newcastle. Still public – but for how long?

the number of accidents fell dramatically, down by 44 per cent.[2] In an interview with *Time* magazine just before his death, Monderman explained that removing signs forces people 'to look each other in the eye, to judge body language and learn to take responsibility – to function as normal human beings'. His stunt of walking backwards into oncoming traffic was designed to prove how well his concept of 'shared space' works. In the schemes even traffic lights are removed, to create 'naked' junctions where cars, cyclists and pedestrians all pass each other in what *Time* describes as a 'polite quadrille of nods and hand gestures'.[3]

Monderman's first foray into 'shared space' came during the late 1970s, after he was appointed traffic safety officer for the northern Dutch province of Friesland. At that time the Dutch government was alarmed by the rising number of accidents. Seeking to reduce traffic speed in the village of Makkinga but hampered by budget cuts, Monderman was unable to use traditional calming measures, so he decided to follow a hunch, based on accident analysis looking at human rather than technical factors. He took away road signs, traffic lights and kerbs and within two weeks speed on the road had dropped by more than half.[4] There are now more than 120 examples of 'shared space' in places across Holland, with the approach spreading to Germany and Scandinavia. The best-known example is in Drachten in Holland, where in 2004 all traffic lights and road markings were removed from a junction used by 20,000 cars a day, as well as cyclists and pedestrians. As a result people's perception of risk changed, encouraging them to take more care, and there have been no serious accidents since.[5] Now the whole town has removed most of its signs and lights, followed in 2007 by Bohmte in Germany.

In the UK Seven Dials in London's Covent Garden was the earliest example of 'shared space', introduced in 1996, followed by Blackett Street in Newcastle in 2001. In Blackett Street there are no barriers or crossings but accident rates have declined, and at Seven Dials there are no lights; instead pedestrians are encouraged to congregate at the monument, which is used as a roundabout by motorists. Although it has become a busy and well-used meeting place, there has not been a single accident. Kensington High Street is the first of the bigger schemes in the UK, introduced in 2003 by Conservative councillor and deputy council leader Daniel Moylan, who was determined to explode assumptions about road safety and risk, despite opposition from council officials. The idea is now being extended to Exhibition Road, a main London thoroughfare and home to key museums and institutions.

Ben Hamilton-Baillie, a British architect and urban designer, compares the behaviour of people in a busy street to those at an ice rink, where informal social protocols ensure that skaters move in a similar direction and people interact with each other to create a safe environment. 'Part of the pleasure derives from a surprising and enjoyable collective consensus, and the ability of all participants to communicate, anticipate and react in ways that bring to mind the behaviour of shoals of fish or flocks of birds,' he writes.[6] Even motorway driving, which is based on the interaction between drivers, indicating to each other before overtaking, has something of the same collective experience.

When I spoke to Hamilton-Baillie, he described Monderman as 'a very practical, down-to-earth traffic engineer' who towards the end of his life found himself discussing questions of civility in society. 'What Hans helped to discover is how easy it is to foster natural civility – it's almost an obvious observation that people enjoy civility and simple interaction and the exchange and development of social protocols,' Hamilton-Baillie said. Despite opposition from traffic engineers, schooled in a risk-averse culture of safety and litigation, 'shared space' is now starting to be taken up in Britain, with around forty projects around the country, following the lead of continental Europe, where thousands of places have adopted it. Before he died, Monderman said there had never been a fatality in any of his schemes, and the evidence consistently shows that 'shared space' invariably slashes accidents, by as much as 90 per cent in some places.

One of the most important aspects of 'shared space' relates to risk and safety. Research on the 'risk compensation effect' by John Adams, Emeritus Professor of Geography at University College, London, found that if protected from hazards, people simply readjust their risk threshold, with the consequence that improving brakes on cars does not necessarily increase safety, because people drive faster and brake later. Similarly, traffic controls can actually increase accidents because they remove personal responsibility from drivers. Research on children's play reaches the same conclusions, finding that increased safety measures in playgrounds do not reduce accidents and may in fact increase them.[7]

Importantly, Adams agrees that the impact of heightened security on people and places is similar to that of increased control over the environment: it raises the risk threshold and that makes us yearn for ever more security, in turn losing our own individual and collective responsibility for our behaviour. 'The message conveyed is that everything that isn't strictly controlled is to be feared. This creeping paranoia that is used in the name of safety and in the absence of any compelling evidence is reshaping our society. But the effect is that all this security is diluting personal responsibility and our own feelings of control over the environment, making us more scared and paranoid and desiring of more security to protect us. It's a never-ending spiral,' Adams said.

Hans Monderman, like Adams, was clear that the benefits of his ideas on 'shared space' and personal and collective responsibility went far wider than questions of traffic on the high street, impacting on social and political questions of what public space and public life should be about. 'Eye contact and the consultation between civilians in public space is the highest quality you can get in a free country,' he said. If his simple yet counter-intuitive 'hunch' has been shown to work for road safety, then the implications for the city are huge. 'Shared space' is interchangeable with the idea of 'natural surveillance': it relies on the interaction between strangers in public places to ensure safety. Continental European cities tend to have a far more open public life in the squares and streets of the city, with less intrusive security. CCTV remains the exception to the rule. From looking at experience on the Continent, where both high security and fear of crime are lower than in Britain, it is likely that, in the same way that 'shared space' decreases accidents, more emphasis on 'natural surveillance' instead of high security would reduce not only fear of crime but actual crime.

In the government's *Manual for Streets* published in 2007, the guidance encourages 'shared space' and open, well-connected streets which promote social interaction and make it easier for people to move around or stop and chat.[8] Yet the document also states that 'defensible space' should not be compromised, no doubt because it would be impolitic to criticize another aspect of government policy. Neither does it take a view on the growth of private streets. As 'shared space' is starting to be seen as the new way of doing things, privately owned places, like parts of Stratford City, are also embracing the principles. Monderman is no longer around to ask, but it is unlikely that adopting 'shared space' in tightly controlled private places is what he meant when he talked of public space and civic life in a free, democratic society. Incorporating his principles into defensible, private space will do little more than provide another tick-box category to be followed and the essence of the concept, which is about shared, open access for all, will be lost.

Non-Plan and Non-Places

The enthusiasm for 'shared space' is an encouraging new trend which should, if adopted in the spirit in which it was intended, run counter to the privatization, control and segregation of cities. Even so, with its attention directed mainly at road signs and junctions, it is unlikely to have more than a limited impact on public life and public culture unless its principles are taken up more widely. Radical ideas about how to change the way planning is done have been hugely influential in the past, from the centralized planning programmes of the 1950s and 1960s to a very controversial proposal in the late 1960s to get rid of planning altogether – a proposal which provided the intellectual basis for Thatcherism's approach to property and planning.

During the late 1960s, partly as a reaction to the perceived failures of postwar planning, a proposal gathered steam among a group of writers, architects and planners. The idea, which was called 'non-plan', was to get rid of planning in specific areas. In 1969 an essay appeared in the political weekly *New Society* by Peter Hall, Cedric Price, Reyner Banham and the editor of *New Society*, Paul Barker. Called 'Non-Plan: An Experiment in Freedom', it argued that planning had failed.

In 1968 Ronan Point, a tower block in Newham in east London, had collapsed, killing four people. It shook public confidence in the safety of industrialized system building, and this, coupled with the revelations of bribery and corruption in the awarding of building contracts, as revealed by the Poulson affair, which broke towards the end of the 1960s, made people receptive to new ideas. The centralized planning initiatives of the post-war years were not standing up to scrutiny. Looking at cities through history, the authors recalled how planning everywhere rides roughshod over the people who live there, from Haussmann's Paris, which was cleared by demolition gangs, to American urban renewal projects which uprooted local people with scant compensation. 'What would happen if there were no plan? What would people prefer to do, if their choices were untrammelled?' the essay asked. The authors proposed 'a precise and carefully observed experiment in non-planning' in a few appropriate places. 'At the least, one would find out what people want; at the most, one might discover the hidden style of mid twentieth-century Britain,' they wrote.[9]

At the time, and as the authors had predicted, the essay was very controversial. Yet little more than a decade later, Peter Hall was the originator of the idea of enterprise zones, where this book began, in the old Docklands. Enterprise zones owed much to the 'non-planning' philosophy.[10]

The authors of 'Non-Plan' had argued that most planning is aristocratic or oligarchic, revealing its historical origins, which chimed with Thatcherism's desire to do away with Britain's culture of paternalism. The current arrangements were doctrinaire and rigid, they said. Instead they proposed 'a plunge into heterogeneity', which would free up British style and culture. One example they gave of a hidden style icon was the filling station, lamenting how hard it was to get planning permission for a filling station and forecasting, with accuracy, that petrol stations could turn into shopping centres. Prophetically, the 'Non-Plan' essay went on to predict more out-of-town shopping centres and strip development along main roads, following the American model. This was the model for the future, not in Britain's old cities, but in the immediacy and excitement of the American west, where neon signs were replacing buildings. 'There, in the desert and the Pacific states, creations like Fremont Street in Las Vegas or Sunset Strip in Beverley Hills represent the living conditions of our age,' the text rhapsodized, accompanied by an illustration of petrol-station forecourts, fast-food outlets and low-cost motels. Today, we may not use the word motel for our no-frills business hotels, but, language apart, nearly all the predicted changes have happened.

The essay was full of words like 'spontaneity' and 'vitality', implying that, free of planning restrictions, the choices people made would create exciting and memorable places. But, as this book has revealed, this is not what happened. The lack of local-government involvement and planning controls in places like Docklands, and the removal of planning restrictions on out-of-town development, resulted in the creation of remarkably similar places, wherever they might be. This is because 'non plan' not only made the places developers wanted, but created the 'non places' identified by French anthropologist Marc Auge[11] – malls, airports, conference centres and, in the new century, central parts of the city. These places are everywhere but feel like they're nowhere in particular, devoid of local culture and history and the distinctiveness that brings. Instead they try very hard to import their own culture and vitality, but it doesn't work, creating fake, themed environments where everything is controlled and far from unplanned and spontaneous. This is an approach to cities which reveals that when the market is given free rein to make places, the result is not the freedom and vitality that people want.

The essay glossed over the fact – wilfully or not – that removing planning does not free up people to make choices; it allows the market to make choices. When it comes to places, the market rarely reflects public demand, because the enhancement and creation of genuinely successful places cannot function in the same way as a classic market, like the car market, where supply is able to meet demand far more effectively. Jane Jacobs sees cities as bodily entities of 'organized complexity', where the streets and public places are the 'vital organs'.[12] Such a complex organism, which constantly interacts with the conscious and unconscious emotions and desires of its inhabitants, cannot even begin to function like a pure market.

'Non-Plan' was written more than forty years ago and contributed to the cracks in state socialist planning. The essay also came out long before the dominance of the car was challenged, reflecting a vision which was reliant on cars to travel between its out-of-town malls and motels. Today, planning has shifted, in terms of rhetoric if nothing else, towards a far greater focus on the needs of the environment and local people, in keeping with the ill-defined phrase 'sustainable development'. The Brundtland Commission is responsible for the most widely accepted definition of this vague term, describing sustainable development as development which 'meets the needs of the present without compromising the ability of future generations to meet their own needs'.[13] Effectively this means development which balances the needs of the economy with the needs of the environment, taking into account economic, environmental and social priorities.

The other aspect of planning which has come to the fore in recent years is its relationship to local democracy. Following the disasters of the 1950s and 1960s centralized planning had many of its powers removed, but local government, as the agent of the post-war grand plans, lost even more, as planning restrictions were simply lifted and quangos such as the Conservatives'

Urban Development Corporations ushered in a new era of private-sector planning. This paid even less regard to local democracy. Planning is at the centre of local government in a democratic society. The planning system is complex and riddled with jargon, but in a well-functioning democracy it allows people to voice what they believe the city is for and to stand up for the kind of places they want to live in. Schools, hospitals, roads and housing developments – like the Pathfinder programme – are all voted on by locally elected councillors who are on the planning committee. It is planning committee meetings which are at the heart of local government and are invariably the best-attended public meetings, where local councillors, answerable to the electorate, have to strike a balance between the wishes of local people and the public good, which are often in conflict. But in recent years local protestors claim the system is deliberately cutting them out, with meetings taking place unannounced and crucial decisions kept secret.

Over the last decade the meaning of the public good has shifted in the UK, despite the rhetoric of sustainable development, to emphasize economic needs, a shift which is reflected in planning legislation. Similar changes have taken place in the US, in contrast to the rest of Europe, where the public life and culture of cities continues to be a priority. There has been huge opposition to these obscure changes to planning in Britain, like Pathfinder, documented in Chapter 5, where they have forced people out of their homes and businesses to make way for the new private places. Yet time and again local people complain they have not been listened to and not informed of critical meetings and decisions. The current situation is making a mockery of government pledges to strengthen civic involvement and increase trust in politicians.

Flexible Places

'Non-Plan' did not address environmental concerns or the undermining of democracy, which are contemporary planning issues and were hastened by the Thatcherite approach to the city, continued so enthusiastically by New Labour. Written in a different context, this is a document of its time, which helps to explain how Britain's cities changed after 1979. But although it gave intellectual credibility to Thatcherism's desire to free up the market, it did contain within it a strain of more progressive thinking, still relevant in today's changing economic climate.

Peter Hall agreed that 'Non-Plan' had more in common with the New Right than the New Left, but he also claimed that the essay had an affinity with anarchism, arguing that 'right and left met around the back of the stage'.[14] In its bid to free the market, 'non plan' was also in favour of not knowing how things were going to turn out when a project began, with the authors complaining how, under the system then, 'nothing must be allowed simply to "happen"', and praising plans which had not turned out as the planner had intended. Erasing the psychedelic painting on the Beatles' former Apple boutique in London's Baker Street was put forward as an example of how planning suppressed British culture, showing that 'non plan' was not that concerned about private-property rights in the face of graffiti which might be considered culture.

On the other side of the Atlantic, Kevin Lynch, a planner and urban designer who became a professor at MIT during the 1960s, was also very interested in creating environments which were not planned, where everything was 'fluid and open'.[15] In contrast to non-plan, he was particularly interested in open spaces which operated outside the market, the parts of the city which had not been committed by the planning system and which were free for people to use and enjoy as they liked, where, he claimed, 'the individual has a chance to demonstrate mastery'. In this way his work clearly chimes with the evidence of 'shared space' that personal responsibility grows when external controls over the environment diminish.[16] Lynch felt that these fluid places were the most free parts of the city, making room for growth and change and providing places for choice and social experiment.

Forty years later a research project funded by the European Union confirmed what had long been suspected: areas which may appear empty and abandoned often provide the most fertile ground for artistic subcultures which begin organically to nurture creative and exciting places. The research was led by a Berlin-based multi-disciplinary group of architects, planners, lawyers and sociologists called Urban Catalyst. They looked at the impact of spontaneous, temporary uses which transformed everyday places, often in former industrial areas, into breeding grounds for new forms of art, music and pop culture. Although the project ranged all over Europe, it singled out Manchester as a place where temporary activities around a music subculture and gay subculture took over former industrial buildings and transformed the image of the city.

This is a process they call 'unplanned urbanism' and it is quite different from classical planning, which is based on ideas of permanence and control.[17] Implicitly it seems to have far more in common with the vision that the 'Non-Plan' authors hoped for when they condemned planning 'as the only branch of knowledge purporting to be some kind of science which regards a plan as fulfilled when it is merely completed'.[18] 'Non-Plan' praised plans which turned out to succeed for quite unforeseen reasons and similarly Urban Catalyst state: 'It is necessary to think of planning as a process that occurs over time and to think not only in terms of a desired end result, but rather in development steps ... which might unfold in several directions, where the end result is never defined.'[19] But where 'unplanned urbanism' and 'Non-Plan' part company is in relation to the market. Urban Catalyst point out that in contrast to classical planning, which depends on bringing in large amounts of public or private money, especially in places where property prices are low, this flexible type of planning thrives in places with little commercial value, which is precisely what attracts creative activities, in search of free spaces or limited rent.

It's quite obvious that during the 1990s this unplanned, spontaneous process worked, not only in Manchester but in former industrial areas all over Europe, from Mitte and later Friedrichsrain in Berlin to Shoreditch and Hoxton in London. In the part of Athens called Gazi, which means gasworks, art galleries, nightclubs and outdoor restaurants have sprung up in old factories and warehouses, in the shadow of the imposing and atmospherically illuminated gasworks. The question is how to support and nurture the process. The danger is that, as happened in Manchester, once the artistic revival has transformed the image of the city, property developers move in and take over, displacing the most exciting cultural activity, which leads to such changes as the morphing of the famous Hacienda nightclub into Hacienda Apartments.

Urban Catalyst believe the answer is to allow the planning system greater flexibility, with councils encouraged to let exciting, temporary uses flourish on vacant land and buildings. This way of doing things could be built into the planning system, but the challenge is that it would need a very significant shift in mindset to recognize 'the importance of values beyond monetary ones',[20] which is where classical planning has a role. These activities rarely have any money behind them, but even more challenging than the idea of allowing parts of the city to be used for activities which are not guaranteed to make a profit is the possibility that once an area has taken off, with the accompanying increase in property prices, it will not all be sold to the highest bidder. For it to retain its character, creativity and benefit to the local community, at least part of it has to be ring-fenced for these sorts of spontaneous, unplanned activities and for affordable housing for local people.

This is what so manifestly failed to happen in old industrial areas all around the UK, with Hoxton, which became the centre for London's art scene in the 1990s, a classic example. As the area took off, local people and local businesses were displaced, creating a far more bland, commercialized part of the city, in place of the excitement of a few years previously. It is still a more interesting and diverse place than many nearby areas, but most of the artists who moved in and made the area take off can no longer afford to live there, as artists' warehouses and local cafés are replaced by sleek lofts and pricey cocktail bars. To some, this is gentrification and is positive because it raises property prices. Others, like Urban Catalyst, point out that maintaining a more authentic and inclusive environment also sustains greater excitement. As a result of this debate, there has been an awful lot of talk about the 'creative city' and the importance of 'creativity' in places over the last few years. But rather than creating a climate where genuine creativity flourishes, all the agencies and 'partners' working in British cities have institutionalized 'creativity', which has become little more than a meaningless buzzword to be 'delivered'. A look at how post-industrial places have changed, in Manchester, Berlin or Hoxton, shows us what creative cities look like. They are places in the throes of change and the issue for policymakers is that, to retain their creativity, they need to continue to sustain a diverse economy, with elements that operate outside or on the fringes of the market.

Despite all the interest in the 'creative city', this mindset couldn't be further from the government's way of looking at things. Councils and developers appreciate that artists and creative people seem to have a good effect on places, but rather than allowing parts of the city to remain open and flexible, the rapid sell-off of public land and buildings discussed in the first part of the book continues, in the constant bid to raise revenue and property values. As for artists, the government tries to harness their energy by insisting that new developments employ artists to work with local communities. For residents affected by some of the more controversial new schemes, particularly in the housing market renewal areas, this can seem like a patronizing way of diluting their opposition and unsurprisingly it fails to generate the kind of excitement experienced in Manchester or in London a few years later.

There is one man who is able to generate real excitement in places. Eric Reynolds is a property developer with a difference. With his shock of blond hair and well-cut suits, he is known to be a shrewd businessman who is not shy of making money. He also knows a thing or two about creating cutting-edge places and was responsible for kick-starting the transformation of Camden Town in the 1970s by setting up the market at Camden Lock and the rock venue Dingwalls. Later he painted the shopping centre at the Elephant and Castle pink and was at the heart of the campaign to save Spitalfields, the east London market on the border with the City. For ten years Eric worked with temporary creative outfits and nurtured a thriving music and arts scene, which included an opera house, recording studios, indoor pitches for football and cricket and the very successful music venue The Spitz. In the end they lost the campaign and the new Spitalfields Estate was built. While The Spitz has closed, some of the activities survive.

More recently Eric was involved in another battle to save part of Smithfield, the old meat market in central London, which the Corporation of London hoped to sell to a private developer planning to build a shopping and office complex. When I spoke to Eric during the bitter public inquiry, he said he feared that 'instead of a network of medieval streets which people feel is common, it will become a sealed place'. He is a property developer happy to make a lot of money, but he is driven more by the culture and atmosphere of the places he helps to create than by the 'bottom line'. I've never known Eric to be involved in a loss-making scheme, but he would certainly have generated far better returns if he had chosen to work on the type of scheme planned by the Corporation. As far as he's concerned, their proposals are 'cancerous'. 'It's not good, although they would say we're the cancer because we're eating into their profits,' he said. He was delighted when the secretary of state ruled that the buildings should remain (although as of March 2009 the developer is still planning to put in a new application). As for Eric, he has put forward an alternative scheme including a market, restaurants, artists' studios and offices.

Eric's company, Urban Space Management, is involved in boosting temporary uses and creative organizations all around the country, but his main project is in Docklands and it is probably the only part of the whole area to retain an element of the more anarchic side of the non-plan spirit. Trinity Buoy Wharf, which has the only lighthouse in London, is far from a non-place, where over 190 creative businesses work out of ships' containers designed by Eric, attracting sculptors, painters, bronze workers, musicians, architects and furniture makers. In one of its more far-sighted moments the Urban Development Corporation responsible for Docklands drew up a 120-year lease for Trinity Buoy Wharf and sold it to Urban Space Management for £1, creating a trust to ensure the place is used for artistic and creative purposes.

This model, which allowed one small part of Docklands to create a flexible environment not based solely on profit, shows what can be done. As Kevin Lynch pointed out in the 1960s, if a new mindset can look beyond the market, leaving places 'fluid and open', then anything can happen. The type of culture which flourished in Manchester emphasized music and clubs and fed into the brief branding of the UK as 'Cool Britannia', which coincided with the hope that greeted New Labour when they came to power. The flexible city is well suited to artists, musicians and bohemians, but it shouldn't only foster 'cool' uses and 'cool' places.

The economic downturn may provide some of that flexibility again, not just for artists and bohemians, but across the social and economic spectrum. With the recession combining with concerns over climate change and with growing interest in locally produced food, the National Trust, which is the biggest private landowner in the country, is behind a drive to create new allotments and community gardens around Britain.[21] Allotments have always been a barometer of social and economic change, with former New York mayor Rudy Guliani causing outrage when he vowed to sell the city's community gardens to make way for economic development. With the recession, interest in allotments is returning, mirroring the depression of the 1930s, when the US government encouraged community gardening.

On the high street, while the closure of thousands of businesses is forcing more small shops out of business alongside larger chains, developers like Eric, voluntary groups and social enterprises are talking to the administrators of companies and drawing up plans to put new, temporary uses into empty places, which will hopefully stimulate their own local economies. At the same time, the move away from a profit-orientated city is likely to encourage what Karen Franck, professor of architecture at the New Jersey Institute of Technology, and Quentin Stevens, urban design lecturer at the Bartlett School of Planning, describes as 'loose space', stimulated by the increased presence of 'open persons' such as children and the elderly, who are more likely than busy shoppers to engage in unplanned social encounters.[22] These alternatives are small scale and nothing like the grand plans of the 1980s. They cannot entirely reverse the economic pain but they show how this part of the economic cycle can bring about a different kind of change.

Open Spaces

The 1950s are often stereotyped as a golden age of social cohesion, where deference and a 'curtain twitching' culture kept bad behaviour in check. Reading Kevin Lynch's writings on the importance of open space for young people, I was suddenly struck by the idea that the bomb sites which littered cities after the Second World War might, inadvertently, have contributed to cohesion by giving children and young people unusual and exciting places to explore. Lynch believed open spaces, on the margins of city life, were places which contributed to community control by allowing young people to take risks and develop a sense of mastery. Today, many parks provide pleasant environments but there are very few open spaces for young people to discover, as Chief Inspector Neil Wain, commander of Stockport police, pointed out when I spoke to him about antisocial behaviour. He even claimed that much of his own youthful behaviour would be considered antisocial in a culture where it is even a criminal offence for a group of boys to go into school buildings after hours to play football. Instead schools and playing fields are heavily fortified, according to Secured by Design principles (with many playing fields sold off to developers), and there are few places to discover and explore in a culture where fearful parents increasingly keep their children close to home.

'Respect' policies are intended to make young people respect their elders and make the majority feel safer, as Chapter 7 shows. They don't work, the most compelling evidence of their failure being the fact that fear of crime has risen steeply since this agenda was introduced. Based on American ideas about zero tolerance, 'Respect' is part of the problem rather than the solution.

That is not to say that the 'Respect' agenda is the only cause of antisocial behaviour, but every youth worker I spoke to believed that if the large amount of funding channelled into punitive policies was put back into youth services, a lot could be done. In Salford I heard how the council spends twice as much money on ASBOs as it does on youth services, and when I visited it was immediately obvious that there just wasn't anything for young people to do, a situation replicated across Britain. In contrast, in continental Europe, and in particular in the Netherlands, Germany and Scandinavia, a culture of 'social pedagogy' thrives. With its roots in German progressive education, this is sometimes translated as 'community education' and its reach spans youth work, crèches and nurseries, day-care centres, work with young offenders and parenting education. Based on ideas of group work and social responsibility, this tradition failed to take hold in Britain, which has followed the American trend of looking at problems of individual adjustment,[23] most recently reflected by the vogue for teaching happiness techniques in schools.

In Salford, not only is there nothing constructive for young people to do, the few pubs in the area do not allow entry to under twenty-fives, dispersal orders stop them from gathering on the street, and they are frequently stopped and searched for no reason. Even so, I met people like Graham Cooper who devote their lives to working with young people, particularly those who are classified as 'NEETs'. Often it is people like Graham, who may have had a chequered youth themselves, who are the most gifted when it comes to working with so-called 'hard to reach' groups. If this were recognized and youth workers from diverse backgrounds encouraged, social community and cohesion could grow.

Everywhere I went I heard how young men, often in white working-class communities, were among the most vulnerable, often falling into the NEET category and the most likely to enter the criminal justice system. These are young men who would once have found secure jobs in heavy industry. For years I have been hearing how more apprenticeships are needed and, although promises of schemes were frequently made, the reality was rarely forthcoming. Now, the economic downturn is again providing an opportunity to boost apprenticeships, with the government promising an extra 20,000 guaranteed places in the public sector and aiming to create 250,000 apprenticeships,[24] which would create a more balanced economy in the process – if it actually happens.

The 'Respect' agenda is mainly aimed at young people and those on the margins of society, such as the homeless and mentally ill, who have also been disproportionately targeted by ASBOs. At the same time there is continuous hand-wringing when report after report finds that children in Britain are the most unhappy, not just in Europe but in the western world, with the United Nations Children's Fund concluding that this was because of lack of social cohesion in the UK.[25]

Partly because of the way ASBOs work, with the breach of an order leading to prison, Britain locks up more young people than any other country in western Europe. That's at the most extreme end of the punitive spectrum. On an everyday level, the lack of things to do and policies such as stop-and-search and dispersal orders, which seem like harassment, make many young people feel stigmatized and discriminated against. If this punitive control agenda could make way for proper youth services, which are the norm in many European countries, greater cohesion would follow. Sweden, for example, has a long tradition of government-sponsored sports clubs, libraries, meeting halls and youth clubs, to the extent that they embrace the lives of most young people.[26] According to the United Nation's Children Fund, Sweden is also at the top of the list when it comes to children's happiness, along with the Netherlands and Denmark. They find it quite unnecessary to teach happiness.

Ironically, the concern in Sweden is that the youth system may be too extensive, limiting young people's freedom to pursue unstructured leisure.[27] Obviously a balance needs to be struck between forcing young people to sign up to activities and providing environments where they can experiment and challenge themselves and each other. Flexible places and open spaces are the ideal environments. As Graham Cooper said, 'They'd far rather be flying through the countryside on mountain bikes than breaking windows.'

Reinventing the Public

Imagine trying to privatize a piazza. So many genuinely public places in towns and cities all over southern and northern Europe, in Italy, Spain, Greece, France, Holland, Germany and Scandinavia, are thriving. Families and groups of people stroll arm in arm taking the *passeggiata*, children run around and old people sit together on benches. These places do not follow the American Clean and Safe agenda of the shopping mall, but they are not dirty and dangerous as a result. Far from it, they are healthier and happier. It is no coincidence that rates of mental illness in continental Europe are half those in Britain and America.

Our politicians claim that the 'urban renaissance' has created a continental café lifestyle, but although outdoor cafés have sprung up, a great many of them are not in truly public places, because for the last decade all we have been building are private places based on shopping, finance centres and apartments, with rigid rules about who is or is not allowed in and what they can do there. And even when the places themselves remain public, an increasingly private form of government, based on the American model, controls the area, as Chapter 3 describes. We do still have public places in the centres of cities. Trafalgar Square in London or Grey's Monument in Newcastle have not been privatized, but it is only a matter of time. In Newcastle controversy accompanied plans by the city centre management company to discourage young people, street performers and protestors from the area.[28]

This is a relatively new phenomenon, which has only taken off in the last decade, under New Labour. Before that, finance centres such as Canary Wharf and the Broadgate Centre in London followed this model of development, but they were singular places created specifically to meet the needs of business. During the 1990s development continued and the private sector invested in places all around the country, but the idea of selling off entire parts of the city remained in the future. This book has tracked the story of how the privatization of large parts of the city became the property industry's entrenched way of doing things, with the full encouragement of the government, which created helpful policies and legislation.

This has been an American approach to the city, which ironically has gone much further than America in many respects, especially with regard to the growing private ownership of city streets and the use of surveillance technologies like CCTV. In European cities, on the other hand, the locally distinctive, public culture of places, expressed through public streets, squares, public buildings and shops, has been protected to a far greater degree against the pressures of globalization. Planning policies favouring small shops and restricting larger stores have been at the heart of this.

Along with streets and public places, thousands of public buildings have been sold to private landlords in Britain. From Manchester's Free Trade Hall, the emblem of democracy and public life in the city since Peterloo, to

Crossland's Holloway Sanatorium, these public buildings, which are part of our national heritage, have been removed from the public realm. This policy of selling off land and buildings is gathering pace, with the sale of what are known as 'local-authority assets' a key aim of the government.

There is a lot of uncertainty about the way in which cities in Britain have changed. There is widespread dislike of the sameness of the high street and the unaffordability of property. Yet few people are really aware of what has happened, because so many of the areas this book deals with are mired in jargon. This is a plague which affects much of the domestic policy agenda, with multiple 'partnerships' between numerous agencies spawning ever more obscure acronyms. Even so – with the exception of finance – planning, housing and regeneration, the policy areas which determine life in cities, seem to be particularly badly affected. Compulsory purchase, Section 106, Pathfinder, even the use of the word 'assets' are just a few of the terms which mean nothing to most people. The spread of jargon is a very effective distancing mechanism, undermining our understanding of policies which profoundly affect the culture of our cities and the way we live.

When it comes to creating new places, the architect Adam Caruso – whose practice Caruso St John is involved with public building projects such as the modernization of Tate Britain – believes one of the reasons why Britain's cities have changed so much is down to the disempowerment of the public sector, in contrast to the rest of Europe. 'The public sector is no longer an active client the way it is in most northern European countries,' he explained, contrasting Britain with Holland and Germany, where, he said, the public and private sectors work together. 'It's win-win, but the private sector has to play ball, it's part of the culture,' he said. In Switzerland, which he finds a particularly interesting example because it is 'no left-wing country', he describes how 'because of its culture the private sector is supposed to deliver for the public good'.

Hans Van der Heijden, the Dutch architect who worked on the award-winning extension to the Bluecoat Arts Centre in Liverpool, agrees. 'It is really one of our frustrations working in Britain. The public sector is very weak compared to the Netherlands. It has a very low ethos and low self-awareness. We were really surprised about it. When we work in Europe, municipal government works with us, looking at what is best for the city as a whole,' he said. In Rotterdam, where his practice BIQ is based, and in Zurich, both cities with a number of post-industrial areas, the city works with landowners and developers to decide what should remain in public hands for what Caruso describes as 'the benefit of place'. In Britain, rather than looking to do everything possible for the benefit of place, policies have developed along the same lines as in the US. Today the 'public good' is what makes the most money.

American-style policies like compulsory purchase mean developers can build big and create economies of scale. It is more than a question of efficiencies, however, with big plans and grandiose visions repeatedly proving seductive to those who create and recreate cities. In the post-war period it was planners and politicians, today it is property developers and politicians, with the market renewal policies for millions of homes across the north underpinned by another grand vision. But big plans and grandiose visions very often contain within them the seeds of their own destruction. Recently the tendency has been to return to grand plans and big schemes which aim first and foremost to maximize the value of land and property. Smaller interventions, on a more human scale, which are based on a wider set of values than the single-minded ideology of increasing property prices, are more likely to bring with them a more diverse and public-spirited culture, which is in tune with local people and creates more successful places as a result.

One of the most important aspects of public life in cities today relates to shopping. Jan Gehl is the Danish urbanist and architect who is credited with transforming Copenhagen. Seen as something of a guru, his public lectures pack in hundreds and sell out instantly. At an event at the Royal Society of Arts I heard him describe how he turned Copenhagen around, quite simply by realizing that shopping should never be the main reason for coming into the city. His achievement is that four times as many people come into the centre of Copenhagen as did so in the past. 'If you asked people twenty years ago why they came into the city, they would have said it was to shop. But if you ask them today, they would say it was because they wanted to go to town.' Today, people of all ages come into town simply to stroll around and take in the atmosphere, perhaps to meet up with friends, and perhaps to shop, if they feel like it.

Wandering around the streets of a city, allowing space for walking and lingering, window shopping and people watching, is one of the real pleasures of city life, harking back to the tradition of the Parisian *flâneur*, the idler or loafer who walks around seeking experiences and chance encounters in the city. Writing about learning in the 1960s, Kevin Lynch wrote that 'the best learning happens by surprise' and that surprising things happen in cities often when we have 'nothing better to do' – waiting for someone or something or just hanging around. More recently the research on public space by the Joseph Rowntree Foundation emphasized how important it was to have places where it is possible to 'do nothing'.[29]

This is a very European way to enjoy life, window shopping, wandering around, doing nothing, going to the market, taking in the café society of the continental squares and piazzas. Our politicians claim this is the type of city they want to see, but the obsession with the micro management of the environment, geared only to making the maximum profit out of places, is not the way to achieve it. Rather than spending our way out of recession, we need to look at real alternatives, based on a more European rather than an American model, which will moderate the architecture of extreme capitalism, contemplate ways of doing things which do not always depend on the market, and create happier and healthier places in the process.

Every chapter in this book includes implicit suggestions for how things can be done differently and this chapter hopes to provide more than just a summary of that. But when it comes to a plea for reinventing a more public culture, it is important to emphasize that the only way the privatization of every aspect of the city can be halted is by slowing the transfer of land and property to large private landlords. It is, in particular, important to ensure that control over the streets and traditional rights of way remains in public hands. Trusts, similar to the model at Trinity Buoy Wharf, which ensure that places are used in ways that benefit the public good are another important alternative; it could become a contemporary version of the civic-minded Victorian approach that saw land and buildings left to local communities in perpetuity.

When I started working on this book, I thought its message was likely to be a gloomy one. It seemed that the privatization, control and segregation of every aspect of city life, which began with Docklands, was spreading inexorably across Britain, following the American model. Now the era of falling back on the argument that 'There is No Alternative' is over. It is possible that this heralds a chance for a real alternative which could open the door to a healthier, continental approach to the city, which celebrates public life, public culture and democracy. It would also reinvigorate civic engagement in Britain.

Notes

The Olympics and the public good

1. Matthiason, Nick, 'Preparing to raise our games', *Observer*, 2/4/06
2. Armstrong G., Coaffee J., Fussey P., Hobbs, D., *Securing and Sustaining the Olympic City: Reconfiguring London for 2012 and Beyond*, Ashgate, 2011
3. Bishop, Tom, 'A year in the shadow of Westfield', *BBC News*, London, 30/10/09
4. Commission for Architecture and the Built Environment: Audit of Conflicts of Interest, June 2004. http://webarchive.nationalarchives.gov.uk/20040722015354/http://www.culture.gov.uk/global/publications/archive_2004/cabe_audit_june2004.htm
5. Simpkins, Edward, 'Olympic bid under threat as village developers fall out, *Daily Telegraph*, 12/6/05
6. Matthiason, Nick, 'Livingstone joins the battle of Stratford', *Observer*, 26/3/06
7. Public letter from the Reuben Brothers on the Stratford City Development, www.reubenbrothers.com
8. London & Continental Railways statement, www.reubenbrothers.com, 22/3/06
9. The budget for the London 2012 Olympic and Paralympic Games, House of Commons Public Accounts Committee, Fourteenth Report of Session 2007–8
10. Ibid.
11. Matthiason, Nick, 'Billionaire tycoon accused of tax evasion', *Guardian*, 17/7/08
12. Prynn, Jonathan, 'Westfield given £200m to help build roads around mall', *Evening Standard*, 16/9/11
13. The media and broadcast centre has also been subject to complicated

deals with consortia of financiers which collapsed. The future of the Olympic Stadium has also witnessed the collapse of the deal for West Ham United to buy it following a legal challenge from rival clubs Tottenham Hotspur and Leyton Orient.

14. Interview with Simon Jenkins, *The Today Programme*, 27/7/11

15. 'Olympic chiefs pay themselves £1.7m bonuses despite rising costs', *Daily Mail*, 27/7/11

16. Beard, Matthew, 'Make Olympic site a royal park', *Evening Standard*, 24/7/11

17. Following the collapse of the deal the government said the stadium would remain in public ownership and would be leased out to the private sector.

18. The Wellcome Trust, http://www.wellcome.ac.uk/News/Media-office/Press-releases/2011/WTVMo52331.htm

19. Kortekaas, Vanessa, 'Ministers reject Wellcome £1bn Olympic bid', *FT.com*, http://www.ft.com/cms/s/0/1ca575fe-bdf7-11e0-ab9f-00144feabdco.html#axzz1ZoeXhHko, 3/8/11

20. *Securing and Sustaining the Olympic City.*

21. It was claimed that the Wellcome Trust bid would necessitate starting a new tender for the whole park, including the village, which would delay development in the park after the Olympics.

22. At the time of writing talks were ongoing between the London Mayor, Newham Council and the OPLC about the possibility of siting a Community Land Trust in the Olympic Park although no agreement had been reached. The possibility of setting aside 80 of the first 800 new homes planned for a CLT was under discussion. With regard to a living wage, the pledge to designate the Lower Lea Valley a 'living wage zone' has not been met but according to London Citizens 93 per cent of workers on the Olympic site are receiving a 'living wage'.

23. *Securing and Sustaining the Olympic City.*

24. Muir, Hugh, 'Protestors picket London Olympics body in pay row', *Guardian*, 21/9/06

25. Beard, Matthew, 'Olympic marathon chief quits and attacks Coe's "appalling" team', *Evening Standard*, 4/4/11

26. Norman, Paul, 'Exclusive legacy interview with OPLC chiefs', *Estates Gazette*, http://www.estatesgazette.com/blogs/olympics/2010/07/exclusive-legacy-interview-with-oplc-chiefs.html, 26/7/10

27. Garlick, Richard, 'Legacy leader', *Planning*, 8/4/11

28. Olympic legacy supplementary planning guidance, consultation draft, Greater London Authority. http://www.london.gov.uk/publication/olympic-legacy-supplementary-planning-guidance, 8/9/11

29. At the time of writing local authorities are still required to discharge their duty to house homeless people by placing them in social housing. But under changes proposed by the Localism Bill councils will be able to discharge this duty by placing homeless people in the private rented sector where there is no security of tenure.

30. Rugg, Julie, Rhodes, David, The Private Rented Sector: Its contribution and Potential', Centre for Housing Policy, University of York, 2008

31. 'Shapps promises "no more red tape" for private landlords', Communities and Local Government, http://www.communities.gov.uk/newsstories/newsroom/1611643, 10/6/10

32. 'Boris Johnson won't accept "Kosovo-style social cleansing", BBC News, 28/10/10

33. Fenton, Alex, 'Housing Benefit reform and the spatial segregation of low-income households in London', Cambridge Centre for Housing and Planning Research, University of Cambridge, January 2011

34. There are more changes planned which Shelter warn will make the situation worse, in particular cuts to the Single Room Allowance which will mean that only people over 35, rather than 25 as at the time of writing, will be eligible. Shelter is also very concerned that because the cuts will mean most people will not receive enough benefit to cover the rent evictions will become commonplace.

35. Brunton, Michael, 'Signal Failure', Time, 30/1/08

36. Securing and Sustaining the Olympic City

37. Ibid.

38. Ibid.

39. Graham, Steve, 'From Helmand to Merseyside: Unmanned drones and the militarisation of UK policing', Open Democrac, http://www.opendemocracy.net/ourkingdom/steve-graham/from-helmand-to-merseyside-military-style-drones-enter-uk-domestic-policing, 27/9/10

40. Minton, Anna, 'Expect the drones to swarm on Britain in time for 2012', Guardia, 22/2/10

41. 'A Manifesto for Public Space: London's Great Outdoors', Mayor of London, http://www.london.gov.uk/greatoutdoors/docs/londons-great-outdoors.pdf, 2009

42. 'Public life in private hands: Managing London's public space', London Assembly planning and housing committee, May 2011

43. Sir John Sorrell, Commission for Architecture and the Built Environment, valedictory speech, Tate Modern, http://webarchive.nationalarchives.gov.uk/20110118095356/http:/www.cabe.org.uk/articles/delight, 17/9/10

44. http://webarchive.nationalarchives.gov.uk/20110118095356/http://www.cabe.org.uk/design-review/tesco-bromley-by-bow-2

45. 'Should local councils reclaim ownership of the public realm?' Debate between Anna Minton and Crispin Kelly, *Building Design*, 3/6/11

46. Draft National Planning Policy Framework: Consultation, Communities and Local Government, 2011

1 Docklands: The Birth of an Idea

1. Furbey, Robert, 'Urban Regeneration: Reflections on a Metaphor', *Critical Social Policy*, vol. 19 (4), issue 61, 1999

2. London Borough of Tower Hamlets, *Ward Data Report*, May 2007. Figures quoted refer to the 'workless', defined as unemployment claimants, those out of work and looking for a job or economically inactive.

3. Jackson, Nicola, 'Docklands: Canary Wharf', in *Architecture & Commerce: New Office Design in London*, ed. Peter Murray, Wordsearch, 2004

4. Hall, Peter & Ward, Colin, *Sociable Cities: The Legacy of Ebenezeer Howard*, Academy Press, 1999

5. Imrie, Rob & Thomas, Huw, eds, *British Urban Policy and the Urban Development Corporations*, Sage, 1993. The authors write: 'The UDCs [Urban Development Corporations] were forerunners in re-orientating urban policy towards new economic imperatives in urban regeneration with the objective of pump-priming inner-city land values.'

6. 'Attracting Investment, Creating Value', *Establishing a Property Market in London Docklands*, LDDC Monograph, 1998

7. Robson, Brian, *Those Inner Cities: Reconciling the Economic and Social Aims of Urban Policy*, Oxford University Press, 1989

8. Hunt, Tristram, 'Why Cities Can Thank the Tories', *Guardian*, 16/5/04

9. 'Regeneration Statement', LDDC, 1998

10. 'Attracting Investment', LDDC

11. Ibid.

12. Moye, Catherine, 'Property in Docklands: Quays to the Future', *Daily Telegraph*, 23/4/08

13. James, Oliver, *Affluenza*, Vermillion, 2007. In Appendix 2, James' analysis of World Health Organization data, published with Richard Wilkinson and Kate Pickett, reveals that the mean prevalence of

emotional distress in English-speaking nations, including the US and UK, is 21.6 per cent, compared to 11.5 per cent for mainland Western Europe and Japan. In Appendix 3, the US is cited as having the highest percentage of the population suffering from emotional distress.

2 The Death of the City

1. Graham, Stephen & Marvin, Simon, *Splintering Urbanism: Networked Infrastructures, Technological Mobilities and the Urban Condition*, Routledge, 2001. The authors use the phrase 'malls without walls' to describe Business Improvement Districts in the US, but commentators have adopted the phrase to critique the new open-air private places as well.
2. Olsen, Donald, *Town Planning in London*, Yale University Press, 1982
3. Ibid.
4. Atkins, P. J., 'How the West End was Won: The Struggle to Remove Street Barriers in Victorian London', *Journal of Historical Geography*, vol. 19, 1993
5. Ibid.
6. Cahill, Kevin, *Who Owns Britain: The Hidden Facts behind Landownership in the UK and Ireland*, Canongate Books, 2002
7. The Land Registry has records of 60 per cent of titles in England and Wales but, because they are not aggregated, it is impossible to find out how much individual landlords own. Councils are supposed to be drawing up lists of their holdings but even the best estimates suggest this could take years, while in the meantime they are selling off their property at an unprecedented rate. So, while we know there is a huge shift in landownership taking place beneath our feet, we cannot actually quantify it.
8. Clover, Charles, 'Old Timers Versus City Slickers: The Fight Goes On', *Daily Telegraph*, 10/5/02
9. Caruso, Adam, *The Emotional City*, www.carusostjohn.com, 2000
10. The row over Quiggins continued in Liverpool, with Grosvenor claiming that a suitable site was available for the market outside Liverpool One. A new Quiggins has opened, but without most of the original businesses.
11. Brindley, Madeleine, 'Cardiff Bay 2003: Where Deprivation Shivers in the Shadow of Prosperity', *Western Mail*, 4/1/03
12. Steel, Carolyn, *Hungry City*, Chatto & Windus, 2008

13. Shearing, C. & Stenning, P., eds, 'Private Policing', *Criminal Justice Systems Annuals*, vol. 23, 1987

14. Ball, Kirstie & Wood, David Murakami, eds, 'A Report on the Surveillance Society: For the Information Commissioner', *Surveillance Studies Network*, 2006

15. 'Britain's Protection Racket', BBC *Panorama*, 21/1/08

16. Gaines, Sarah, 'Liverpool is England's Most Deprived District', *Guardian*, 30/4/08

17. Ibid.

18. Ford, Adam, 'Liverpool 2009: Capital of Crisis?' *Nerve Magazine*, www.catalystmedia.org.uk, 7/1/09

3 'Clean and Safe'

1. Jamieson, Alastair, 'Britain Suffering from a Buy-to-Let Blow Out', *Daily Telegraph*, 27/9/08

2. Florida, Richard, *Boho Britain Creativity Index*, Demos, 2003

3. Hochleutner, Brian R., 'BIDs Fare Well: The Democratic Accountability of Business Improvement Districts', *New York University Law Review*, vol. 78, no. 2, 2003

4. MacDonald, Heather, 'Why Business Improvement Districts Work', *Civic Bulletin*, no. 4, Manhattan Institute for Policy Research, 1996

5. Graham, Stephen & Marvin, Simon, *Splintering Urbanism: Networked Infrastructures, Technological Mobilities and the Urban Condition*, Routledge, 2001

6. Lambert, Bruce, 'Ex-Outreach Workers Say They Assaulted Homeless', *New York Times*, 14/4/95

7. Travers, Tony & Weimar, Jeroen, *Business Improvement Districts: New York and London*, Corporation of London, 1996

8. Ward, Kevin, 'Policies in Motion, Urban Management and State Restructuring: The Trans-Local Expansion of Business Improvement Districts', *Imaging Futures*, Working Paper 1, Geography, School of Environment and Development, University of Manchester, 2007

9. Ward, Kevin, 'Business Improvement Districts: Policy Origins, Mobile Policies and Urban Liveability', *Geography Compass*, vol. 1, issue 3, 2007

10. Police Reform Act, 2002

11. Frith, Maxine, 'Big Brother Britain, 2004', *Independent*, 12/1/04. Report on international conference on CCTV, Sheffield University, where Professor Clive Norris presented research findings.

12. Koster, Olinka, 'I Dropped a Morsel of My Daughter's Sausage Roll and the Litter Police Fined Me £75', *Daily Mail*, 25/4/08

13. Smith, Neil, 'Which New Urbanism? New York City and the Revanchist 1990s', in R. Beauregard & S. Body-Gendrot, eds, *The Urban Moment: Cosmopolitan Essays on the Late-20th-Century City*, Sage, 1999

14. Lambert, Bruce. 'Ex-Outreach Workers Say They Assaulted Homeless'

15. Smith, 'Which New Urbanism?'

16. Mitchell, Don & Staeheli, Lynn A., 'Clean and Safe? Property Redevelopment, Public Space, and Homelessness in Downtown San Diego', in Neil Smith & Setha Low, eds, *The Politics of Public Space*, Routledge, 2005

17. Benjamin, Alison, 'Cleaned Out', *Guardian*, 24/9/08

18. Figures for 2008 from the Department for Communities and Local Government for homeless people in temporary accommodation stood at 77,510. This represents a fall, compared to a high of 101,070 in 2005, but as Chapter 6 describes, this is a contentious area, with claims that in order to meet targets on reducing homelessness, the government is pressurizing local authorities not to accept people as homeless.

19. Ottewell, David, 'Marks in Free Speech Storm', *Manchester Evening News*, 17/7/04

20. Ibid.

21. Clark, Andrew, Holland, Caroline, Katz, Jeanne & Peace, Sheila M., *Social Interactions in Urban Public Places*, Open University, published for the Joseph Rowntree Foundation by the Policy Press, 2007

22. Wiseman, Eva, 'Is he a Sinner or a Winner?', *Guardian*, 5/5/06

23. Lefebvre, Henri, *The Production of Space*, trans. D. Nicholson-Smith, Blackwell, 1991, originally published 1974

24. Andrews, Robert & Brown, Jules, *The Rough Guide to England*, Rough Guides, 2004

25. Kofman, Eleonore & Lebas, Elizabeth, eds, *Writings on Cities: Henri Le-febvre*, Blackwell, 1996. Includes a translation of Lefebvre's *Le Droit à la ville*, published in 1968.

26. Kaufman, Gerald, 'Teaching the Big Apple', *Building Magazine*, issue 40, 2001

4 Secured by Design

1. Arnott, Chris, 'Laager Toffs', *Guardian*, 30/1/02

2. Blakely, Edward J. & Snyder, Mary Gail, *Fortress America: Gated*

Communities in the United States, Brookings Institution Press, 1997

3. Atkinson, R., Blandy, S., Flint, J. & Lister, D., *Gated Communities in England*, Office of the Deputy Prime Minister, 2004. This report estimated that there were at least 1,000 gated communities. Since then author Sarah Blandy estimated in discussion that there are likely to be many more.

4. Mulholland, Helene, 'Blunkett calls for spread of gated communities', *Guardian*, 22/1/04

5. Savills Weybridge promotional material, 2006, www.savills.co.uk

6. Brooks, Libby, 'Latter-Day Diggers Claim Piece of an Upmarket Golf Course', *Guardian*, 5/4/99

7. Monbiot, George, 'Still digging', BBC *History*, 2000

8. Edwards, Adam, 'Why the World Wants a Piece of London', *Daily Telegraph*, 9/2/07

9. Sinclair, Iain, *London Orbital*, Penguin, 2003

10. 'A Magnificent Lifestyle in a Parkland Setting', Octagon Developments Limited, 1998

11. Thomas, Lisa, 'Disconnection: The Perceptions of Gated Community Residents in the UK', unpublished MSc Environmental Psychology dissertation, University of Surrey, 2006

12. Communities and Local Government, *Live Tables on House Building*. Figures from the Department for Communities and Local Government reveal UK housing stock was 26,652,000 homes in 2007, while housing completions stood at 214,110 for 2007/8.

13. Van der Heijden, Hans, 'Whose Space is Public Space?', address for *Free Thinking 2008, Festival of Ideas*, BBC Radio 3, unpublished paper

14. Newman, Oscar, *Defensible Space: People and Design in the Violent City*, Architectural Press, 1973

15. Hillier, Bill, *The Common Language of Space: A Way of Looking at the Social, Economic and Environmental Functioning of Cities on a Common Basis*, Space Syntax Laboratory, Bartlett School of Graduate Studies, University College London, 1998

16. *Design Guide for Residential Areas*, Essex County Council, 1973

17. Quoted in Colquhoun, Ian, *Design Out Crime: Creating Safe and Sustainable Communities*, Architectural Press, 2004

18. Jacobs, Jane, *The Death and Life of Great American Cities*, Random House, 1961

19. Hillier, *The Common Language of Space*

20. *Manual for Streets*, Department for Transport, 2007

21. Burney, Elizabeth, *Crime and Banishment: Nuisance and Exclusion in Social Housing*, Waterside Press, 1999

22. *Securing the Nation: The Case for Safer Homes*, Association of British Insurers, 2006

23. Minton, Anna, *Building Balanced Communities: The US and UK Compared*, Royal Institution of Chartered Surveyors, 2002

24. Low, Setha, *Behind the Gates*, Routledge, 2003

25. Blakely & Snyder, *Fortress America*

26. Low, *Behind the Gates*

27. Blandy, Sarah & Lister, Diane, 'Gated Communities: (Ne)gating Community Development?' *Housing Studies*, vol. 20, no. 2, pp. 287–302

28. Atkinson, Rowland, Blandy, Sarah, Flint, John & Lister, Diane, *Gated Communities: A Systematic Review of the Research Evidence*, University of Glasgow, 2003

29. Low, *Behind the Gates*

30. Atkinson, et al., *Gated Communities*

31. Blakely & Snyder, *Fortress America*

32. Thomas, *Disconnection*

33. Atkinson, Rowland & Flint, John, 'Fortress UK?', *Gated Communities: The Spatial Revolt of the Elites and Time-Space Trajectories of Segregation*, Department of Urban Studies, University of Glasgow, 2003

34. Giddens, Anthony, *The Consequences of Modernity*, Stanford University Press, 1991

5 Housing Market Renewal

1. Department for Communities and Local Government, *Housing Market Renewal*, report by the Comptroller and Auditor General, National Audit Office, November 2007

2. Robert McCracken, QC, 'Derker Compulsory Purchase Order', Final Submissions, 2007, www.publicinterestlawyers.co.uk

3. At the time of writing, the Community Action Group was appealing to the High Court, having lost its case on compulsory purchase for phase 1 of the plans. However, even if they lose, they have vowed to fight on, as Maureen's home is part of phase 2 of the development.

4. Clover, Charles, 'Prescott's "Social Cleansing" Faces Court Challenge', *Daily Telegraph*, 25/3/06

5. High Court of Justice, 'Elizabeth Susan Pascoe and the Secretary of

State for Communities and Local Government', Claim no. CO/30114/2006

6. Department for Communities and Local Government, *Housing Market Renewal*

7. Office of the Deputy Prime Minister, *Empty Homes and Low-Demand Pathfinders*, Housing, Planning, Local Government and the Regions Committee, Eighth Report of Session 2004/5, vol. 1, 2005

8. Jenkins, Simon, 'Once They Called It Rachmanism, Now It's Being Done with Taxpayers' Money', *Guardian*, 16/3/07

9. Office of the Deputy Prime Minister, Select Committee on Housing, Planning, Local Government and the Regions, Written Evidence, 'Memorandum by the Derker Community Action Group' (AH 17), 2006

10. Kelo et al. v. City of New London et al. (04-108), Supreme Court of the United States, 22/2/05

11. Select Committee on Transport, Local Government and the Regions, 'Memorandum by the Centre for Urban and Regional Studies', Birmingham University (EMP 47), 2001

12. Ibid.

13. Wainright, Hilary & Wainright, Martin, 'Street Drama', *Guardian*, 13/9/00

14. Minton, Anna, *Northern Soul*, Demos & Royal Institution of Chartered Surveyors, 2003

15. Wainwright & Wainwright, 'Street Drama'

16. Cameron, Stuart, 'From Low Demand to Rising Aspirations: Housing Market Renewal within Regional and Neighbourhood Regeneration Policy', *Housing Studies*, 21 (1), 2006

17. 'Agenda Setters', *Guardian*, 3/9/03

18. Wilkinson, Adam, *Pathfinder*, SAVE Britain's Heritage, 2006

19. Email from Jonathan Brown, including paragraphs 2.3, 4.1.1, 4.2.1, 8.1, 8.2, 8.3, 8.4 and 8.5 of the 'Overarching Agreement'.

20. Wilkinson, *Pathfinder*

21. New Heartlands, *Business Plan 2008–11*, www.newheartlands.co.uk

22. Jenkins, 'Rachmanism'. Jenkins quotes developers boasting that £5 billion of public money would be matched by £20 billion from the private sector. So far, less than half this money has been pledged by the government and the amount from the private sector is very uncertain following the financial collapse.

23. Wilkinson, *Pathfinder*

6 Housing: The Untold Story

1. *Ward 4 Area Profile*, Community Planning, Lothian & Borders Police, Edinburgh City Council, NHS, Scottish Enterprise, www.edinburghnp. org.uk/UserFiles/Files/Ward04-Forth.pdf

2. Minton, Anna & Jones, Sarah, *Generation Squalor: Shelter's National Investigation into the Housing Crisis*, Shelter, 2005

3. Sampson, Adam, 'Private Renting for Public Good', *The Future of the Private Rented Sector*, eds P. Bill, P. Hackett & C. Glossop, Smith Institute, 2008

4. Minton & Jones, *Generation Squalor*

5. Rugg, Julie & Rhodes, David, *The Private Rented Sector: Its Contribution and Potential*, Centre for Housing Policy, University of York, 2008

6. Crew, Debbie, *The Tenants' Dilemma: Warning, Your Home is at Risk if You Dare Complain*, Crosby, Formby and District Citizens Advice Bureau, 2007

7. Hills, John, *Ends and Means: The Future Roles of Social Housing in England*, Economic and Social Research Council, Research Centre for Analysis of Social Exclusion, CASE report 34, 2007

8. Shelter's input into the review of the private rented sector, Shelter Policy Library, 2008

9. Rogers, Emily, 'Heffernan Explained', *Inside Housing*, 16/1/09

10. Rogers, Emily, 'Rental Areas Changed to Duck Lords' Ruling', *Inside Housing*, 8/1/09

11. 'Housing Benefit Change Makes Mockery of Consultation Process', British Property Federation, press release, 26/11/08

12. Best, Richard, 'Time to Regulate', *Future of the Private Rented Sector*

13. The Poverty Site. UK site for statistics on poverty and social exclusion, produced by the New Policy Institute with support from the Joseph Rowntree Foundation, www.poverty.org.uk

14. Kenway, P., MacInnes, T. & Palmer, G., *Monitoring Poverty and Social Exclusion 2008*, Joseph Rowntree Foundation, 2008

15. Poverty statistics, like crime figures, are notoriously difficult to reach consensus on, with so many different variables and indicators. According to the Poverty Site, www.poverty.org.uk, in absolute terms the number of working-age adults in poverty is 400,000 greater than in 1997, but Labour has lifted more children and pensioners out of poverty. The most commonly used threshold for low income is 60 per cent or less of average income, and according to this the number of people

on low income is less than a decade ago. However, with a threshold of 40 per cent of average income, the picture is reversed.

16. The Poverty Site, www.poverty.org.uk

17. Communities & Local Government Housing Research & Statistics, *Live Tables*, Table 241: 'Permanent Dwellings Completed By Tenure, United Kingdom, Historical Calendar Year Series'

18. The United Nations Convention on Human Rights 1948 enshrines the right to adequate housing.

19. 'Council tenants will have "right to buy"', BBC, *On This Day*, 20/12/79

20. Holmans, A., Monk, S. & Whitehead, C., *Homes for the Future*, Cambridge Centre for Housing and Planning Research, University of Cambridge, Shelter, 2008

21. Ibid.

22. *Housing Completions in Great Britain*, Communities & Local Government Housing Research & Statistics, dated 30/5/08. In 1997 15.5 per cent of total completions were in the social sector, compared to 12.5 per cent in 2007.

23. House of Commons Select Committee on Public Administration, Minutes of Evidence, 'Supplementary Memorandum by Defend Council Housing' (CVP 05 (a)), Point 2: Holding ballots early to wrong foot opponents, and Point 3: Obstruction and intimidation, 2004

24. Duckworth, Lorna, 'Council Tenants Vote Against Housing Transfer Plans', *Independent*, 9/4/02

25. Barker, K., 'Review of Housing Supply, Interim Report', 10/12/03, www.hm-treasury.gov.uk/press_barker_03.htm

26. Pickard, Jim, 'Developers Put Faith in their Imagination', *Financial Times*, 19/2/05

27. Randhawa, Kiran, '£1 Million Council Home Sparks Review of Benefits', *Evening Standard*, 10/10/08

28. www.orchard-shipman.com

29. Rogers, Emily, 'Prime Minister Plays it Safe', *Inside Housing*, 10/10/08

7 Fear of Crime, 'Respect', Trust and Happiness

1. Van Dijk, Jan, Manchin, Robert, van Kesteren, John & Hideg, Gergely, 'The Burden of Crime in the EU: Research Report, *A Comparative Analysis of the European Crime and Safety Survey* (EU ICS), 2005

2. James, Oliver, *Affluenza*, Vermillion, 2007. Appendix 2 shows that the mean prevalences of emotional distress in six English-speaking nations

is 21.6 per cent, compared to a mean of 11.5 per cent for nations in mainland Western Europe, plus Japan. The US tops the league for emotional distress, followed by the UK and Australia.

3. Duffy, Bobby, Wake, Rhonda, Burrows, Tamara & Bremner, Pamela, *Closing the Gaps: Crime and Public Perceptions*, Ipsos MORI, 2007

4. Ibid.

5. Van Dijk, et al., 'Burden of Crime in the EU'

6. The World Values Survey is compiled at the Institute of Social Research, University of Michigan, www.worldvaluessurvey.org

7. Waterhouse, Keith, 'The British Crime Survey: It's All Lies, Damned Lies and Crime Figures', *Daily Mail*, 20/7/08

8. *A Summary of Recorded Crime Data from 2002/3 to 2007/8*, Home Office research development statistics, www.homeoffice.gov.uk/rds/pdfs08/recorded-crime-2002-2008.xls

9. *Crime in England and Wales 2007/8*, Chapter 3 on violent and sexual crime, Home Office research development statistics, www.homeoffice.gov.uk/rds/pdfs08/hosbo708chap3.pdf

10. 'BBC's Misleading Crime Headlines', press release, www.mediahell.org, 24/4/07

11. Email exchange with Tom Chatfield, *Prospect*, 20/10/08. Tom wrote that the data used 'shouldn't really have been compared, or should have been more carefully qualified'.

12. Duffy, et al., *Closing the Gaps*

13. Hurley, Bevan, 'Nick Ross under Fire after Accusing Media of Distorting Crime Figures', *Daily Mail*, 21/7/07

14. Glassner, Barry, *The Culture of Fear: Why Americans are Afraid of the Wrong Things*, Basic Books, 2000

15. Davenport, Justin & Brierley, Danny, 'Another Knife Victim: Stabbed 16-Year-Old Dies after Begging for his Mother', *Evening Standard*, 4/4/08

16. Mulgan, Geoff & Leadbetter, Charles, 'Face of Our Future Leader', *Guardian*, 13/7/94, quoted in Peter Oborne, *The Rise of Political Lying*, Simon and Schuster, 2005

17. *Crime in England and Wales 2007/8*, Chapter 6: 'Geographic Patterns of Crime', Home Office research development statistics.

18. Quoted in Coleman, Roy, Sim, Joe & Whyte, Dave, 'Power, Politics and Partnerships: The State of Crime Prevention on Merseyside', in Gordon Hughes & Adam Edwards, *Crime Control and Community: The New Politics of Public Safety*, Willan Publishing, 2002

19. Gaines, Sarah, 'Liverpool is England's Most Deprived District', *Guardian*, 30/4/08

20. Low, Setha, *Behind the Gates*, Routledge, 2003
21. Crawford, A., Lister, S., Blackburn, S. & Burnett, J., *Plural Policing: The Mixed Economy of Visible Patrols in England and Wales*, Policy Press, 2005
22. Ibid.
23. Jacobs, Jane, *The Death and Life of Great American Cities*, Random House, 1961
24. Sennett, Richard, *The Fall of Public Man*, Alfred A. Knopf, 1977
25. Newman, Oscar, *Defensible Space: People and Design in the Violent City*, Architectural Press, 1973
26. 'UK Politics: Jack Straw Speech in Full', BBC *News*, 30/9/99, http://news.bbc.co.uk/1/hi/uk_politics/461967.stm
27. *Respect and Responsibility: Taking a Stand against Anti-Social Behaviour*, Home Office, 2003
28. 'Ain't Misbehavin'' campaign, press release, British Institute for Brain Injured Children, 2007. 'Over 30 per cent of youths receiving ASBOs have a diagnosed mental health disorder or an accepted learning difficulty.'
29. Hope, Christopher, 'Two out of Three Breach Their First ASBO', *Daily Telegraph*, 27/5/08. Figures obtained by the Conservatives and quoted in this piece revealed 67 per cent breached their ASBOs in 2006.
30. Collins, Scott & Cattermole, Rebecca, *Anti-Social Behaviour: Powers and Remedies*, second edition, Sweet & Maxwell, 2006. Evidence of Barnardo's to Home Affairs Select Committee on Anti-Social Behaviour, quoting Lord Ashley.
31. Stop-and-search without reasonable suspicion is permissible for limited periods under Section 60 of the Criminal Justice and Public Order Act 1994 and Section 44 of the Terrorism Act 2000. However, a spokesperson for human-rights group Liberty confirms that in designated areas it continues on a rolling basis.
32. Collins & Cattermole, *Anti-Social Behaviour*
33. Kelling, George L. & Wilson, James Q., 'Broken Windows', *Atlantic Monthly*, March 1982
34. *Respect and Responsibility*, Home Office
35. Harcourt, Bernard E., *Illusion of Order: The False Promise of Broken Windows Policing*, Harvard University Press, 2001
36. Levitt, Steven D. & Dubner, Stephen J., *Freakonomics*, Penguin Books, 2006
37. Harcourt, Bernard E. & Ludwig, Jens, 'Broken Windows: New Evidence

from New York City and a Five-City Social Experiment', *University of Chicago Law Review*, vol. 73, 2006. For a summary of American critics see also Daniel Brook, 'The Cracks in Broken Windows', *Boston Globe*, 19/2/06

38. Harcourt, Bernard E., 'The Broken Windows Myth', *New York Times*, 11/9/01
39. 'Allegations against Police Rise', BBC *News Online*, 25/9/08
40. Harcourt & Ludwig, 'Broken Windows'
41. Collins & Cattermole, *Anti-Social Behaviour*
42. Duffy, et al., *Closing the Gaps*
43. Harcourt, *Illusion of Order*
44. Smith, Neil, 'Which New Urbanism? New York City and the Revanchist 1990s', in R. Beauregard & S. Body-Gendrot, eds, *The Urban Moment: Cosmopolitan Essays on the Late-20th Century City*, Sage, 1999
45. Etzioni, A., 'Common Values', *New Statesman and Society*, 12/5/95. Cited in Sarah Hale, 'Communitarian Influence? Amitai Etzioni and the Making of New Labour', unpublished paper, 2005
46. Muncie, John, *Youth & Crime*, second edition, Sage, 2004
47. Vallely, Paul, 'He Visited in Glory Days of '97 but Has Blair Kept His Vow to Aylesbury Estate?' *Independent*, 12/5/05
48. Blair, Tony, 'The Will to Win', speech delivered at the Aylesbury Estate, London, 2/6/97
49. Hale, Sarah, *Blair's Community: Communitarian Thought and New Labour*, Manchester University Press, 2006
50. Hale, Sarah, 'Communitarian Influence? Amitai Etzioni and the Making of New Labour', unpublished paper, 2005
51. Etzioni, Amitai, *The Third Way to a Good Society*, Demos, 2000
52. Burney, Elizabeth, *Making People Behave: Anti-Social Behaviour, Politics and Policy*, Willan Publishing, 2005
53. Ford, Richard, 'Cut Petty Crime by Grassing on Your Neighbours, Urges Straw', *Times*, 23/9/98
54. Wheeler, Brian, 'Who are the Liberati?' BBC *News Online*, 7/7/04
55. Burney, *Making People Behave*
56. Labour Party, *A Quiet Life: Tough Action on Criminal Neighbours*, 1995
57. Field, Frank, *Neighbours from Hell: The Politics of Behaviour*, Politico's Publishing, 2003
58. 'Ain't Misbehavin'', British Institute for Brain Injured Children
59. Gil-Robles, Alvaro, 'Report by Mr Alvaro Gil-Robles, Commissioner for Human Rights on his Visit to the United Kingdom 4th–12th

November 2004', Office of the Commissioner for Human Rights, 2005
60. Schlesinger, Fay, '"Death Knell" of the ASBO', *Manchester Evening News*, 29/8/08
61. Ibid.
62. Wain, Neil, with Burney, Elizabeth, *The ASBO: Wrong Turning, Dead End*, Howard League for Penal Reform, 2007
63. National Audit Office, *Tackling Anti-Social Behaviour*, The Stationery Office, 2006
64. Wain, *The ASBO*
65. Crawford, Adam & Lister, Stuart, *The Use and Impact of Dispersal Orders: Sticking Plasters and Wake-Up Calls*, published for the Joseph Rowntree Foundation, Policy Press, 2007
66. Ibid.
67. 'The fight for Salford's future', *Salford Star*, 10/8/06
68. Crawford & Lister, *Use and Impact of Dispersal Orders*
69. Straw, Jack, Crime and Disorder Bill, second reading, *Hansard*, 8/4/98
70. Straw, Jack, 'Crime and Old Labour's Punishment', *Times*, 8/4/98
71. 'Deal for Anti-Gang Sonic Device', BBC *News Online*, 15/5/06
72. Greater Manchester Police, CJPOA Stop and Search Data 2006-07, S44 www.gmp.police.uk/mainsite/pages/stopaccount08.htm
73. 'Truancy Mother Sent to Jail Again', BBC *News Online*, 23/3/04
74. 'Ratboy: A Fourteen-Year-Old Becomes a Byword for Trouble', *Independent*, 9/10/93. Quoted in Muncie, *Youth & Crime*
75. Hare, Bernard, 'Going Under', *Guardian*, 13/9/06
76. Richardson, Celia & Halliwell, Ed, *Boiling Point: Problem Anger and What We Can Do About It*, Mental Health Foundation, 2008
77. Harcourt, *Illusion of Order*
78. Figures from Liberty, the human-rights organization for England and Wales, www.liberty-human-rights.org.uk/issues/3-privacy/32-cctv/index.shtml
79. Ditton, Jason, 'Crime and the City, Public Attitudes towards Open Street CCTV in Glasgow', *British Journal of Criminology*, vol. 4, no. 4, 2000
80. Ibid.
81. Giangrande, Richard, Haldenby, Andrew, Lundy, Lawrence, Parsons, Lucy, Thornton, Daisy & Truss, Elizabeth, *The Lawful Society*, Reform, 2008
82. Batty, David, 'Profile: Government Crime Adviser Louise Casey', *Guardian*, 16/6/08
83. Casey, Louise, *Engaging Communities in Fighting Crime*, Cabinet Office, 2008

84. Gilligan, James, 'Shame, Guilt and Violence', *Social Research*, vol. 70, no. 4, 2003
85. Collins & Cattermole, *Anti-Social Behaviour*
86. Putnam, Robert D., *Bowling Alone: The Collapse and Revival of American Community*, Simon & Schuster, 2001
87. Arneil, Barbara, *Diverse Communities: The Problem with Social Capital*, Cambridge University Press, 2006
88. Fischer, Claude, 'Bowling Alone: What's the Score?', *Social Networks*, 27, 2005
89. Ibid.
90. World Values Survey
91. Lloyd, John, 'Study Paints a Bleak Picture of Ethnic Diversity', *Financial Times*, 8/10/06
92. Putnam, Robert D., 'E Pluribus Unum: Diversity and Community in the 21st Century', 2006 Johann Skytte Prize lecture, Nordic Political Science Association, 2007
93. Davis, Mike, *City of Quartz*, Verso, 1990
94. Duffy, et al., *Closing the Gaps*
95. Sennett, Richard, 'The Search for a Place in the World', in *Architecture of Fear*, ed. Nan Ellen, Princeton Architectural Press, 1997
96. Neuberger, Julia, 'Unkind, Risk Averse and Untrusting: If This is Today's Society Can We Change It?' *Viewpoint*, Joseph Rowntree Foundation, 2008
97. Grubin, Don, *Sex Offending against Children: Understanding the Risk*, Policing and Reducing Crime Unit, Police Research Series, Home Office, 1998
98. Duffy, et al., *Closing the Gaps*
99. Layard, Richard, *Happiness: Lessons from a New Science*, Penguin, 2005
100. James, *Affluenza*
101. Scitovsky, Tibor, *The Joyless Economy: The Psychology of Human Satisfaction*, revised edition, Oxford University Press, 1992
102. Titmuss, Richard, *Problems of Social Policy*, HMSO, 1950

8 Moving Forwards

1. Brunton, Michael, 'Signal Failure', *Time*, 30/1/08
2. Jenkins, Simon, 'Rip out the Traffic Lights and Railings: Our Streets are Better without Them', *Guardian*, 29/2/08
3. Brunton, 'Signal Failure'

4. Clarke, Emma, 'Shared Space – the Alternative Approach to Calming Traffic', *Tec*, 2006

5. Hamilton-Baillie, Ben, 'Streets and the Public Realm', in Nick Cavill, ed., *Building Health: Creating and Enhancing Places for Healthy Active Lives*, National Heart Forum, 2007

6. Hamilton-Baillie, Ben, 'Shared Space: Reconciling People, Places and Traffic', *Built Environment*, 34 (2), 2008

7. Gill, Tim, *No Fear: Growing up in a Risk-Averse Society*, Calouste Gulbenkian Foundation, 2007

8. *Manual for Streets*, Department for Transport, 2007

9. Banham, Reyner, Barker, Paul, Hall, Peter, Price, Cedric, 'Non-Plan: An Experiment in Freedom', *New Society*, 20/3/1969

10. 'Modern Docklands: Modern Commercial Developments, Poplar, Blackwall and Isle of Dogs', *Survey of London*, vols 43 and 44, 1994, www.british-history.ac.uk/report.aspx?compid=46549

11. Auge, Marc, *Non-Places*, Verso, 1995

12. Jacobs, Jane, *The Death and Life of Great American Cities*, Random House, 1961

13. *Our Common Future*, report of the United Nations World Commission on Environment and Development, Oxford University Press, 1987

14. Hall, Peter, review of *Non-Plan: Essays on Freedom, Participation and Change in Modern Architecture and Urbanism*, eds. Jonathan Hughes & Simon Sadler, Architectural Press, 2000, www.arplus.com/book/reviews/aug2000onplan.htm

15. Lynch, Kevin & Carr, Stephen, 'Grounds for Utopia', in *City Sense and City Design: Writings and Projects of Kevin Lynch*, eds Tridib Bannerjee & Michael Southworth, MIT Press, 1995

16. Lynch, Kevin, 'The Openness of Open Space', in *City Sense*, eds Bannerjee & Southworth

17. Oswalt, Philipp, Misselwitz, Philipp, Overmeyer, Klaus, 'Patterns of the Unplanned', in *Loose Space: Possibility and Diversity in Urban Life*, eds Karen Franck & Quentin Stevens, Routledge, 2006

18. Banham, et al., 'Non-Plan'

19. Oswalt, et al., 'Patterns of the Unplanned'

20. Ibid.

21. 'Creating 1,000 New Allotments', National Trust, 2009, www.nationaltrust.org.uk/main/w-global/w-news/w-latest_news/w-news-growing_spaces.htm

22. Franck, Karen A. & Stevens, Quentin, 'Tying Down Loose Space', in *Loose Space: Possibility and Diversity in Urban Life*, Routledge, 2006

23. Smith, M. K., *Social Pedagogy: The Encyclopaedia of Informal Education*, 2009, www.infed.org/biblio/b-socped.htm

24. Wintour, Patrick & Addley, Esther, 'Brown's £140 Million Plan for 35,000 Apprenticeships', *Guardian*, 8/1/09

25. UNICEF, Report Card 7, *Child Poverty in Perspective: An Overview of Child Well-Being in Rich Countries*, 2007

26. Bradford Brown, B., Larson, Reed W. & Saraswathi, T. S., *The World's Youth: Adolescence in Eight Regions of the Globe*, Cambridge University Press, 2002

27. Ibid.

28. Müge, Akkar. 'The Changing "Publicness" of Contemporary Public Space: A Case Study of the Grey's Monument Area, Newcastle upon Tyne', *Urban Design International*, vol. 10 (2), 2005

29. Clark, Andrew, Holland, Caroline, Katz, Jeanne & Peace, Sheila M., *Social Interactions in Urban Public Places*, Open University, published for the Joseph Rowntree Foundation, Policy Press, 2007

Bibliography

Anderson, Stanford, ed., *On Streets*, MIT Press, 1986

Arendt, Hannah, *The Human Condition*, University of Chicago Press, 1958, second edition with an introduction by Margaret Canovan, 1998

Armstrong, Stephen, *War plc: The Rise of the New Corporate Mercenary*, Faber and Faber, 2008

Arneil, Barbara, *Diverse Communities: The Problem with Social Capital*, Cambridge University Press, 2006

Auge, Marc, *Non-Places: Introduction to an Anthropology of Supermodernity*, Verso, 1995

Barrett, Wayne, *Rudy! An Investigative Biography of Rudolph Giuliani*, Basic Books, 2001

Baudelaire, Charles, *The Painter of Modern Life*, 1863; *The Painter of Modern Life and Other Essays*, translated and edited by Jonathan Mayne, Phaidon, 1995

Bauman, Zygmunt, *Liquid Modernity*, Polity Press, 2000

Baumgartner, M. P., *The Moral Order of Suburbs*, Oxford University Press USA, 1991

Bill, Peter, Hackett, Paul & Glossop, Catherine, *The Future of the Private Rented Sector*, Smith Institute, 2008

Blakely, Edward & Snyder, Mary Gail, *Fortress America: Gated Communities in the United States*, Brookings Institution Press, 1997

Boddy, Trevor, 'Underground and Overhead: Building the Analogous City', in *Variations on a Theme Park: The New American City and the End of Public Space*, ed. Michael Sorkin, Hill & Wang, 1992

Boyer, Christine M., 'X Marks the Spot: Times Square Dead or Alive?' in *A Companion to the City*, eds Gary Bridge & Sophie Watson, Blackwell Publishing, reprinted 2004

Bradbury, Ray & Anderton, Frances, eds, *You are Here: The Jerde Partnership International*, Phaidon Press, 1999

Bridge, Gary & Watson, Sophie, eds, *A Companion to the City*, Blackwell Publishing, reprinted 2004

Bridge, Gary & Watson, Sophie, eds, *The City Reader*, Blackwell Publishing, reprinted 2004

Burney, Elizabeth, *Crime and Banishment: Nuisance and Exclusion in Social Housing*, Waterside Press, 1999

Burney, Elizabeth, *Making People Behave: Anti-Social Behaviour, Politics and Policy*, Willan Publishing, 2005

Cahill, Kevin, *Who Owns Britain and Ireland?*, Canongate Books, 2002

Coleman, Roy, *Reclaiming the Streets: Surveillance, Social Control and the City*, Willan Publishing, 2004

Coleman, Roy, Sim, Joe & Whyte, Dave, 'Power, Politics and Partnerships: The State of Crime Prevention on Merseyside', in *Crime Control and Community*, eds Gordon Hughes & Adam Edwards, Willan Publishing, 2002

Collins, Scott & Cattermole, Rebecca, *Anti-Social Behaviour: Powers and Remedies*, second edition, Sweet & Maxwell, 2006

Crawford, Adam, Lister, Stuart & Blackburn, Sarah, *Plural Policing: The Mixed Economy of Visible Patrols in England and Wales*, Policy Press, 2005

Davis, Mike, *City of Quartz*, Verso, 1990; Pimlico edition, 1998

Ellin, Nan, ed., *Architecture of Fear*, Princeton Architectural Press, 1997

Engels, Friedrich, *The Condition of the Working Class in England*, 1845; edited with an introduction by David McLellan, Oxford University Press, 1993

Etzioni, Amitai, *The Third Way to a Good Society*, Demos, 2000

Field, Frank, *Neighbours from Hell: The Politics of Behaviour*, Politico's Publishing, 2003

Flusty, Steven, 'Building Paranoia', in *Architecture of Fear*, ed. Nan Ellin, Princeton Architectural Press, 1997

Foucault, Michel, *Discipline and Punish: The Birth of a Prison*, 1975, reissued by Vintage, 1995

Franck, Karen & Stevens, Quentin, *Loose Space: Possibility and Diversity in Urban Life*, Routledge, 2006

Furedi, Frank, *Culture of Fear*, Continuum, 2002

Garland, David, *The Culture of Control: Crime and Social Order in Contemporary Society*, Oxford University Press, US, 2001

Gehl, Jan, *Life between Buildings: Using Public Space*, Danish Architectural Press, fifth edition, 2003

Giddens, Anthony, *The Consequences of Modernity*, Stanford University Press, 1991

Glassner, Barry, *The Culture of Fear: Why Americans are Afraid of the Wrong Things*, Basic Books, 2000

Graham, Stephen & Marvin, Simon, *Splintering Urbanism: Networked Infrastructures, Technological Mobilities and the Urban Condition*, Routledge, 2001

Hale, Sarah, *Blair's Community: Communitarian Thought and New Labour*, Manchester University Press, 2006

Hall, Peter & Ward, Colin, *Sociable Cities: The Legacy of Ebenezeer Howard*, Academy Press, 1999

Harcourt, Bernard, *Illusion of Order: The False Promise of Broken Windows Policing*, Harvard University Press, 2001

Harrison, Fred, *Boom Bust: House Prices, Banking and the Depression of 2010*, Shepheard-Walwyn, 2005

Harvey, David, 'The Right to the City', in *Divided Cities: The Oxford Amnesty Lectures, 2003*, ed. Richard Scholar, Oxford University Press, 2006

Hayden, Dolores, *The Power of Place: Urban Landscapes as Public History*, MIT Press, 1997

Hillier, Bill, *The Common Language of Space: A Way of Looking at the Social, Economic and Environmental Functioning of Cities on A Common Basis*, Space Syntax Laboratory, Bartlett School of Graduate Studies, University College London, 1998

House, Richard & Loewenthal, Del, *Against and for CBT: Towards a Constructive Dialogue?*, PCCS Books, 2008

Imrie, Rob & Thomas, Huw, eds, *British Urban Policy: An Evaluation of the Urban Development Corporations*, Sage, 1999

Jackson, Tim, Jager, W. & Stagl, S., 'Beyond Insatiability: Needs Theory, Consumption and Sustainability', in *The Ecological Economics of Consumption*, eds Lucia Reisch & Inge Ropke, 2004

Jacobs, Jane, *The Death and Life of Great American Cities*, Random House, 1961

James, Oliver, *Affluenza*, Vermillion, 2007

Jefferies, Tom & Swanson, Neil, 'Living with the Fear of Crime', in *Shrinking Cities*, vol. 1, ed. Philipp Oswalt, International Research, Kulturstiftung des Bundes, 2006

Jenks, Charles, 'Hetero-Architecture for the Heteropolis: The Los Angeles School', in *Architecture of Fear*, ed. Nan Ellin, Princeton Architectural Press, 1997

Jones, Phil & Evan, James, *Urban Regeneration in the UK: Theory and Practices*, Sage, 2008

Jones, Trevor & Newburn, Tim, eds, *Plural Policing: A Comparative Perspective*, Routledge, 2006

Klein, Norman M., 'The Electronic Baroque: Jerde Cities', in *You are Here: The Jerde Partnership International*, eds Ray Bradbury & Frances Anderton, Phaidon Press, 1999

Kohn, Margaret, *Brave New Neighbourhoods: The Privatization of Public Space*, Routledge, 2004

Layard, Richard, *Happiness: Lessons from a New Science*, Allen Lane, 2005

Levitt, Steven D. & Dubner, Stephen J., *Freakonomics*, Penguin Books, 2006

Lofland, Lyn H., *The Public Realm: Exploring the City's Quintessential Social Territory*, Aldine Transaction, 1998

Low, Setha, 'The Edge and the Center: Gated Communities and the Discourse of Urban Fear', in *The Anthropology of Space and Place*, eds Setha Low & Denise Lawrence-Zuniga, Blackwell Publishing, 2003

Low, Setha, *Behind the Gates*, Routledge, 2003

Lynch, Kevin, Bannerjee, Tridib & Southworth, Michael, *City Sense and City Design: Writings and Projects of Kevin Lynch*, MIT Press, 1995

Maslow, Abraham, *Motivation and Personality*, Harper & Bros, 1959

Massey, Doreen, *Docklands: A Microcosm of Broader Social and Economic Trends*, Docklands Forum, 1991

Massey, Doreen, *World City*, Polity Press, 2007

Merrifield, Andrew, *Henri Lefebvre: A Critical Introduction*, Routledge, 2006

Mitchell, Don & Staeheli, Lynn A., 'Clean and Safe? Property Redevelopment, Public Space and Homelessness in Downtown San Diego', in Neil Smith & Setha Low, eds, *The Politics of Public Space*, Routledge, 2005

Mitchell, Don, *The Right to the City: Social Justice and the Fight for Public Space*, Guilford Press, 2003

Muncie, John, *Youth and Crime*, second edition, Sage, 2004

Munck, Ronaldo, ed., *Re-inventing the City?*, Liverpool University Press, 2003

Murray, Peter, ed., *Architecture and Commerce*, Wordsearch, 2004

Newman, Oscar, *Defensible Space: People and Design in the Violent City*, Architectural Press, 1973

Oborne, Peter, *The Rise of Political Lying*, Simon and Schuster, 2005

Olsen, Donald, *Town Planning in London*, Yale University Press, 1982

Oswalt, Philipp, ed., *Shrinking Cities*, vol. 1, International Research, Kulturstiftung des Bundes, 2005

Oswalt, Philipp, ed., *Shrinking Cities*, vol. 2, Interventions, Kulturstiftung des Bundes, 2006

Oswalt, Philipp, Misselwitz, Philipp, Overmeyer, Klaus, 'Patterns of the Unplanned', in *Loose Space: Possibility and Diversity in Urban Life*, ed. Karen Franck & Quentin Stevens, Routledge, 2006

Parenti, Christian, *Lockdown America: Police and Prisons in the Age of Crisis*, Verso, 2000

Poole, Steven, *Unspeak: How Words Become Weapons, How Weapons Become a Message and How That Message Becomes a Reality*, Grove Press, 2006

Power, Anne & Mumford, Katherine, *Boom or Abandonment? Resolving Housing Conflicts in Cities*, Chartered Institute of Housing, 2002

Putnam, Robert D., *Bowling Alone: The Collapse and Revival of American Community*, Simon & Schuster, 2000

Robson, Brian, *Those Inner Cities: Reconciling the Economic and Social Aims of Urban Policy*, Clarendon Press, 1988

Sampson, Adam, *Private Renting for Public Good, in the Future of the Private Rented Sector*, ed. P. Bill, P. Hackett & C. Glossop, Smith Institute, 2008

Schoon, Nicholas, *The Chosen City*, Spon Press, 2001

Scitovsky, Tibor, *The Joyless Economy: The Psychology of Human Satisfaction*, 1976, revised edition, Oxford University Press, 1992

Sennett, Richard, 'Growth and Failure: The New Political Economy and Its Culture', in *Spaces of Culture: City, Nation, World*, ed. Mike Featherstone & Scott Lash, Sage, 1999

Sennett, Richard, 'The Search for a Place in the World', in *Architecture of Fear*, ed. Nan Ellin, Princeton Architectural Press, 1997

Sennett, Richard, *The Fall of Public Man*, Alfred A. Knopf, 1977, republished Penguin Books, 2002

Shearing, Clifford & Johnston, Les, *Governing Security: Explorations in Policing and Justice*, Routledge, 2003

Sinclair, Iain, *London Orbital*, Granta, 2002

Smith, Neil & Low, Setha, eds, *The Politics of Public Space*, Routledge, 2005

Smith, Neil, 'Which New Urbanism? New York City and the Revanchist 1990s', in R. Beauregard & S. Body-Gendrot, eds, *The Urban Moment: Cosmopolitan Essays on the Late-20th Century City*, Sage, 1999

Smith, Neil, *The New Urban Frontier: Gentrification and the Revanchist City*, Routledge, 1996

Sorkin, Michael, ed., *Variations on a Theme Park: The New American City and the End of Public Space*, Hill & Wang, 1992

Steel, Carolyn, *Hungry City*, Chatto & Windus, 2008

Titmuss, Richard, *Problems of Social Policy*, HMSO, 1950

Wain, Neil, with Burney, Elizabeth, *The ASBO: Wrong Turning, Dead End*, Howard League for Penal Reform, 2007

Wilkinson, Richard, *The Impact of Inequality: How to Make Sick Societies Healthier*, Routledge, 2005

Zukin, Sharon, *The Cultures of Cities*, Blackwell Publishing, 1995

Reports

Ball, Kirstie & Wood, David Murakami, eds, 'A Report on the Surveillance Society: For the Information Commissioner', *Surveillance Studies Network*, 2006

Crawford, Adam & Lister, Stuart, *The Use and Impact of Dispersal Orders: Sticking Plasters and Wake-Up Calls*, University of Leeds, published for the Joseph Rowntree Foundation, Policy Press, 2007

Department for Communities and Local Government, *Housing Market Renewal*, National Audit Office, 2007

Department for Transport, *Manual for Streets*, 2007

Design Guide for Residential Areas, Essex County Council, 1973

Duffy, Bobby, Wake, Rhonda, Burrows, Tamara & Bremner, Pamela, *Closing the Gaps: Crime and Public Perceptions*, Ipsos MORI, 2007

Eades, Chris, Grimshaw, Roger, Silvestri, Arianna & Solomon, Enver, *'Knife Crime': A Review of Evidence and Policy*, Centre for Crime and Justice Studies, second edition, 2008

Hills, John, *Ends and Means: The Future Roles of Social Housing in England*, Economic and Social Research Council, Research Centre for Analysis of Social Exclusion, CASE report 34, 2007

Holland, Caroline, Clark, Andrew, Katz, Jeanne & Peace, Sheila, *Social Interactions in Urban Public Places*, Open University, published for the Joseph Rowntree Foundation, Policy Press, 2007

Hough, Mike, Millie, Andrew, Jacobson, Jessica & McDonald, Eraina, *Anti-Social Behaviour Strategies: Finding a Balance*, Policy Press, 2005

Labour Party, *A Quiet Life: Tough Action on Criminal Neighbours*, 1995

LDDC Monograph, 'Attracting Investment, Creating Value', *Establishing a Property Market*, 1998

Minton, Anna & Jones, Sarah, *Generation Squalor: Shelter's National Investigation into the Housing Crisis*, Shelter, 2005

Minton, Anna, *Building Balanced Communities: The US and UK Compared*, Royal Insitution of Chartered Surveyors, 2002

Minton, Anna, *Mind the Gap: Tackling Social Polarization through Balanced Communities*, Royal Institution of Chartered Surveyors, 2004

Minton, Anna, *Northern Soul*, Demos & Royal Institution of Chartered Surveyors, 2003

Minton, Anna, *What Kind of World are We Building? The Privatization of Public Space*, Royal Institution of Chartered Surveyors, 2006

Neuberger, Julia, 'Unkind, Risk Averse and Untrusting: If This is Today's Society Can We Change It?' *Viewpoint*, Joseph Rowntree Foundation, 2008

Page, David, *Respect and Renewal: A Study of Neighbourhood Social Regeneration*, Joseph Rowntree Foundation, 2007

Rugg, Julie & Rhodes, David, *The Private Rented Sector: Its Contribution and Potential*, Centre for Housing Policy, University of York, 2008

Wilkinson, Adam, *Pathfinder*, SAVE Britain's Heritage, 2006

Worple, Ken & Knox, Katherine, *The Social Value of Public Spaces*: *Summary of Research Projects*, Joseph Rowntree Foundation, 2007

Journals and Selected Articles

Adams, Richard E. & Serpe, Richard T., 'Social Integration, Fear of Crime and Life Satisfaction', *Sociological Perspectives*, vol. 43 (4), 2000

Alessandro, Annigi & Graham, Stephen, 'Virtual Cities, Social Polarization and the Crisis in Urban Public Space', *Journal of Urban Technology*, vol. 4 (1), 1997

Atkins, P. J., 'How the West End was Won: The Struggle to Remove Street Barriers in Victorian London', *Journal of Historical Geography*, vol. 19, 1993

Atkinson, Rowland & Blandy, Sarah, 'Panic Rooms: The Rise of Defensive Home Ownership', *Housing Studies*, vol. 22 (4), 2007

Banham, Reyner, Barker, Paul, Hall, Peter & Price, Cedric, 'Non-Plan: An Experiment in Freedom', *New Society*, 20/3/69

Blackmore, Lisa, 'Different Experiences of the Anti-Social Behaviour Process', *Social Work Monographs 226*, School of Social Work and Psychosocial Studies, University of East Anglia, 2007

Blandy, Sarah & Lister, Diane, 'Gated Communities: (Ne)gating Community Development?' *Housing Studies*, vol. 20 (2), 2005

Boland, Philip, 'Unpacking the Theory-Policy Interface of Local Economic Development: An Analysis of Cardiff and Liverpool', *Urban Studies*, vol. 44 (5/6), 2007

Cameron, Stuart, 'From Low Demand Housing to Rising Aspirations: Housing Market Renewal within Regional and Neighbourhood Regeneration Policy', *Housing Studies*, vol. 21 (1), 2006

Coleman, Roy, 'Reclaiming the Streets: Closed Circuit TV, Neoliberalism and the Mystification of Social Divisions in the UK', www.surveillance-and-society.org

Cook, Ian R., 'Mobilizing Urban Policies: The Policy Transfer of US Business Improvement Districts to England and Wales', *Urban Studies*, vol. 45 (4), 2008

Cozens, Paul, Hillier, David & Prescott, Gwyn, 'Crime and the Design of Residential Property: Exploring the Theoretical Background', *Property Management*, vol. 19 (2), 2001

Dear, M. & Flusty, S., 'Postmodern Urbanism', *Annals of the Association of Urban Geographers*, vol. 88 (1), 1998

Ditton, Jason, 'Crime and the City: Public Attitudes Towards Open Street CCTV in Glasgow', *British Journal of Criminology*, vol. 40 (4), 2000

Dixon, John & Durrheim, Kevin, 'Displacing Place-Identity: A Discursive Approach to Locating Self and Other', *British Journal of Social Psychology*, vol. 39 (1), 2000

Furbey, Robert, 'Urban Regeneration: Reflections on a Metaphor', *Critical Social Policy*, vol. 19 (4), 1999

Gray, Emily, Jackson, Jonathan & Farrell, Stephen, 'Reassessing the Fear of Crime', *European Journal of Criminology*, vol. 5 (3), 2008

Hamilton-Baillie, Ben, 'Shared Space: Reconciling People, Places and Traffic', *Built Environment*, vol. 34 (2), 2008

Harcourt, Bernard E., 'The Broken Windows Myth', *New York Times*, 11/9/01

Hillier, Bill, 'Can Streets be Made Safe?' *Urban Design International*, vol. 9 (1), 2004

Hillier, Bill, 'City of Alice's Dreams', *Architects' Journal*, 9/7/86

Hochleutner, Brian R., 'BIDS Fare Well: The Democratic Accountability of Business Improvement Districts', *New York University Law Review*, vol. 78, no. 2, 2003

Imrie, Rob & Thomas, Huw, 'The Limits of Property-Led Regeneration', *Environment & Planning C: Government and Policy*, vol. 11 (1), 1993

Jones, Trevor & Newburn, Tim, 'Urban Change and Policing: Mass Private Property Reconsidered', *European Journal on Criminal Policy and Research*, vol. 7 (2), 1999

Kelling, George L. & Wilson, James Q., 'Broken Windows', *Atlantic Monthly*, March 1982

Kempa, Michael, Carrier, Ryan, Wood, Jennifer & Shearing, Clifford, 'Reflections on the Evolving Concept of Private Policing', *European Journal on Criminal Policy Research*, vol. 7 (2), 1999

Loader, Ian, 'Consumer Culture and the Commodification of Policing and Security', *Sociology*, vol. 33 (2), 1999

Low, Setha, 'New Scope for the Public Realm', in *The Future of New York: An International Perspective*, Zicklin School of Business, Urban Center Books, 2006

Marcuse, Peter, '"Dual City": A Muddy Metaphor for a Quartered City', *International Journal of Urban and Regional Research*, 1989

Merrifield, Andy, 'Integration and Exclusion in Urban Life', *City*, vol. 1, issues 5 & 6, 1996

Mitchell, Don, 'The End of Public Space? People's Park, Definitions of the Public Realm and Democracy', *Annals of the Association of American Geographers*, vol. 85 (1), 1995

Müge, Akkar, 'The Changing "Publicness" of Contemporary Public Space: A Case Study of the Grey's Monument Area, Newcastle upon Tyne', *Urban Design International*, vol. 10 (2), 2005

Noaks, Lesley, 'Diversification of British Policing: The Citizen Experience', *Policing: An International Journal of Police Strategies & Management*, vol. 27 (2), 2004

Noaks, Lesley, 'Private Cops on the Block: A Review of the Role of Private Security in Residential Communities', *Policing and Society*, vol. 10 (2), 2000

Pascoe, Tim & Topping, Phil, 'Secured by Design: Assessing the Basis of the Scheme', *International Journal of Risk, Security and Crime Prevention*, Spring/Summer 1997

Seligman, Martin, E. P. & Diener, Ed, 'Beyond Money: Toward an Economy of Well Being', *Psychological Science in the Public Interest*, vol. 5 (1), 2004

Sheptycki, James, 'Insecurity, Risk Suppression and Segregation', *Theoretical Criminology*, vol. 1 (3), 1997

Skair, Leslie, 'Iconic Architecture and Capitalist Globalization', *City*, vol. 10 (1), 2006

Steventon, Graham, 'Defensible Space: A Critical Review of the Theory and Practice of a Crime Prevention Strategy', *Urban Design International*, vol. 1 (3), 1996

Swyngedouw, Erik & Kaïka, Maria, 'The Making of "Glocal" Urban Modernities', *City*, vol. 7 (1), 2003

Thomas, Lisa, 'Disconnection: The Perceptions of Gated Community Residents in the UK', unpublished MSc Environmental Psychology dissertation, University of Surrey, 2006

Van der Heijden, Hans, 'Whose Space is Public Space?' address for *Free Thinking 2008, Festival of Ideas*, BBC Radio 3, unpublished paper

Vandevogel, Franck, 'Private Security and Urban Crime Mitigation: A Bid for BIDS', *Criminal Justice*, vol. 5 (3), 2005

Ward, Kevin, '"Policies in Motion", Urban Management and State Restructuring: the Trans-Local Expansion of Business Improvement Districts', *International Journal of Urban and Regional Research*, vol. 30 (1), 2006

Whyte, Dave, 'Something Rotten in the City State of Manchester', published online by UHC, Manchester, 2004

Williams, Bernard, 'Truth, Politics and Self-Deception', *Social Research*, vol. 83 (3), 1996

Zedner, Lucia, 'Too Much Security?' *International Journal of the Sociology of Law*, vol. 31, 2003

Films

Byker, Amber Films, 1983
Dilapidated Dwelling, Patrick Keiler, 2000
T. Dan Smith, Amber Films, 1987

Acknowledgements

This book has had a gradual genesis, emerging from a number of articles about mixed communities in the *Guardian* in 2001 and 2002. The ideas discussed developed into a series of reports about gated communities and the privatization of public space, published by Michael Chambers when he was director of policy at the Royal Institution of Chartered Surveyors. Michael gave me the platform to explore the subject and I am very grateful to him for that.

In a moment of synchronicity, just when I was hoping to write a book, my agent, Karolina Sutton at Curtis Brown, read a piece of mine in the *Liberal* and approached me. I would like to thank Karolina for her consistent support and encouragement, insightful comments and engagement with the subject. My editor Helen Conford, editorial director at Penguin Press, has been brilliant, dedicated and incisive. I always hoped to find an editor who would make my work better and with Helen I finally did.

John Davies, the photographer who took the pictures which accompany the book, has made a beautiful and resonant set of images. John is an artist who creates images which combine the fragility of the environment with social comment. The discussions I had with Sue Davison informed every part of the book from the beginning to the end and were invaluable. I am grateful for copy editor Daphne Tagg's scrupulous attention to detail and burnishing of the text.

The book is a blend of investigative journalism and research and I owe a lot to the large body of excellent academic work on the subject, which does not get anything like the attention it should. Part of my aim is to make these areas, which are subject to fierce academic debate, more accessible. There is one book in particular I would like to single out for crystallizing many of my ideas. I read *Splintering Urbanism*, by Stephen Graham and Simon Marvin, after I had written about gated communities and ghettoes but before I looked at the privatization of public space, and it was this book which opened my eyes to the ramifications of the subject. In America the work of Setha Low, professor of environmental psychology at the City University of New York, on gated communities and the 'crime complex' in the US was a big influence.

I am indebted to a long list of experts, colleagues and friends who read early drafts and debated many of the topics discussed in the book. Mike Hough, director of the Centre for Crime and Justice Studies at Kings College, London, read and commented on the section on fear and crime. Peter Cosmetatos, director of finance at the British Property Federation, ran his razor eye over my writing on property finance and, where we did not always agree, confirmed there were no errors. My Placeteam colleague Dickon Robinson read and commented on my suggestions for housing policy and Place-team director Julie Cowans helpfully debated the future of housing with me. Jim Meikle, also from Placeteam, sent me useful information on surveillance. Daniel Matlin, Beth Watts, Jane Franklin and Rebecca Fox were all kind enough to read early drafts at various stages.

The book was written at the British Library, which is a fantastic place to work. In keeping with the themes dealt with, it seems apt that the book was written in such an inspiring public building. I was disappointed when, half way through the writing, security guards and bag checks were introduced, but little can diminish my enthusiasm for the British Library. Working there, I had long discussions, not just about our books, with Susanna Kleeman, with whom it has been great to share this experience. There are two other writers with whom I shared the trials and tribulations. Carolyn Steel, author of *Hungry City*, was always a year ahead of me in this process and able to show me what to expect and to share the uncertainties which come with writing a book. With Selina Mills we navigated book proposals, agents and editors and Selina is now embarking on her book.

This could have been an international book, with many of the themes it deals with equally relevant in societies from Dubai to Denmark. But I chose to base it loosely on a journey around Britain, to focus on the impact of specific policies on communities all around the country. It relies on interviews with a wide range of people, from property developers, lawyers and estate agents to alienated young people and the police. I owe a huge thank you to all of them, especially the people who didn't agree with me but talked to me anyway. The aim of the book is to raise a debate and I am very grateful to all who sat down and discussed the issues.

I would like to thank all my friends and family, who've heard far too much about the book over the last two years. Andrea Eisenhart, Polly Staple and Cressida O'Shea have all talked through ideas. Arthur Norton and Les Poyner have both, in their different ways, been part of the process. My brother Aris Minton gave me his take on private environments and was supportive during the final throes of editing. My boyfriend Martin Pickles has borne the brunt, especially in the final few months, and he has been patient, interested, kind and a great morale booster. And he came up with the subtitle. Finally I want to thank my parents: my mother, from whom I inherit my politics, and my father, to whom I owe any talent I may have for writing.

*

For the 2012 edition of the book, I would like to thank Tamasin Cave, from Spinwatch, for assisting me in mapping the bewildering array of companies, quangos, agencies and government bodies involved in the Olympic project.

Index

Italic page numbers refer to illustrations
'n' indicates references to end-notes (e.g. 210n37)

He just wanted a decent book to read ...

Not too much to ask, is it? It was in 1935 when Allen Lane, Managing Director of Bodley Head Publishers, stood on a platform at Exeter railway station looking for something good to read on his journey back to London. His choice was limited to popular magazines and poor-quality paperbacks – the same choice faced every day by the vast majority of readers, few of whom could afford hardbacks. Lane's disappointment and subsequent anger at the range of books generally available led him to found a company – and change the world.

'We believed in the existence in this country of a vast reading public for intelligent books at a low price, and staked everything on it'
Sir Allen Lane, 1902–1970, founder of Penguin Books

The quality paperback had arrived – and not just in bookshops. Lane was adamant that his Penguins should appear in chain stores and tobacconists, and should cost no more than a packet of cigarettes.

Reading habits (and cigarette prices) have changed since 1935, but Penguin still believes in publishing the best books for everybody to enjoy. We still believe that good design costs no more than bad design, and we still believe that quality books published passionately and responsibly make the world a better place.

So wherever you see the little bird – whether it's on a piece of prize-winning literary fiction or a celebrity autobiography, political tour de force or historical masterpiece, a serial-killer thriller, reference book, world classic or a piece of pure escapism – you can bet that it represents the very best that the genre has to offer.

Whatever you like to read – trust Penguin.